Scarecrow Studies in Young Adult Literature
Series Editor: Patty Campbell

Scarecrow Studies in Young Adult Literature is intended to continue the body of critical writing established in Twayne's Young Adult Authors Series and to expand it beyond single-author studies to explorations of genres, multicultural writing, and controversial issues in YA reading. Many of the contributing authors of the series are among the leading scholars and critics of adolescent literature, and some are YA novelists themselves.

The series is shaped by its editor, Patty Campbell, who is a renowned authority in the field, with a thirty-year background as critic, lecturer, librarian, and teacher of young adult literature. Patty Campbell was the 2001 winner of the ALAN Award, given by the Assembly on Adolescent Literature of the National Council of Teachers of English for distinguished contribution to young adult literature. In 1989 she was the winner of the American Library Association's Grolier Award for distinguished service to young adults and reading.

1. *What's So Scary about R.L. Stine?* by Patrick Jones, 1998.
2. *Ann Rinaldi: Historian and Storyteller,* by Jeanne M. McGlinn, 2000.
3. *Norma Fox Mazer: A Writer's World,* by Arthea J.S. Reed, 2000.
4. *Exploding the Myths: The Truth about Teens and Reading,* by Marc Aronson, 2001.
5. *The Agony and the Eggplant: Daniel Pinkwater's Heroic Struggles in the Name of YA Literature,* by Walter Hogan, 2001.
6. *Caroline Cooney: Faith and Fiction,* by Pamela Sissi Carroll, 2001.
7. *Declarations of Independence: Empowered Girls in Young Adult Literature, 1990–2001,* by Joanne Brown and Nancy St. Clair, 2002.
8. *Lost Masterworks of Young Adult Literature,* by Connie S. Zitlow, 2002.
9. *Beyond the Pale: New Essays for a New Era,* by Marc Aronson, 2003.
10. *Orson Scott Card: Writer of the Terrible Choice,* by Edith S. Tyson, 2003.

Orson Scott Card

Writer of the Terrible Choice

Edith S. Tyson

Scarecrow Studies in Young Adult Literature, No. 10

The Scarecrow Press, Inc.
Lanham, Maryland, and Oxford
2003

 # 52047345

SCARECROW PRESS, INC.

Published in the United States of America
by Scarecrow Press, Inc.
An imprint of The Rowman & Littlefield Publishing Group
4501 Forbes Boulevard, Suite 200, Lanham, Maryland 20706
www.scarecrowpress.com

PO Box 317
Oxford
OX2 9RU, UK

Copyright © 2003 by Edith S. Tyson

British Library Cataloguing in Publication Information Available

Library of Congress Cataloging-in-Publication Data

Tyson, Edith S.
   Orson Scott Card: Writer of the Terrible Choice / Edith S. Tyson.
        p. cm. — (Scarecrow Studies in Young Adult Literature; 10)
   Includes bibliographical references and index.
   ISBN 0-8108-4790-6 (alk. paper)
   1. Card, Orson Scott—Criticism and interpretation.   2. Young adult
fiction, American—History and criticism.   I. Title.   II. Series.
PS3553.A655Z88 2003
813'.54—dc21
                                                         2003005730

∞™ The paper used in this publication meets the minimum requirements of
American National Standard for Information Sciences—Permanence of
Paper for Printed Library Materials, ANSI/NISO Z39.48-1992.
Manufactured in the United States of America.

This book is dedicated to the subject,
Orson Scott Card,
and
to the person whom I hereby solemnly nominate as
"The World's Most Patient Editor,"
Patty Campbell.

Contents

Acknowledgments   ix

Preface: "In the Hands of the Savior"   xi

Introduction: Orson Scott Card, the Making of a Writer   xiii

**Part I: *Ender's Game*, The Shadow Books,
and The Speaker Trilogy**

1   *Ender's Game*   3

2   The Shadow Books   15

3   The Speaker Trilogy   27

Part II: The Other Great Series

4   The Tales of Alvin Maker   41

5   The Homecoming Series and More   57

**Part III: Card the Explicit Christian, and
Card the Explicit Mormon**

6   Stories from the Bible   79

7   Stories from Mormon Life   97

Part IV: Novels That Stand Alone (Not in a Series), and Shorter Works and Poems

8	Four Early Novels	115
9	Fantasy/Mysteries in the Present Age	125
10	Moving in Time	135
11	Shorter Fiction and Poems	145

Conclusion: What Card Is Telling Us — 157

Chronology of Events in the Life of Orson Scott Card — 165

Appendix: "God's Army" by Geoffrey Card — 169

Index — 171

About the Author — 187

Acknowledgments

Almost every chapter in this book owes something to the monumental work by Michael R. Collings, *Storyteller: The Official Orson Scott Card Bibliography and Guide*, Overlook Connection Press, PO Box 526, Woodstock, GA 30188, (2001).

Collings lists, summarizes, and discusses book-length works by Orson Scott Card to the year 2000, and lists book reviews of each with quotations from a sample of them; lists by title, date, and printings every piece of fiction shorter than book-length, poetry, plays, essays, reviews of the books of others, letters to editors, and nonfiction about computers, and gives a summary of awards to the year 2000. Collings also reprints an essay by Card and an essay of his own about Card.

Collings and I both approve of Orson Scott Card. Collings sees Card as a fellow Mormon of genius and imagination. I see Card as a writer with a powerful ethical grounding and a Christian outlook, who is, among other things, a Mormon. I am a Christian outside the Mormon tradition. To me, the Mormon element in Card's work is virtually invisible unless he is writing specifically about Mormons. So Collings and I often select and discuss from different angles, and express ourselves very differently.

That said, the debt that I owe Collings is enormous. He shows the way for me to discover reviews, to find lesser-known works, and to point out controversy. His book has helped mine to be far more complete than it otherwise would be. Thank you, Mr. Collings.

Thanks are also due to Hatrack River, the special website for fans of Orson Scott Card (www.hatrack.com) that lists upcoming publications, often with advance glimpses of the opening chapters. The website also keeps up with current reviews.

And many thanks to Orson Scott Card himself, not only for the gracious interview he gave me on September 12, 2000, but also for his critique of chapter 7. Also, there was meaningful help from his wife, Kristine, and from his assistant, Kathleen Bellamy.

My heartfelt gratitude to one and all!

Preface

"In the Hands of the Savior"*

ORSON SCOTT CARD'S STATEMENT ABOUT THE PURPOSE OF HIS WRITING

I believe that speculative fiction is the one literary tradition available today to writers who would like to deal seriously with great moral, religious, cosmological, and eschatological issues without confining themselves to . . . a particular religious group. . . . I can deal with religious, theological, and moral issues with greater clarity in science fiction [and fantasy] than anywhere else, precisely because [they] allow . . . the writer to set these issues at one remove, freeing writer and reader from biases and issues relating to particular religions or philosophies in the present. . . . And, in fact, most [speculative] fiction writers are doing exactly the same thing. . . . Isaac Asimov, though an avowed atheist, consistently wrote about people caught up in fulfilling (or flouting) the will of a quasi-divine character who has plans and purposes for the human race: in other words, God. . . . all the great questions and issues are still available within . . . [speculative] fiction. . . . There is nothing I have written, in my entire career, which I would not gladly place in the hands of the Savior, knowing that he will understand the intention . . .

---

*Selections from an eleven-page online document, "An Open Letter from Orson Scott Card to Those Who Are Concerned about Plagiarism in *The Memory of Earth*." Copyright 2000. Hatrack River Enterprises, Inc. Used with permission.

of all that is in my work. . . . [H]e might chide me for this or that error of judgment . . . but . . . he will know that . . . my intention was one that I promised long [ago]: that all my work, in one way or another, will contribute to the cause of good in the world.

Introduction

Orson Scott Card, the Making of a Writer[1]

In 1893, in a village of whites living near a Canadian Indian tribe, a two-year-old boy had fever and difficulty breathing, and was dying. It may have been pneumonia. Indians who knew the baby's father well came by. Food and assistance was always available at the house of this white "brother," who was a practicing member of The Church of Jesus Christ of Latter-Day Saints (Mormons).

The Indians offered their medicine tent, steam-laced with herbs, to treat the child. Whatever the herbs were, the steam was probably as good for the little lungs as any treatment in a modern hospital. The boy survived, and eventually became a father and a grandfather. One grandson was the writer Orson Scott Card.

The dedication to Card's book *Red Prophet* reads: "In memory of my grandfather, Orson Rega Card (1891–1984), whose life was saved by the Indians of the Blood tribe when he was a child on the Canadian frontier."[2] There is no story by Orson Scott Card in which the life of a child is saved by the Other People using their unique methods. But again and again, throughout his fiction, we meet variations on this theme: It is *essential* for people of different kinds to try to understand each other!

THE INTERVIEW

I am sitting in the kitchen of Scott[3] and Kristine Card. It is a warm, bright September afternoon. Sunlight is streaming through the glass-paneled doors. One or another of the four telephone lines, all with extensions in the kitchen, rings from time to time. Kristine takes the calls. She also listens to the interview attentively. Once, when Scott Card failed to remember a detail from one of his stories, *she* remembered that detail.

I was careful to wear a dress, not a pantsuit. "Everyone knows" that Mormons are conservative about clothes, especially clothes for women. But Scott and Kristine are each comfortable in shorts and short-sleeved shirts. So much for stereotypes! I have a glass of orange juice in front of me. I am so mesmerized by what I have been hearing that I have only been sipping it.

I had telephoned a few weeks ago, offering to postpone this scheduled interview.

The death of their second son, Charlie Ben, had been suddenly posted on Scott Card's website. But Kristine had encouraged me to come, just as planned. "We are all right," she had said. And they are. There has been real laughter in this interview. Would anyone believe that these are parents in mourning, who loved their child as much as a child was ever loved? Yes, there are some convinced Christians who would believe it.

Scott Card is autographing a copy of *Sarah* for me. It is literally just off the press, and it is a substantial book. "Do you know what you are doing to me?" I ask. "I'll be awake all night reading that. I won't be good for anything tomorrow."

"That is not *my* responsibility!" he says quickly, with a grin.

They are going to take me out to a restaurant for supper. Their daughters, Emily and Zina Margaret will join us there. Their elder son Geoffrey is on the West Coast, and I am sorry not to meet him. We are taking two cars since Scott will be directing a musical play of his tonight. He will go straight to the rehearsal after supper, and Kristine will take me back to the hotel.

As we move to the garage, I see that the two cars have personalized license plates.

One says "Ender." One says "Alvin."

EARLY LIFE OF A WRITER

Orson Scott Card was born August 24, 1951, in Richland, Washington, the son of Willard Richards Card and Peggy Jane Park Card. Willard Card was a World War II veteran who had served in the Navy despite back problems. When baby Scott was a month old, the family moved to San Mateo, California. Willard Card started a sign-painting company. But his back problems were increasing. The family could not depend on his sign painting for income, so Willard Card finished college and worked on graduate degrees to become a professor. He continued to paint signs for pay, occasionally even after he had begun college teaching.

The next move, when Scott was three years old, was to Salt Lake City, Utah, where his father was finishing his bachelor's degree. He took walks with his grandmother through Temple Square, the center of Mormonism, and she sang to him. By the time he was four he was harmonizing with her in duets. He loved stories. His retarded Aunt Donna read to him, and even when he couldn't understand her, he knew he was loved. His sister, Janice, read to him from her Nancy Drew books, which puzzled him with the phrase "colored woman." Nonwhites are rare in Utah. He tried to imagine how many different colors that woman had!

The next move was to Santa Clara, California in 1957. Scott Card was now six, and stayed in Santa Clara until he was thirteen. His father was teaching at San Jose State College while working on his master's degree. Scott was in a special "gifted" class, but the music classes mattered more: clarinet first, then French horn.

Most significant of all was the reading that he discovered on his own. Among other things, he read his mother's historical novels, including the Williamsburg series by Elsworth Thane. He read Mark Twain's *The Prince and the Pauper*, which became his favorite book for a long time. He read the family's one-volume encyclopedia, and when they got the multivolume World Book, he read that.

At ten years old, he would bicycle to the Santa Clara Public Library, and read everything on his age level or above in the children's department. Then he sneaked over to the adult side, sure that he would be penalized if he were caught. He discovered short science fiction classics, like Poul Anderson's "Call Me Joe" and the less known "Tunesmith" by Lloyd Biggle Jr., which he credits with changing his life.[4] He learned about good and evil on an international scale from reading *The Rise and Fall of the Third Reich* by William Shirer, an account of Hitler's Germany and the Holocaust.

HIS FIRST STORY

Many writers write about their worst fears. Scott was nonathletic, and he was afraid of bullies and had a distaste for fighting, even in self-defense.

He wrote about a smart kid, beaten up by bullies, who becomes brain-damaged and retarded. He consulted his father's copy of *Writer's Digest*, and submitted the story to two magazines. It was not accepted. However, the Stilson incident in *Ender's Game*, which he would write twenty-four years later, has some details in common with that first story, written at age ten.

EARLY POLITICS

The family moved again, in 1964, to Mesa, Arizona where there were presidential mock debates in junior high. Scott, now thirteen, took the part of Lyndon Johnson, in Goldwater's state. He favored Goldwater, but he took the part because nobody else would. This experience made an impression. Today he is a political maverick, "conservative" on some issues (such as homosexual marriage or abortion) and "liberal' on others (such as the death penalty or gun control.) He and his wife register one as Democrat, one as Republican, so that they can vote in the primary elections.

APPRENTICESHIP IN THEATER

The family left Mesa in 1967 for Orem, Utah, where his father was now on the faculty of Brigham Young University (BYU). Scott was enrolled at the university laboratory school, where a capable student could take individual college classes while still in high school. So his high school and early college years overlapped.

He first wanted to major in archeology, but noticed that he was spending more and more time in the theatre department. All aspects of theatre interested him, but his particular abilities were most needed in scriptwriting. He rewrote plays written by other students, and wrote at least ten plays himself at this time, one in high school (the only one with a science fiction theme) and the rest in BYU (with scriptural themes, or from Mormon history).

He gives credit for his development as a writer to this time of writing playscripts. When a play is being performed "The audience will never lie. By the way they lean forward . . . eyes riveted on the stage they tell you that they are interested. . . . Then [some] shift in their seats, glance at the program . . . you've lost their attention."[5]

MISSION IN BRAZIL

Before finishing his bachelor's degree, Scott left on his mission in 1971, at age twenty. Almost all young Mormon men (and since the 1970s, many young Mormon women) do mission work. He was sent to São Paulo, Brazil, and the effects of this contact with the Brazilian Catholic culture and the Portuguese language can be seen in The Shadow Books, The Speaker Trilogy, and in other writings.

The playscript of *Stone Tables*, about Moses and the Exodus, was written while he was in Brazil, in part because he missed using the English language.

AFTER THE MISSION

He returned to Utah in 1973 after his mission service was over, and finished his bachelor's degree with distinction in 1975, majoring in theater. He served as assistant editor at *The Ensign*, the official Mormon magazine. He resumed writing playscripts based on scripture and on Mormon history and tried creating his own theater company. As a business, the company was a failure. After six months he was in debt, and his job as an editor wasn't paying enough to live on, let alone pay off the costs of the theater venture. He got a second job, as a copyeditor at Brigham Young University Press, but he needed more money.

FIRST COMMERCIAL PUBLICATION

Card dug out, and rewrote, a story that five years he had submitted to an editor, and received a polite, personally written, rejection. It was "The Tinker," and tells of a tinker with the two gifts: healing people's disease and the ability to communicate with birds. When the villagers slaughter some birds, which are the tinker's friends, he withdraws; a winter epidemic kills many people. The villagers blame him for the deaths of their loved ones, and murder the gentle tinker.

He sent the story to the science fiction magazine *Analog*. Psionic powers of all kinds are common in science fiction, and he was imagining the setting as a colony planet. But to Ben Bova, editor of *Analog*, it was fantasy. The rural landscape, the handicraft occupations, all suggested a fantasy in a medieval setting. *Analog* didn't print fantasy. Bova refused this story but encouraged Card to send more.

This experience gave Card a principle in writing speculative fiction: If the story has *trees* it will be seen as fantasy; if a story has *rivets* it will be seen as science fiction, regardless of how impossible, or not, the events may be. (Eleven years later, he wrote *Speaker for the Dead*, in which the trees are significant. But no tree appears on the cover, and no tree appears in the title. The book is accepted as science fiction.)

Card's next submission to *Analog* was accepted at once. It was "Ender's Game," not the novel that we know by that name today, but a novelette. It was selected for anthologies and was nominated for both the Hugo and the Nebula awards of 1977. It did not win either award but it was on the final ballot for the Hugo—not bad for a young writer's first commercially published story.

EARLIEST WRITING AND
CIRCUMSTANCES ON THE WAY

Early in his writing career. Card began experimenting with variations on the theme of star travel. Ships between stars take lifetimes. In Card's earliest stories the solution is the drug *somec*. This drug gives suspended animation but robs a person of memory. However, it is possible to tap a brain, record the memories, and play them back in the brain when the person awakes from somec.

These discoveries have uses beyond star travel. A person can take a one-way trip to the future, years, decades, even centuries ahead. Somec gives an illusion of immortality: One lives just one's normal waking lifespan, but skips over intervening years. Somec is not available to everyone; the people who decide upon the recipients become priestly figures, supposedly incorruptible. In practice, they are *almost* incorruptible.

Card wrote short stories based in this somec-society, showing what might happen to marriage, parent–child relationships, friendships, power-seeking, amusements, competitions, attempts to correct mistakes, and even legal punishments in such a setting. He gathered together five of these somec stories that had been published in various magazines, added six more not yet published, and put them together in a collection he called *Capitol*.[6] Reviews of *Capitol* were patronizing: "On the whole, the cycle while entertaining does not hang together very well. Card is a skilled craftsman and a writer to watch—perhaps his promise will be better realized in his next book."[7]

The next book was his first attempt at a unified *novel*, not a collection of stories. This was *Hot Sleep: The Worthing Chronicle*.[8] In *Capitol*, he had introduced a mutated human race of telepaths (known as *swipes*), who are hated and feared because of their telepathic powers. In *Hot Sleep*, Jason Worthing, a swipe, is manipulated into taking the captaincy of a ship of somec-suspended independent thinkers seeking a new world. The ship is struck by an enemy missile, which explodes in the compartment where the passengers' mindtapes are stored.

Worthing arrives at the new planet with a shipload of sleeping adult bodies with infant brains. They remember nothing but can, eventually, learn anything. Jason is their god. He can try to make them into any society that he chooses. He can bring them a satan. One stored mindtape—that of the most extreme anti-authority rebel—escaped destruction. If he is revived, with his memory intact, he *may* undermine what Jason hopes to do.

In May of 1977, Scott Card married Kristine Allen. Kristine got an early lesson on being married to a writer. Card had been working the night before his wedding on a final revision of *Hot Sleep*. He was so anxious to get it into the mail on time that he was a few minutes late to his own wedding!

For *Hot Sleep* some reviews had praise, such as Fred Niederman's evaluation of "fresh, intelligent and interesting"[9] and some had censure, as with Michael Bishop's: "Weird . . . muzzy religio-political parallels . . . ill conceived characters . . . [no clear depiction] of time or place . . . awkward prose."[10] Of the unfavorable review, Card says "[Bishop] hated [*Hot Sleep*] . . . *intelligently*. He understood what I was trying to do and explained exactly why I failed. . . . Bishop gave me an insight."[11] It is unusual for a writer to react to negative criticism this way.

Over the next four years, Card continued his editorial work, sold about forty stories altogether, published collections of his stories, and edited collections of other peoples' stories. He wrote and published two novels, *A Planet Called Treason* (later revised as *Treason*) and *Songmaster*.

AT THE UNIVERSITY OF NOTRE DAME

By 1981, Scott and Kristine Card had two children: Michael Geoffrey and Emily Janice. All of their children have one name for a relative or family friend and one name for a favorite writer. Geoffrey is named for Geoffrey Chaucer; Emily for Emily Dickinson *and* Emily Brontë. The family moved to South Bend, Indiana, where Scott could work on a doctorate at Notre Dame and teach undergraduates.

Some of his methods of teaching literature were unusual. For instance, he would give the students Robert Cormier's grim book *I Am the Cheese* to read and analyze. Then, he would give them Shakespeare's *King Lear*, strictly ordering them to read no commentaries or notes, just the text.

He rewrote *Hot Sleep: The Worthing Chronicle* and renamed it *The Worthing Chronicle*. He drastically altered the framework and focus of the story. The old story of "The Tinker" is woven into the narrative. This book goes beyond where *Hot Sleep* ends. Jason Worthing's descendants have power to abolish human suffering, and in the process make humans into little more than contented slaves or puppets. *Should* they?

Contrasts of time and place are better managed in *The Worthing Chronicle*. As Lawrence Charters says in his review, "Practice did come close to perfect."[12] Card asked his publisher to withdraw *Capitol* and *Hot Sleep*.[13]

THE RECESSION CHANGES EVERYTHING

If it had not been for the recession of the early 1980s, Card might have continued the academic life. He likes to teach and has often headed workshops for beginning writers. But he could not support his family on his salary at Notre Dame.

By this time he had written or edited eleven books and received the John W. Campbell Award for the Best New Science Fiction Writer (1978) and the Edmond Hamilton/Leigh Brackett award for *Songmaster*. But in the recession the publishers panicked and stopped giving substantial advances for book manuscripts, and sometimes would not buy at all. A third child was on the way.

GREENSBORO, NORTH CAROLINA

In 1983, the family moved to Greensboro, North Carolina. Scott had an opportunity to be an editor at *Compute!* magazine. He found out the hard way that his personality and talents were hopelessly incompatible with cutthroat office politics, rigid scheduling without compromise for family emergencies, and other aspects of business life.

The job did not last the year. Charles Benjamin (for Charles Dickens) was born. The baby had cerebral palsy and would require much care.

Card has portrayed much of this grim time in his book *Lost Boys*. The book shows clearly, among other things, how a marriage can, painfully, gain more resilience from a crisis, how religious faith can help people through anything, and how loving ward (congregation) members support each other emotionally in trying times.

But real success as a freelance writer was just two years ahead.

BREAKTHROUGH

Card's second revision of the Worthing material was in print in 1983, and the next year saw the publication of the first version of *Saints* (titled *A Woman of Destiny*). This book would win Card his third award, this time from the Association for Mormon Letters.

The breakthrough came in 1985. When working on a book that he had tentatively named *Speaker of Death* (later to be called *Speaker for the Dead*) Card realized that he needed Ender Wiggin in the book, a character of his from the novelette of "Ender's Game" written seven years before. It would have to be Ender as a grown man, with a motivation to travel to the stars. He shelved *Speaker* for the moment, and rewrote *Ender's Game* as a novel, with much detail that the original novelette did not have.

Ender's Game, the novel, won both the Nebula and the Hugo awards in 1986. In 1987, *Speaker for the Dead* also won both these awards. This was the first time that any writer had won both awards in consecutive years. In the rest of the 1980s, Card began the series known as The Tales of Alvin Maker, published the novel *Wyrms,* revised previous books, published more collections of his short stories, was asked to do a novelization of a motion picture (*Abyss*) and was asked to write two books about how to write books.[14] He now had an established reputation as an author.

In 1990, he did a final revision of the Worthing stories. In a book titled *The Worthing Saga,*[15] he reprinted the whole of *The Worthing Chronicle,* essentially unaltered. He added six of the short stories from *Capitol,* and three more stories from the "Forest of Waters" group about Jason Worthing's descendants. The book has an author's introduction and an afterword by Michael Collings.

The Worthing Saga is not the fourth book in a series of sequels, but a combination and culmination of four endeavors to tell essentially the same story over a period of eleven years. (Or twenty years, if we count the first version of "Tinker.") Card says: "The Worthing tales are the root of my work in science fiction."[16]

MARRIAGE AND FAMILY LIFE, AND WHAT THEY MEAN TO CARD'S WRITING

Card believes that every writer needs a Wise Reader. Kristine is the one who most often fills this role. She can do for him what the audience did for him in his early playwriting days. Ideally, as Card sees it, the Wise Reader should *not* be trained in literature. Kristine does not diagnose or prescribe. She does not say things like "There is too much description" or "Your characterization is thin." She says things like "I lost interest about *here*" or "I can't remember who that person is."

Just as an audience never lies during the performance of a play, a Wise Reader cannot be mistaken about her own reactions. If she misunderstood the *story* that just shows that there is a problem to be corrected.

Kristine does not have a total veto power over his writing. Card allowed a story to go to print that Kristine found too sickening to finish.[17] What she does is show him just exactly what he has done. Card says, "She is a part of every page I write. Instead of my writing being a point of conflict in our marriage, as it is with some writers, it is one of the places that we are most closely involved with each other."[18]

THE CARDS' CHILDREN TODAY

The eldest child, Geoffrey, has finished his Mormon mission. He is now designing electronic games in Washington State. He also reviews motion pictures and has written a novelization of one. (See the appendix.) Emily, the eldest daughter, is showing promise as an actress. Charlie Ben, born with cerebral palsy, died of natural causes at age seventeen. He never did walk or talk, but he did take real pleasure in life. When he was small, his father would toss him in the air; the child would shriek with delight, starfishing his arms and legs. Card dedicated his collection of shorter fiction, *Maps in a Mirror*, "To Charlie Ben, who can fly."[19]

Since Charlie Ben had a loving elder brother and elder sister, he knew how to be an older brother (within his limitations) when Zina Margaret (named for Margaret Mitchell) was born. Zina is still young.

The fifth child, Erin Louisa (for Louisa May Alcott) died seven hours after her birth.

When the Cards are asked how many children they have had, they always say "five" and do not necessarily explain that only three are still living.

There are duties of an established writer: speaking tours, autograph sessions, attendance at conferences, and such. While Card enjoys meeting his readers—he takes an honest pleasure in being liked—these extra duties take him away from his family more than he would prefer. He has websites by which fans can keep in touch with him. He hasn't stopped all "tours," but his websites help him to keep them under control.

PILGRIM FROM UTAH

Scott Card's parents went to Utah, partly so that they could raise their children as good Mormons. Scott and Kristine Card left Utah partly for that same reason.

The Cards feel that the dangers of hypocrisy, complacency, and financial corruption of the faith are particularly present in the majority church in any given area. Thus, in Utah, these temptations would be strongest among Mormons. In other places, these temptations would be most evident in Methodists, or in Presbyterians, or in Lutherans, or in Catholics, whatever was the most "normal" or accepted church.

As the Cards see it, if almost everyone belongs to one denomination, no one needs to ask himself or herself, "Do I really believe it?" But when one's denomination is a minority, one must ask that question, and answer others who ask it. In a majority denomination, congregations ("wards," as Mormons would say) are identified with neighborhoods: the wealthy ward, the ward for educated people, the ward from the "bad" part of town, and so forth. But in a minority church, the members must associate with people outside their income group or education level. It becomes more democratic, more "broadening" and there are fewer prejudices.

Every lay Mormon adult is supposed to have a "calling," some significant task he or she does for the church. In Utah, the ward leaders didn't know what to do with Card's particular abilities, and there was rarely a calling for him. Kristine, on the other hand, once had five callings at the same time. When the ward leaders offered Kristine a sixth calling, (teaching nine-year-olds), Scott stepped in firmly to save his overburdened wife. *He* insisted on teaching the nine-year-olds, and he loved it. But he would never have gotten it, in Utah, if he hadn't insisted. In Indiana, and in North Carolina, he gets his callings readily, without having to insist. Mormons are in short supply; *everyone* is needed.

Card wrote on this topic in his online column in the interfaith website known as Belifnet.[20] He got responses, pro and con, not all of them from Mormons. An interesting response in agreement is from a New Zealand Jew, who claims that the worst place to be a practicing Jew is in Israel!

FAITH AND WRITING

Card has never stopped writing for the Mormon church. He just stopped depending on such writing as a source of income. Besides revisions of the musical play about Moses, *Stone Tables*, he did the Hill Cummorah Pageant *America's Witness for Christ* in 1988. In 1997, he wrote the musical drama *Barefoot to Zion*. He has composed poetry and hymns. These are just examples. This dimension of his writing is beyond the scope of this book; more detail on his ongoing written work for his church is in *Storyteller: Orson Scott Card*, by Michael Collings.[21]

NOTES

1. Details about the life of Orson Scott Card are scattered in multiple places. He has candidly answered many questions, many times, in face-to-face interviews, online interviews, and in panel participations. He tells many things about himself in a collection of his speeches and essays entitled *A Storyteller in Zion* (Salt Lake City: Bookcraft, 2000). He also recounts significant parts of his life in places in his two books on writing: *Characters and Viewpoint*, (Cincinnati: Writer's Digest Books, 1988) and *How to Write Science Fiction and Fantasy*, (Cincinnati: Writer's Digest Books, 1990.)

Often, there is something personal told in a preface or afterword to one of his stories or books, or even in his comments on other writers' stories in anthologies that he has edited.

A very quick outline of his life can be found in *Orson Scott Card: A Reader's Checklist and Reference Guide*, (Middletown, Conn.: Checkerbee, 1999). Much of what is original in this brief biography comes from an interview at his home on September 12, 2000. Exact citations are given only when the exact words of Card (or of others) are being used.

2. Orson Scott Card, *Red Prophet* (New York: Tom Doherty Associates, Tor, 1988), dedication page.

3. Orson Scott Card has always been "Scott" to family and friends. When reference is made in this chapter to childhood years, he will be called "Scott." As the narrative moves more into his writing and publishing, he will be called "Scott Card" or "Card" (except when speaking of personal matters only indirectly related to his writing).

After this chapter, he will consistently be "Card" for the rest of the book.

4. Orson Scott Card, "How Lloyd Biggle, Jr. Changed My Life," foreword and afterword to "Tunesmith" by Lloyd Biggle, Jr., in *Tor Double #27* (with "Eye for Eye" by Orson Scott Card) (New York: Tom Doherty Associates, Tor, 1987), 99–112 and 181–186.

5. Card, *How to Write Science Fiction and Fantasy*, 122.

6. Orson Scott Card, *Capitol* (New York: Ace, 1979). Out of print.

7. Bradley Sinor, *Science Fiction and Fantasy Book Review,* April 1979, 27.

8. Orson Scott Card, *Hot Sleep: The Worthing Chronicle* (New York: Baronet, 1979; New York: Ace, 1979). Both editions out of print.

9. Fred Niederman, *Science Fiction and Fantasy Book Review,* December 1979, 155.

10. Michael Bishop, *Magazine of Fantasy and Science Fiction,* January 1980, 35.

11. Orson Scott Card, preface to "A Gift from the Greylanders" by Michael Bishop, in *Future on Fire,* ed. Orson Scott Card (New York: Tom Doherty Associates, Tor, 1991), 70.

12. Lawrence I. Charters, *Science Fiction and Fantasy Book Review,* November 1983, 19.

13. Card and his publishers were successful in eliminating *Capitol* and *Hot Sleep.* I made three appeals to book finders to get a copy of *Capitol* and seven to get a copy of *Hot Sleep.*

14. See the two titles on book writing in note 1.

15. Orson Scott Card, *The Worthing Saga* (New York: Tom Doherty Associates, Tor, 1990).

16. Card, *The Worthing Saga,* ix.

17. Orson Scott Card, "A Thousand Deaths," short story in *Maps in a Mirror* (New York: Tom Doherty Associates, Tor, 1990), 140–151; afterword, 263–264.

18. Card, *How to Write Science Fiction and Fantasy,* 123.

19. Card, *Maps in a Mirror,* dedication page.

20. Orson Scott Card, "Mountain Saints and Minority Mormons," www.belief.net/story/35/story_3518_1.html

21. Michael R. Collings, *Storyteller: Orson Scott Card* (Woodstock, Ga: Overlook Connection Press, 2001).

Part I

ENDER'S GAME, THE SHADOW BOOKS, AND THE SPEAKER TRILOGY

Chapter 1

Ender's Game

PREQUELS TO *ENDER'S GAME*

"Polish Boy"[1]

Twice the aliens from space, known as "buggers" have invaded our solar system. In the exigency of war, humanity has united under one rule, that of the Hegemon. The Hegemon tries to limit families to two children, but some whole nations are "noncompliant," especially Catholic ones. Life is hard in these noncompliant nations.

The Wieczorek family, in Poland, home schools its nine children. They don't realize that the seventh, John Paul, is reading college-level books. They think that this child, not quite six, is just pretending to read.

The International Fleet (I.F.) discovers John Paul's precocity. He might be the one who can command the human space fleet against the buggers, succeeding the legendary Mazer Rackham. John Paul is not interested in fighting, but he *is* interested in his family having a better life. In the big cities of America noncompliant Poles can get better jobs. Children can be sent to different schools to avoid awkward questions. John Paul agrees to go to Battle School if his family can go to America.

John Paul will not keep his word. However, Captain Graff of the I.F. will take a long-term gamble: Get the family out of Poland. Change the name to Wiggin, and stake the chances of humanity's survival on the next generation.

"Teacher's Pest"[2]

Theresa Brown, a graduate instructor, has worked hard on her research project, but her name will be removed from it. The work will continue under other authorship. She will get her graduate degree; this university is more independent than most. Her father Admiral Brown, a Mormon, resigned in protest over the Hegemon's population laws. The daughter is being punished for the father's reputation.

She is being courted, persistently and annoyingly, by one of her students. John Paul Wiggin's family came from noncompliant Poland when he was six. He and Theresa have common cause against the population laws. Eventually, Theresa stops considering John Paul to be a pest and gets acquainted. They stimulate each other's thoughts and conclusions. They realize that they may be manipulated tools in someone else's eugenics program, but they don't let that stop them from love.

ENDER'S GAME: THE BOOK THAT BEGAN CARD'S WIDESPREAD REPUTATION

The Wiggin's firstborn is Peter, who is brilliant enough, and certainly ruthless enough, but lacks the integrity and empathy that a commander needs. The next is Valentine, who has brilliance and empathy but is insufficiently ruthless. The Wiggin family receives unusual government permission to have a third.

This is Andrew, called "Ender" from his sister's early pronunciation of his name. He does not like to fight, but when compelled to defend himself at six years old against a bully his age named Stilson, he mercilessly kicks chest, face, and groin when the boy is down. He does this to terrorize Stilson's friends, to *end* all chances of further conflict.

Ender wonders if he is just as bad as his brother Peter, who makes both Valentine and Ender miserable and threatens to kill them. But Colonel Graff of the International Fleet is sure that Ender is the one. The reasons for Ender's ruthless self-defense—to *end* the conflict—are significant. Graff does not tell Ender that Stilson died.

Ender enters Battle School three years younger than most of the other students. Battle School is in orbit above Earth, and there Ender is trained with other recruits in combat without gravity. There are battles (called "games") of one "army" of forty students and their commander, against another army in a zero-gravity battle room. They use weapons that "freeze" the opposing "soldiers." Competent soldiers get promoted to commander by the teachers of Battle School. All must overcome their old gravity-based orientations of direction. Ender does this by saying, "The enemy gate is *down*."[3]

Ender's first commander, Bonzo, will not even let Ender fire his weapon, because he is young and small. But a girl soldier, Petra, teaches Ender how to shoot. There is also help from a Muslim soldier, Alai. Ender gets traded to an army where he has a chance to fight, and is soon at the top of the standings.

Bonzo, who now looks foolish, is Ender's bitter enemy. Most soldiers who fight with or against Ender are his admirers. But admirers are not always friends. Graff and others have isolated Ender to help him develop toughness. Although isolated, Ender is a caring person. He organizes training for new students of the kind he wishes he had had.

Back on Earth, Peter and Valentine are having their own kind of genius growth. The family has moved from a crowded city to Greensboro, North Carolina, where it is still possible to have lakes and woods, rare on Earth now. They hoped that the surroundings might cure Peter of his cruelty, but it has only made him more subtle. Instead of tormenting young children, he secretly torments small animals.

With Valentine, Peter plots his own way to power. They get a reputation on the computer nets, using false names so that no one knows that they are children. Valentine is shocked at her own persuasive power. Graff makes use of her twice, to remotivate Ender, who continues to fear that he is just like Peter.

Ender becomes a Battle School commander. One of his soldiers is a boy even younger and smaller than Ender was when he first arrived at the school. His name is Bean; he is very quick, a sharp soldier, self-confident to the point of being cocky. The teachers set up an "impossible" schedule for Ender's army, with unusual arrangements in the battle room, or unannounced rule changes that stack the odds in favor of the other side. Ender continues to win, with Bean helping him think up dirty tricks to counter the teachers' dirty tricks.

Bonzo's anger at Ender becomes literally murderous. He traps Ender alone in the shower room. Again, when Bonzo attacks, Ender defends himself without restraint. In the midst of self-hatred and depression Ender receives the assignment of another battle, this time against two armies at once! He is ready to quit, but with Bean silently waiting for orders, he decides on a trick instead, which is not quite against the rules; it just "isn't done." He is reproved, and then transferred to Command School. Nobody has ever been sent to Command School before age sixteen.

Bonzo goes home in a body bag. Once again, Ender is not told that his self-defense was lethal. Graff was aware of the situation and chose to remain hands off. Ender must remain self-reliant. Graff and others had felt reasonably sure that Ender could take care of himself, but had not expected death.

On the way to Command School, which is located on an asteroid, Ender learns some important things: The training at Battle School was not to create a force to *defend* humanity against a Third Invasion of our solar system; it is to train officers to command a space fleet to *attack* the buggers' home world. Seventy years ago space ships with fighters were launched. The humans, not the buggers, are the Third Invasion.

These space ships, and the buggers' ships—like everything else in the universe—must travel below the speed of light, but that is no limit to *communication*. The buggers communicate instantly, by telepathy. Humans have a new invention, the "ansible" by which it is possible for a commander to give orders to ships stellar distances away.[4] Graff (who now has full charge of Ender) tells him that the human invasion force will reach the buggers' home world in five years.

Ender asks why humanity is fighting the buggers. Since we are not telepathic they may not even know that we are intelligent life, he argues. Perhaps now they know, and will leave us alone. Graff points out that the buggers struck first. Is it possible to trust a known enemy when one cannot communicate? The buggers don't know what reading, writing, or signals mean; it has been tried. Are they trying to send thoughts? Who knows? Any theory that they will not attack again is gambling the survival of all humanity.

At Command School, Ender receives a special tutor who calls himself Ender's "enemy." The tutor is Mazer Rackham, hero of the Battle of the Asteroid Belt. Twenty years after Rackham's victory he was put in a space ship and sent away from the solar system at a speed near the speed of light. This "relativistic" speed ensured that he would age far more slowly. While he was on the ship only eight years passed for him, although fifty years passed on Earth. This keeps him young enough to train the commander of the Third Invasion. He himself cannot command. He says that Ender has not yet had enough psychology to understand why.

Ender learns more. The buggers are fully insectoid, like ants or bees. A hive is centered around a queen, who communicates with her workers not in telepathic *words* but more in the way that the brain communicates with a hand or foot. A bugger hive does not act in discipline, everyone *obeying* the leader; everyone *is* an extension *of* the leader, with no choice. The only true "person" in each hive is the queen, the only one with independent rational thought, the only one with a genetic future.

Rackham won the Battle of the Belt with a lucky shot, exploding the queen's ship. When the queen was dead, the whole invasion force died. Without that shot, it is likely that Earth would have become a bugger colony. Whether or not they knew they were killing thinking beings, the fact remains that they *were* killing thinking beings. Due to the hive-mind, with the queen as the only "person," it could be said that the buggers killed thousands, but just one of them was killed.

Ender learns of a new weapon, the Molecular Detachment Device (M.D. Device for short, and thus nicknamed "Little Doctor"). Its explosion grows as it encounters matter while exploding. It cannot be used on the surface of a planet (as atomic weapons have been), but it is ideal for attacking a tight swarm of space ships.

Ender is now introduced to a new stage of his training. He will speak orders to unseen squadron leaders through a microphone. These leaders will then each pass on these orders to the ships portrayed on the simulator. This parallels conditions of combat. The squadron leaders are not strangers; they are Petra, Bean, Alai, and all the rest of the best of the other Battle School students. Further, Ender is informed that he will no longer be playing programmed computer games. He will play against Mazer Rackham.

These battles rapidly get harder. As stress mounts, Ender has nightmares. He gnaws his hand. The squadron leaders feel the tension. Petra, his best tactician, collapses during a battle and nearly causes a disastrous loss.

Then one morning he is allowed to sleep late. Today is his final examination in Command School: He will command a battle game staged around a planet. The simulator shows the assignment. It is hopeless! There are thousands of enemy ships for every human one. Ender is about to yield to despair when in his earphones he hears Bean say, "Remember, the enemy gate is *down*."[5]

That's it! Make a suicide plunge right down toward the planetary surface. Then launch the Little Doctor and blow up the planet. This will also destroy all the enemy fleet as the Little Doctor expands; (it will also destroy the rest of the human fleet.) This is improper, unfair, and not allowed! Ender doubts that the simulator is equipped to show an exploding planet. It will end any hope of getting a real command.

It is like his last fight in Battle School; if Mazer gives him an unfair challenge, he will win unfairly. Then he will go home and drift on a lake near Greensboro.

He instructs his squadron leaders to form a thick cylinder. This cylinder is dodged, switched, and feinted (with heavy losses) through the enemy fleet; then the surviving fighters drop straight in. The Little Doctor is launched. The planet explodes, taking all remaining space ships of both sides.

Graff, Rackham, and other adults are cheering, praying, or weeping. Ender is embraced. Now he is told the truth. He has never played a game against Mazer Rackham. For months now, he has been the commander of the I.F. space forces, fighting the buggers. It was real human pilots he sent to their deaths. It was real, thinking beings, all the queens and all their children, that he has exterminated.

Graff explains why the trick was necessary. Anyone with empathy enough to win loyalty from his followers and to understand the enemy could never be the merciless killer that was needed. Mazer explains that they needed a child's quick reflexes without the caution of experience. "Any decent person who knows what warfare is can never go into battle with a whole heart. . . . We made sure you didn't know."[6] Nothing that anyone can say matters to Ender. He is in collapse. At age eleven, he is a world-destroyer.

The end of the bugger menace brings war between humans. Both sides want Ender, either to lead them or to destroy before the others get him, but Ender is in a coma for the whole five days of the war and is closely guarded.

When it is over, Peter is on the way to being the world dictator. He has made a proposal through his Net identity, Locke, that has ended the war on Earth. It delays a world war that could have lasted for lifetimes. The irony is not lost on Ender. Peter, the cruel and sadistic brother has saved millions of lives, while Ender has killed billions.

Graff is tried for the deaths of Stilson and Bonzo, but acquitted on a plea of wartime necessity. Ender finally learns about these deaths. They weigh heavily too.

Ender gradually realizes that if he returns to Earth he would be Peter's tool. Ender and Valentine emigrate, with many others, to one of the former bugger colonies. Ender studies the buildings and artifacts of the buggers to learn what he can.

One day, telepathically guided, he finds something carefully hidden: the pupa of a queen bugger, fertilized, ready to hatch a hundred thousand baby buggers. The queen-mind has within it all the history of the species. In his mind, Ender can see his invasion of the home planet as the hive queen saw it, the terrible fighters coming through the dark. He feels the feeling, not in words, but he can translate it into words: "They did not forgive us . . . we will surely die" and also "We thought we were the only thinking beings in the universe. . . . Never did we dream that thought could arise from lonely animals who cannot dream each other's dreams. How were we to know? We could live with you in peace. Believe us, believe us."[7]

Like Ender, they had unknowingly killed thinking beings. He perceives in his mind the recipe for bringing the pupa to life, to bring back the species. He can't do it; humanity would kill them again. He makes a promise that he will travel from world to world until he finds a place where the hive queen can be safely brought to life.

He writes a book, *The Hive Queen*, telling the story of the buggers, with all its greatness and all its failures. He signs it "Speaker For The Dead." The book is read all over Earth. Almost no one knows that the author is the same person as the boy hero (or boy villain) Ender, who killed all the hive queens. Ender's book gives rise to a semi-religious practice. A Speaker for the Dead will stand by the grave and tell the truth about the deceased, hiding no faults, pretending no virtues, yet trying to speak from the deceased's point of view.

Peter Wiggin, Hegemon of Earth, now elderly while Ender is still young due to the relativistic effect of space travel, guesses who wrote *The Hive Queen*. He asks Ender to write a book to Speak for him. Ender truthfully writes of his brother's crimes and virtues. This book is also signed "Speaker For The Dead." The two books become bound in one volume, *The Hive Queen and the Hegemon*, which become revered as sacred volumes.

Ender resumes his quest to find a home for the hive queen.

SOME MEANINGS OF THE STORY

There are equal, and opposite, meanings that can be taken from this story. One might go like this:

> For the survival of humanity, anything is justified. It is bad to lie to children; it is bad to destroy another intelligent species. But if it is to be them or us that survives, we must do what we must. We should give *ourselves* and our descendants the benefit of any doubt.

This we might call the position of the Patriot. Another person might say this:

> There are things so evil that even the survival of humanity cannot justify them. If we become the destroyers of children's innocence, if we wipe out another intelligent species (when we are not even sure that they know what they are doing) we are no better than they, possibly worse. As long as there is any doubt, we should give our potential *victims* the benefit of the doubt. And, if we perish, we perish.

This we might call the position of the pacifist.

So, which one is "right"? Card has quite deliberately raised the stakes on each side to the highest point. The staunchest patriot, the most devoted pacifist, might each tremble at what his position forces him to defend. Of one thing, Card is certain. If this situation ever becomes real, those in charge *will* make the patriot's decision. As Graff puts it, "Nature can't evolve a species that hasn't a will to survive. Individuals might be bred to sacrifice themselves, but the race as a whole can never decide to cease to exist."[8]

What, then, shall we say of the unknowing tool, such as Ender, who works horrors without knowing it? Is he guilty? Is he responsible?

In Battle School, Ender, acting in defense of a student who was persecuted, signed himself "God." This was just a piece of whimsy; he meant nothing. But, in regard to Stilson, Bonzo, and the buggers, Ender *was* a god. He had, although he did not know it, taken on himself the awesome right of life or death, survival or extinction.

A person who "plays God" is left with two choices: He can become utterly hardened to all suffering and dreadful consequence, justifying his right to cause it. This is the decision to become a Satan. This is the position of Nero, Ghengis Khan, Hitler, or Stalin. The other choice is to take on himself the burden of the suffering he has caused, without any quibbles about his own degree of guilt. Instead of being a Satan, he becomes a Christ-bearer, or, at least a Christian martyr, devoting his life to healing and rebuilding, regardless of the cost to himself. This choice is developed in the last books of the series, *Speaker for the Dead, Xenocide*, and *Children of the Mind*.

Card evokes comparisons to World War II; for example, "Battle of the Belt" echoes "Battle of the Bulge." The most controversial aspect of World War II was the dropping of atomic bombs on Japan. At the time, it seemed right. It seemed that the only other way to get Japan to surrender was to make an invasion that would cost the lives of thousands of Allied soldiers.

The bombs caused suffering of a kind never experienced before. The crew that dropped the first bomb exclaimed: "My God! What have we done?" The pilot of the advance airplane later became a pacifist, active in the anti-nuclear movement after the war. One of the scientists who developed the bomb said, "The scientists have now known sin!" and quoted from an ancient Hindu writing, "I am become the destroyer of worlds."

But the British prime minister, Winston Churchill, called the bombs "a miracle of deliverance"—there are many who would agree. The Axis powers were evil and strong. If they had conquered the world we would all have suffered. Did we become something almost as bad as they, in defeating them? Or not?

The immediate result was a Cold War nuclear standoff with the Soviet Union. Did we really accomplish anything? Or, on the other hand, was it the horror of the nuclear weapons that kept the standoff mostly Cold, instead of Hot? In Ender's universe, ending the buggers meant human war, ending in a world dictatorship. Was the extinction of the buggers worth it? Or not?

In some degree, these same questions are asked, after even a small war, or even when the police open fire on the street. People will say, "Did we *really* need to do that?" Card will not give you an easy answer. But he says to both the patriot and the pacifist: "Will you pay the *full* price of your position? It may be higher than you think."

THE ROOTS OF THE STORY[9]

In 1967, Orson Scott Card's older brother went off to boot camp to prepare for the possibility of fighting in Vietnam. This put military subjects on Card's mind. He had read novels about training pilots in World War I and the problems of teaching them to look for enemy planes in three dimensions. Card, in his middle teens at this time, knew that he wanted to be a science fiction writer. How could one train for combat in *space*? Without gravity there is no clear up and down. He imagined a gravity-free battle room, trainees with handheld weapons that could "freeze" soldiers of the other army.

Years later, when he was waiting for a friend who was taking children to the circus, he realized that the trainees should be children, since they would not have so much to unlearn. He took out a notebook and jotted: "Remember, the enemy gate is *down*."

Even later, he wrote a novelette, "Ender's Game," printed in *Analog Science Fact and Fiction* in August 1977. The novelette won second place for the Hugo award for short fiction of 1977 and Card received the John W. Campbell award for "Best New Writer." Card had no idea, at this time, of expanding the story to a novel or of doing any sequels.[10]

In 1980, Card was trying to write a book that would become *Speaker for the Dead*. It wasn't working well. He needed a lead character of a particular type, and he didn't have it. (We will have more to say about this in chapter 3.) Then he realized it was Ender that he needed. But the novelette didn't tell enough about Ender.

So Card went back to "Ender's Game." He gave Ender a family, with an older brother and sister. Card patterned them after his own older brother and sister as he remembered them at age ten, and then exaggerated wildly. He gave Ender two enemies to kill before he became a planet-killer.

Most significantly of all, he gave a name, face, and characteristics to the enemy of humanity. In the novelette, the aliens are simply "the enemy," and the enemy has neither name nor description. Nothing is said in the novelette about the impossibility of communication. The novel changes this. In the novel, when fighting the enemy, they are the "buggers." When Ender tries to rescue a survivor and her brood, the name is "the hive queen." The reader can now relate to these beings.

The novel *Ender's Game* was published in 1984. First reviews were mixed; it was a problem giving the story a fair review without giving away the significant surprise. A fairly typical review summarized the story down to Command School, then said: "This sounds like the synopsis of a grade Z . . . science-fiction-rip-off. . . . But Mr. Card has shaped this . . . material into an affecting novel full of surprises that seem inevitable once they are explained."[11]

The book won both the Hugo and the Nebula, the two most prestigious awards in science fiction. It appeared on the recommended lists of young adult literature published by the American Library Association. In spite of this, (teens are often biased against recommended books) it was, and is, a hit with teens. Over the years it has been translated into at least twenty different languages. Although Card had already published some books, this was the book that began his national, and international, reputation.

THE TWO DIFFERENT BRANCHES OF THE STORY

The "Speaker Trilogy" Branch

Card continues Ender's story in three more books: *Speaker for the Dead, Xenocide,* and *Children of the Mind.* In these books Ender is a grown man, and the action takes place in worlds far from Earth. These books are discussed in chapter 3.

The "Shadow Books" Branch

First, in *Ender's Shadow,* a parallel book to *Ender's Game,* we see Battle School, Command School, and the victory from Bean's viewpoint. We see Ender as Bean sees him, but do not hear Ender's thoughts. Then in the next three books (*Shadow of the Hegemon, Shadow Puppets,* and *Shadow of the Giant*) we follow a narrative of the Earth and humanity in turmoil, with former Battle School students in the middle. After the first Shadow Book, Ender is not present except as a memory.

NOTES

1. Orson Scott Card, "Polish Boy," in *First Meetings: Three Stories from the Endervrse* (Burton, Mich.: Subterranean Press, 2002), 9–53.

2. Orson Scott Card, "Teacher's Pest," in a paperback edition of *First Meetings* (forthcoming).

3. Orson Scott Card, *Ender's Game: The Definitive Edition* (New York: Tom Doherty Associates, Tor, 1985, 1991), with an introduction by the author, 64. This phrase is often repeated.

4. Along with other science fiction writers, Card borrowed the idea of the ansible from the books of Ursula K. LeGuin. He gives her credit in Orson Scott Card, *How to Write Science Fiction and Fantasy* (Cincinnati: Writer's Digest Books), 44.

5. Card, *Ender's Game,* 205.

6. Card, *Ender's Game,* 209.

7. Card, *Ender's Game,* 223–224.

8. Card, *Ender's Game,* 178.

9. The biographical data and publishing history of this section is compiled from "Orson Scott Card: Jack of Many Trades," *Locus* 20, no. 6 (June 1987): 5, 56–58; Card, *How to Write Science Fiction and Fantasy,* 27; Orson Scott Card, *Maps in a Mirror: The Short Fiction of Orson Scott Card* (New York: Tom Doherty Associates, Tor, 1990), endnote to the novelette "Ender's Game," 665, 667–668; an introduction to the author's definitive edition of *Ender's Game,* pages not numbered; "Orson Scott Card: Creative Chaos," an article based on an interview, *Locus* 28, no. 1 (January 1992): 5, 75; Orson Scott Card, "The Ender Series," a foreword to his novella "Investment Counselor," in *Far Horizons,* ed. Robert Silverberg (New York: Avon Books, 1999), 89–91; Orson Scott Card, preface to *Ender's Shadow* (New York: Tom Doherty Associates, Tor, 1999), 11–12.

10. Card included the original novelette of "Ender's Game" in collections of his own short fiction: *First Meetings,* 97–149; *Maps in a Mirror,* 541–566; and in his audiotape, *Elephants of Posnan and Other Stories* (San Bruno, Calif.: Fantastic Audio, 2001).

11. Gerald Jonas, Science Fiction Department, "New York Times Book Review." *New York Times,* July 16, 1984, section 7.

Chapter 2

The Shadow Books

Ender's Shadow, Shadow of the
Hegemon, and *Shadow Puppets*

BEAN AND HIS RELATIONSHIPS

Bean and Poke

Bean is the product of an illegal experiment in genetic engineering, although he knows nothing about this. He is small; at four years old he looks to be two. He speaks like a ten-year-old. His powers of deduction would do credit to a mature adult. To survive, he joins a "crew" (juvenile gang) on the streets of Rotterdam in the Netherlands. This crew is led by Poke, a nine-year-old girl, too tenderhearted to turn away a starving baby, yet tough enough to protect her crew from the bullies, the older children of twelve or thirteen.

Poke and the other children of the crew take down a bully named Achilles (so named because of a limp) to recruit him as their protector. Bean distrusts Achilles and wants Poke to kill him. But Achilles wins over the crew, calls them his "family," and eventually kills Poke. Bean never quite forgives himself for not preventing Poke's death.

Bean and Ender

Sister Carlotta of the Order of Saint Nicholas, is a recruiter for the International Fleet. She finds unusual children who can be trained to fight the fearsome alien species, the buggers (the scientific name is "the

Formics") in the event of a Third Invasion. Sister Carlotta discovers Bean's intelligence and gets him into Battle School.

There, Bean is compared to a student called Ender Wiggin, also bright and young, but not quite so small. Bean is helped by a girl soldier named Petra, about four years older than he. Bean hacks the computer system, hides in the ducts, spies on the teachers' conferences, and uses his "desk" (laptop) *only* for what he wants the teachers to read. Bean's creed is straightforward: "Know, Think, Choose, Do."[1]

Bean, at first, is suspicious of Ender. Achilles was idolized by Poke's crew; Ender is greatly admired by younger students that he helps. Is this Ender just another Achilles? When Bean finds otherwise, he becomes Ender's greatest admirer.

Bean is assigned to select an army for Ender to command in the battle games. Bean includes himself on the roster. Bean needs only one practice to learn that "The enemy gate is *down*,"[2] in his instincts. As the battle games escalate, Ender appoints Bean to direct a special squad to employ dirty tricks to counter the teachers' dirty tricks.

Ender is in danger from his old commander Bonzo, who had traded him away and now looks foolish. Bean and Petra try different ways to protect Ender. But when the attack comes, neither Bean nor Petra is there. Ender defends himself without restraint, and Bonzo is killed. Bean is humbled. If only Poke had had Ender, not Bean, to protect her!

When the teachers give Ender's army a battle game against two armies at once, Bean and Ender devise a trick that technically wins the game. Ender is then sent to Command School. No one has gone there before age sixteen. Ender is not yet eleven.

When Bean (and all the rest of the best of Ender's other allies and opponents in Battle School) eventually join Ender in Command School, Bean is made Ender's secret backup. If Ender cannot, or will not, "pass his final examination" (i.e., totally destroy the world of the Formics) command of the fleet will pass to Bean.

Bean has deduced that these computer "games" at Command School are not training exercises. Real humans are dying as a result of the orders that these children send out by ansible. Real intelligent beings will have their very world destroyed. Ender has not realized this, at least not consciously. Bean hopes strongly that Ender, the unknowing one, will be the world-destroyer, if it must be so. It must be Ender's game.

The day of the final battle comes, and the human ships face overwhelming odds from the Formics. Ender, at first, does nothing. Bean can see no solution either. In ironic despair, Bean says, "Remember, the enemy gate is *down*."[3]

Ender, then, devises the suicide plunge to the planet with the Molecular Detachment Device that destroys the Formics' world, fleet, and surviving human ships.

When the secret is revealed, the rest of Ender's army feels anguish almost as much as Ender himself does. For Bean, it is different. He experienced extreme anguish *during* the last "game," fully aware that he was helping to destroy a world and send fellow humans to certain death. He did it simply because there was nothing else that could be done. Afterward, Bean is empathetic to the feelings of Ender and the others.

Human war breaks out almost at once after the Formics are defeated. It is ended by the proposals of Ender's brother, Peter, using his Net identity, "Locke." Ender and his sister Valentine leave for colonies in space. None of the Battle School children ever see Ender again. They return to their respective families.

Bean and Sister Carlotta

Bean also has a family. Sister Carlotta discovers the couple whose genetic material had been stolen for the illegal experiment. Bean's genetic parents take him into their arms with benediction, but he doesn't have long to stay with them.

The Battle School children are being kidnapped, especially the ones who formed Ender's "jeesh" or private army. Petra is the first. There is an attempt to murder Bean and his family, an attempt that takes the lives of their unsuspecting neighbors.

Bean goes in a separate direction from his genetic parents, accompanied by Sister Carlotta. They use assumed names and Sister Carlotta poses as Bean's grandmother.

Achilles is behind the kidnappings. Bean had tricked confessions out of him and gotten him into an asylum for the criminally insane. Achilles has escaped. He sells his tactical skills to Russia first, then India. Achilles is always really working for himself.

Bean and Sister Carlotta meet with Peter Wiggin but don't really trust him. Yet, they form an alliance. Peter, too, is out for himself, but he does not commit whimsical murders as Achilles does. Peter wants to be Hegemon of Earth. This is now a nominal office, but he hopes to make it powerful again and secure world peace under himself. Bean wants to rescue Petra, whom Achilles took with him when he fled to Russia.

Sister Carlotta has feared for Bean's soul, not because he is unbaptized or because he does not profess a creed, but because he has seemed to have no goal higher than his own survival. Now that he has a goal, she is anxious that Bean not become Peter's tool. To Carlotta, ends do *not* justify means. Compromise is necessary, but the heart must remain fixed on the noblest goal. She consistently takes the long view, the perspective of Eternity.

Shortly after Bean and Sister Carlotta make an alliance with Peter, they all go in separate directions. Bean senses that Sister Carlotta knows something about his origins and nature that she has not told him. He tells her that he cannot fully trust her.

Bean ends up in Thailand, helping to plan strategy against invasion from India, where Achilles holds Petra. Bean finds his life in immediate danger from a Thai superior who is suborned by Achilles. Bean, with a loyal Thai comrade, escapes from a building just before it is blown up. He gets out a message on the Net to Peter and Sister Carlotta. The message explains the situation, and says that he and his comrade will come out of hiding when they can see Sister Carlotta and a high official of the Thai government.

Sister Carlotta is halfway around the world at this moment, but she goes into action with her Vatican contacts. The Prime Minister of Thailand gets a personal telephone call from the Pope. Bean's treacherous superior is driven away under police escort. Then Sister Carlotta flies to Thailand. Achilles, furious that Bean has escaped him, arranges to have Sister Carlotta's airplane shot down. All on board are killed.

She had prepared an encrypted letter for Bean on the Net to be released in the event of her sudden death. Along with many expressions of love for this son of her heart, she urges him to forego vengeance. "Anger makes people stupid, even people as bright as you. Achilles must be stopped because of what he is, not because of anything he did to me."[4] Then, she tells Bean about his genetic alteration, known as "Anton's Key."

Bean's brain will continue to develop, his body will continue to grow. His body will never stop growing until it gets so massive that his heart fails, or his spine collapses. Then he will die. Death will probably happen between ages fifteen and twenty. He is about nine now. She urges Bean not to be reckless with the time remaining, but not to be over-careful either. "Death is not a tragedy. To have wasted life, that is the tragedy."[5] In heaven, she will still pray for him.

The news of his inescapable early death is, of course, highly significant to Bean. But this evidence of Sister Carlotta's love is overwhelmingly powerful, more so than he realizes at the time. Her advice about revenge sinks into his very being and influences all decisions he makes from that moment on.

Bean feels guilty for the death of Sister Carlotta, just as he did for that of Poke. He raises a cenotaph with their names on it in his new home town in Brazil. He vows that a dear friend will never again die when he could and should have prevented it.

Bean and Peter

From the moment the kidnappings of former Battle School students begins, Bean remembers that there is one sibling of Ender and Valentine left on Earth, and gets his help. Peter has accumulated worldwide respect through his Net persona of "Locke" and he is vital in breaking the alliance that Achilles has in Russia and causing Achilles to flee to India, taking Petra with him.

However, Peter decides for himself when, and how, to use his influence. Achilles likes to think of himself as "Machiavellian." But it is Peter, not Achilles, that (at least as far as Bean can see) lives by the philosophy of Niccolò Machiavelli, the fifteenth-century writer. Machiavelli taught that it is a *disadvantage* to a ruler to be "merciful, faithful, humane, religious or upright,"[6] but that it is essential that a ruler *appear* to have these qualities. Ruthless acts must be done indirectly.

World War II is frequently referred to in the Shadow Books. Hitler was a "madman" ruthlessly sending men, women, and children into poison gas chambers by the millions. Achilles is much like Hitler. Stalin was the slow, calculating Machiavellian who instituted "reforms" that led, indirectly, to the deaths by starvation of men, women, and children by the millions.

Peter, in his attempts to become a powerful Hegemon of Earth, seems much like a Stalin. At one point, he deliberately withholds information that, if he had published it promptly, would have shortened a war in Asia. Protecting his reputation, Peter releases the data at a time that suits his interests. When he does release it, Achilles goes to China.

Bean leaves Asia, having rescued Petra. He brings with him a commando force, all volunteers, to put at the disposal of Peter, the Hegemon, now headquartered in Brazil. This commando force is similar, on a grander scale, to the "dirty tricks" squad he once organized for Ender in Battle School. It is an important addition to Peter's slender power. Bean despises Peter, but knows that he is the best powerful alternative in the world to Achilles. He makes the decision, as the Allies did in

World War II, to work with the Machiavellian in order to defeat the madman.

Years pass, and China swallows up India and Thailand, but Vietnam is halted on the western frontier by the solidarity of the Islamic nations. Bean grows, and is now tall. Then it appears that China (like Russia and India before her) will no longer trust or use Achilles; they are planning to imprison him. Peter decides that perhaps *he* can use Achilles. He uses the commando force that Bean gave him to rescue Achilles and bring him to Hegemon headquarters in Brazil.

Bean cannot accept this. He and Petra leave Peter and go their own way. But Peter is a more complex person than Bean realizes and has some changes ahead of him.

Bean Versus Achilles

Achilles can deceive almost everyone. But Bean, though sometimes taken in by Achilles' tactics, is never for a moment deceived about Achilles' goals or his character.

Even Sister Carlotta is briefly deceived. In Rotterdam, she had thought, at first, that Achilles was the extraordinary one in Poke's crew, until she discovered more about Bean. Through her, the I.F. finds out about Achilles. Part of the reason for Sister Carlotta sending Bean to Battle School is to keep him far from the danger of Achilles.

After Ender goes to Command School, the I.F. sends Achilles to Battle School (over Sister Carlotta's protests). His crippled leg is corrected by surgery. Bean, with the help of others, entraps Achilles and forces a recorded confession of how Achilles had killed Poke and six other people, including the surgeon who repaired his leg. (He could not forgive the surgeon for having seen him helpless.) This recording is enough to get Achilles expelled and into custody as criminally insane.

But Achilles is convinced that the universe ultimately bends to his wishes. He escapes, sells himself to one government after another, betraying where he chooses, killing casually. For a time, he has all of Ender's jeesh kidnapped and under his control. But, when Peter Wiggin makes Achilles' identity and history public, Achilles flees from Russia to India, and he takes Petra with him.

After the death of Sister Carlotta, Bean arrives in India with his Thai commando force to rescue Petra and others. Bean momentarily has a chance to kill Achilles. If Bean does this, at this time and place, other lives will be lost, including Petra's. Petra is willing to be sacrificed to rid the world of a monster and Bean knows this. But Bean remembers

Sister Carlotta's words about vengeance making people stupid. He chooses to save Petra. Achilles escapes to China.

As far as Achilles is concerned, honorably keeping one's word, sparing the life of an enemy in order to save a friend, is simply a sign of weakness. He is sure that Bean is weak, and that he can easily deceive and defeat him. This turns out to be a disastrous miscalculation on Achilles' part. Achilles eventually discovers that, under different circumstances, Bean can be ruthless and deadly.

Bean and Petra

When Petra and the others are kidnapped by Achilles, Bean deciphers a concealed coded message and enlists Peter's help. He puts messages on the Net about women in bondage to warriors, such as Briseus, captive of Achilles in the *Iliad*. Petra's computer can send nothing out now, but "each message [is] a cool kiss to her fevered brow."[7]

Twice, Petra misses a chance to kill Achilles. If her instincts had been just a bit more ruthless she might (or might not) have been able to push him out the door of a flying airplane, or, later, to break his neck with a karate chop. She regrets that she lacks Ender's unrestrained killer instinct. Yet Ender could hardly bear to live with himself because of that killer instinct. Bean tells Petra that no one but Achilles is responsible for the evil that Achilles is doing. It is easier for Bean to say such things than to believe them himself.

Bean and Petra are married. Bean wants to make certain that their children will not have Anton's Key. Volescu, the scientist who originally, and illegally, created Bean, assures them that he has a test that will make sure of that. Petra is implanted with hers and Bean's *in vitro* embryo, and becomes pregnant.

Petra deceives Bean by silence. She realizes that Volescu is untrustworthy. She doubts that an embryonic genetic test for Anton's Key exists. But since she wants Bean's baby and knows that Bean won't live long, she does not mention her insights to Bean. By the time she confesses her passive manipulation, Bean has begun to bond with his unborn child and wants the child to survive, Anton's Key or not.

But not just *that* child. There were five more of their embryos *in vitro* and they were stolen from the hospital. When Bean stops Achilles forever, Achilles does not have the embryos with him. Are they stored somewhere? Sold? Discarded? Implanted? By the end of *Shadow Puppets*, the world is recovering from Achilles and his wars, but Bean and Petra do not know where their other five potential children are.

PETER AND HIS RELATIONSHIPS

To Ender and Valentine, Peter has rarely been anything but a mean and sadistic bullying elder brother. To Bean, he is a despicable Machiavellian whose only virtue is that he does not commit casual murders as Achilles does. To his parents, Peter has always been their least favorite child, and now he is the only one they have left. Ender and Valentine, out in space, are effectively dead to them, due to time dilation.

But Peter is unlike Achilles in that he *is* capable of learning and changing. He makes a ludicrous mistake thinking that he can safely bring Achilles into his Hegemony and this mistake almost gets Peter killed. To save himself, he is compelled to admit that he was wrong and that his friends and his parents were right. Acknowledging error, especially to his parents, is a new and humbling experience to Peter. Like many another penitent, once he *does* accept correction he finds that it is not impossibly painful. Indeed, it is almost refreshing to admit that he is not always right.

This paves the way for other changes. One of Achilles' tools is caught trying to help kill Peter and his parents. Peter discovers that the man acted because his own family was being held hostage by Achilles and he asks for mercy for the failed killer. Peter learns that one of Ender's jeesh, a Muslim named Alai, has become Caliph of a new and more peaceful Islam and united all the Muslim countries. Peter wonders if he, Peter the Hegemon, is really needed to save the world; maybe Alai should do it. The "old Peter" would never have thought of that.

Sometimes writers think about their characters as if they had their own free wills. Card says, "I'm happy about how [Peter] comes out at the end of [*Shadow Puppets*]"[8] almost as if he had not caused this!

Peter and His Parents

In *Ender's Game,* the parents of Peter, Valentine, and Ender had been placeholders at most, without even first names, just "Father" and "Mother." Now, John Paul Wiggin and Theresa Wiggin emerge as strong, intelligent people trying to understand Peter, and to give him the emotional support and practical advice that he will not admit he needs. Indeed, they become so important to the narrative that Card was motivated to write short stories—"Polish Boy" and "Teacher's Pest"—set a generation earlier.[9]

In addition to the main stars discussed here, there is a whole constellation of supporting characters in The Shadow Books, some almost worth books in their own right.

A SAGA OF LOVE

Care and protectiveness, and the response to them; true friendship; hero worship; the enjoyment of being a part of a team; families that will forgive, persist, and try to understand and hope for growth; care for children, even for children that are still unborn, or embryos not implanted yet—all of these are a part of that complex emotion, *love*.

A zeal to save a comrade, a zeal so complete that one can not only risk one's life but sacrifice a long overdue vengeance; a devotion to one's spouse so great that one can lay down one's fear of passing on a mutation for the love of her—that is *heroic* love.

Bean's original creed of "Know, Think, Choose, Do" was a fine creed for survival, but not for love. At Battle School, Bean tries to make sense of people like Poke, Sister Carlotta, and Ender, who use free time to train younger students. He studies scholarly explanations of altruism, service, and self-sacrifice and is still bewildered. Something here is *not* logical, or is beyond logic. It is easy to explain why society needs heroes, but what explains the heroes?

Bean becomes a loving person, not by logic, but by conversion. He doesn't reason himself into love; love finds him, and claims him.

For Peter, the process is different. He had felt rejected by his parents, as if he could do no good compared to Valentine and Ender. His need is to cease trying to prove that he is the best, the smartest, the one who can handle everything. He must accept his parents' unconditional love without even asking if he deserves it. At the moment that he does so, he begins to deserve it.

Self-centeredness, whether it is "I must survive" or "I must be the best," leaves no room for love, given or received. When love finds a way, self-centeredness is gone.

A SAGA OF IRONY

It is Bean, the convert to love, who *knowingly* destroys the world of the Formics, and knowingly sends humans to certain death in doing so. It is Ender, the child of respectable middle class parents, who twice commits manslaughter in self-defense, while it is Bean, the urchin of the streets, who entraps his enemy and gets a confession without killing. It is Ender, the sensitive brother, who kills and wipes out species; it is Peter, the one too ruthless for Battle School, who gets a reputation on the Net for wisdom and moderation.

In the ins and outs of the world in turmoil, there are betrayals, counter-betrayals, and divided loyalties of people who would rather be loyal to their country than loyal to what they know is right. The Chinese occupation of India is slowed by such a simple thing as people putting lines of stones across the road, a "Wall of India." Anything that the mighty military Chinese do about it just makes them look foolish.

There are people who are not quite ruthless enough (like Petra) and people whose decency and honor unleashes a monster (as when Bean spares Achilles to save Petra). Even so, we can't quite bring ourselves to wish that these people had less honor or more ruthlessness. Card forces us to face difficult questions.

This same interesting mix of love and irony can be seen in a short story of Card's: "50 WPM."[10] This story has nothing whatever to do with the Shadow Books, or anything else in The Ender Saga. However, Card was writing it at about the same time he was writing *Shadow Puppets*. A World War II veteran insists that his son learn to type at least fifty words per minute to keep himself safe behind the lines in wartime. In Vietnam, "safely" in Saigon, this typist–soldier is nearly blown to bits by a child–saboteur; he is saved by a comrade who sacrifices himself. The Vietnam veteran teaches *his* son how to type *and* how to shoot. Love and irony, indeed! Nick Gevers calls this fictional tale "a brilliant essay in moral scrutiny."[11]

THE ROOTS AND THE FUTURE
OF THE SHADOW BOOKS

Card originally followed the novel *Ender's Game* with The Speaker Trilogy. However, he could not help noticing that *Ender's Game* was far more popular with teens than The Speaker Trilogy. Card had not been deliberately writing for teens, but he certainly had no objection to that audience.

He returned to that setting, asking, "What becomes of the other Battle School students after Ender leaves Earth?" First, he retold *Ender's Game* from Bean's perspective, then began branching off from there. At once, there were both good sales and critical acclaim. Craig Engler, reviewing *Ender's Shadow* feared that "[this book] like Bean himself will always be eclipsed by the myth of Ender . . ."[12] but that seems not to be so. The saga of Bean, Petra, Peter, and Achilles is strong enough not to be eclipsed. Another reviewer compares the Shadow Books to Isaac Asimov's Foundation stories as a "series that appeals to young readers smitten with the notion of hidden power."[13]

What is next in the Shadow Books? There will be at least one more, *Shadow of the Giant*. There are still loose ends to tie up in this saga. Then, there is to be a book that links The Shadow Books and The Speaker Trilogy together.[14]

In the meantime, Ender is out in space, traveling from world to world, looking for a place for the hive queen. The relativistic effect of time travel keeps him young while centuries pass on Earth. What becomes of Ender? The books discussed next, The Speaker Trilogy, tell us about that.

NOTES

1. Orson Scott Card, *Ender's Shadow* (New York: Tom Doherty Associates, Tor, 1999), 111.

2. Card, *Ender's Shadow*, 198.

3. Card, *Ender's Shadow*, 368.

4. Orson Scott Card, *Shadow of the Hegemon* (New York: Tom Doherty Associates, Tor, 2000), 279.

5. Card, *Hegemon*, 284.

6. Niccolò Machiavelli, chapter 18 of *The Prince* (1513), as translated by W. K. Marriott, in *Great Books of the Western World*, vol. 23, *Machiavelli and Hobbes* (Encyclopedia Britannica and University of Chicago, 1952), 25.

7. Card, *Hegemon*, 201.

8. On the website of Orson Scott Card, www.hatrack.com, an audio interview about Orson Scott Card, *Shadow Puppets* (New York: Tom Doherty Associates, Tor, 2002).

9. See chapter 1.

10. Orson Scott Card, "50 WPM," in *In the Shadow of the Wall: An Anthology of Vietnam Stories That Might Have Been*, ed. Byron R. Tetrick (Nashville, Tenn.: Cumberland House, Tekno, 2002), 13–25.

11. Nick Gevers, review of *In the Shadow of the Wall*, *Locus*, November 2002, 57.

12. Craig Engler, editorial reviews at www.amazon.com, under *Ender's Shadow*.

13. Gary K. Wolfe, "Reviews by Gary K. Wolfe," *Locus*, September 2002, 71.

14. "Casting Shadows," *Locus* 49, no. 6 (December 2002): 7–9, 71–72.

3

✝

The Speaker Trilogy

"INVESTMENT COUNSELOR"[1]

More than 400 years after the Third Bugger War, Ender is only twenty subjectively, because of time dilation traveling between worlds. A female "talking head" appears in his computer, calling herself Jane and showing him that the tax collector is cheating him. Ender eventually Speaks the death of this tax collector, showing the man's greed but making it more understandable. This is his first public Speaking.

THE SPEAKER TRILOGY: *SPEAKER FOR THE DEAD,* *XENOCIDE,* AND *CHILDREN OF THE MIND*

Conflict, Change, and Cooperation in the Family of Novinha and Ender

More than 3,000 years since humanity fought the buggers, Andrew ("Ender") Wiggin, a Speaker for the Dead, is called to Speak a death on the planet of Lusitania, a world settled by Brazilian Catholics. Humans share this world with another intelligent species, *porquinhos,* or piggies. On this world Ender finds a home for the hive queen.

He will stay on Lusitania. He has fallen in love with Novinha, the widow of a man whose death he Spoke, and she with him. He becomes a stepfather to six children.

Miro, a son, the eldest, is a xenologer, a scientist who studies the lifestyle of intelligent nonhuman species. When Miro wants something, he wants it passionately. His impetuousness leads him into desperate actions that result in an accidental electrocution that leaves him paralyzed. Jane, who has been Ender's computer companion, now becomes Miro's companion. This helps; but Miro becomes cynical.

Ela, the eldest daughter is a xenobiologist; that is, a scientist who studies the biology of alien species. Ela is calm, does her work carefully, and is ready to learn. This is fortunate, for she has a tender heart that could lead her down mistaken paths without her scientific objectivity.

Quim, the second son, has found the Catholic Church to be a refuge. On Lusitania all humans must at least pretend to be devout Catholics; with Quim it is real. He becomes a priest, missionary to the piggies. At one point, in a quarrel, the paralyzed Miro throws himself on Quim in fury, knocking them both to the ground. Quim then clasps his suffering, angry brother in his arms and prays eloquently for his healing. Miro marvels at Quim's relationship with God.

Quim's priestly compassion leads to martyrdom, when he tries to save a renegade piggy tribe from their own violence. Ender declines to Speak the death of his martyred stepson. "Quim was always exactly what he seemed to be . . . I have nothing to add to his story. He completed it himself."[2]

Olhado is a boy with artificial eyes (replacing those lost in an accident). These eyes can record, store, and replay past events that they have seen. There is a remoteness about him, as if he were always just observing. He becomes a businessman with a family.

Quara, the youngest girl, never tries to be obliging, even when (literally) her life depends upon it. She becomes a biologist and is particularly contrary to her sister Ela. She would spare the lives of disease microbes that *might* be intelligent. Later, she favors using the planet-wrecking Little Doctor weapon on a world of intelligent nonhumans.

Grego, a boy, the youngest child of the family, is a cauldron of violence. Ender's first encounter with him comes when little Grego comes rushing at him with a knife aimed at Ender's groin. (Ender disarms him, both physically and emotionally.) When he is a grown man, a physicist, Grego incites mob violence, but cannot control it. As he meditates in jail he finally matures.

And there is Novinha, their mother, whom Ender marries. She can be self-pitying, like Miro, and like Miro, she has reason. She has experienced the tragic deaths of her parents, her foster father, her lover (who is father of all six of her children) and a painful life with an abusive husband-in-name. She kept secrets about the death of her foster father in the hope of protecting his son (her lover) from dying in the same dreadful way. But he did die, in exactly that way, and her secrecy may have been to blame.

Like Ela, she is a brilliant scientist. Like Olhado, she can be remote. Like Quara, she can be contrary. Like Grego, she has a potential for anger, not with physical violence, but with cruel words. Most of Novinha's children have an exaggerated aspect of their mother.

The one who resembles her the least is Quim, and (perhaps for that reason) he is her favorite. She tries to forbid his dangerous missionary journey. Quim replies with the words of Jesus when His mother and brothers tried to interrupt Jesus' teaching of those who needed it: "These [suffering sinners, not you] are my mother and my brothers."[3]

Perhaps Quim resembles his true father and true grandfather. They were not missionaries, but xenologers. But each one was faithful to his calling until death.

Ender must work with this diverse group and help to make them into a family of people who support each other, a team who can work together for the good of all Lusitania. He perceives that there is genuine love in this family that he can nurture.

Almost everyone is changed over the years. When real crises come and every hand and brain is needed, Miro can rise above self-pity and cynicism. Ela can accept the self-sacrifice of others when it is needed. Quim's piety tempts him to reject his mother when he first learns of her adultery but he overcomes that. Olhado can become involved with others. Grego can turn his brilliant mind to problem solving instead of creating problems. Even Quara can sometimes cooperate with Ela, at least until the crisis is over.

Novinha has the biggest challenge. She, who has lost so much, must speak to Ender, giving him her permission to die his natural death. His death at this time will ensure the life of others. It may even ensure Ender's own continued existence, as a part of another body and personality (but not as Novinha's husband.) Sustained by others, she speaks the necessary loving words that release Ender. Ender's body dies; a portion of his spirit and memory continues in another.

Conflict, Change, and Cooperation between Ender and Valentine

These events interact with the relationship between Ender and his sister Valentine. When Ender leaves for Lusitania, Valentine stays behind with her husband and baby. This is the first time since they began their travels from world to world that they have been separated. Because of time dilation, Valentine will be decades older before they meet again, and Ender will be only months older. It is like a death. Their parting is almost bitter.

But later, when Valentine has aroused Starways Congress and is wanted as a traitor, she and her family go into space to join Ender on Lusitania. Starways Congress has planned the destruction of Lusitania; she and Ender will meet their fates together. The great age difference matters less than one might think. Valentine is again his comrade and ally; she is an aunt to his stepchildren and a valuable citizen of Lusitania.

The relationship is tested. The desperate experiment to save Lusitania has an unintended byproduct: Two human beings come into physical existence from images in Ender's mind. They are his brother Peter, the Hegemon, long dead, just as Ender remembers him in all his childhood nastiness, and his sister Valentine, as he remembers her: gentle, loving—and *young*! "Old" Valentine must learn to live with *that*! She does.

Conflict, Change, and Cooperation in a Family on the World of Path

A family on another world has power to assist the destruction of Lusitania, or to help prevent it. On the world of Path, where the population is descended from the Chinese, a girl, Qing-jao ("Gloriously Bright"), raised by her widowed father, is "godspoken." That is, she is a part of an elite, honored, and powerful minority who feel compelled to perform certain repetitive acts. In her case, this means tracing the grains of bare wooden floors.

Qing-jao, with her father, is using her computer skills to help Starways Congress destroy the wicked, disobedient world of Lusitania. She has a maid, Wang-mu. The two are almost as close as sisters, but Wang-mu is contemptuous of Starways Congress and condemns the forthcoming destruction.

Then Qing-jao's father, Han Fei-tzu, discovers that the "godspoken" are victims of obsessive compulsive disorder (OCD) deliberately spliced into their genes by Starways Congress, as an attempt to keep a super-genius experiment under control. Han Fei-tzu reverses his allegiance, opposes Starways Congress, and helps Lusitania. Wang-mu becomes his ally in this, becoming more of a daughter to him than Qing-jao.

Qing-jao remains loyal to Starways Congress. "I'll serve the man [my father] was when he was strong and good" she says.[4] This is also faithfulness to her dead mother. She remains loyal to the cult of the "god-spoken," even after an engineered healing virus has been released on Path and nobody has genetically induced OCD any more. She continues to trace wood grains until she dies of old age. No one else repeats old compulsions, and she no longer has an inward urge to do so. She is scorned and pitied. After her death her society makes her a god.

The reader is torn. Is Qing-jao contemptible for persisting in absurdity? Or is it pathetically beautiful that she heroically maintains the best that she knows (or allows herself to know)? Family loyalty, loyalty to the dead, and single-minded religious devotion have all accomplished much good. But they are better based on the truth than on a lie.

Conflict, Change, and Cooperation between Societies

The world of Path and the world of Lusitania are mirror opposites. On Path, there is a lie that is venerated as a faith. On Lusitania, there is a belief that appears to be a baseless myth; yet it turns out to be the literal truth.

The human xenologers on Lusitania follow standard anthropological practice. They pretend to believe what the piggies believe. When the piggies execute their own kind a tree appears in the vivisected corpse. (The humans assume that the piggies planted the tree there.) The piggies then treat the tree as if it were the dead piggy. The piggies speak to an ancestor by drumming on his tree in a fixed pattern. Ender approaches the piggies with an open mind, pretending nothing, willing to learn.

He discovers that the piggies' beliefs are true. On Lusitania, a dreadful disease (called the *descolada* by the humans) wiped out many species long before humans settled there and it still exists on that planet. The surviving species, plants and animals, went into partnership, adapting to the descolada for survival. The piggies and certain trees became one species, existing in animal form for a part of their existence, and in tree form for another part. The piggies who were "executed" by vivisection, with careful placement of organs nearby, were actually being "planted." When the piggies "planted" two human xenologers they honestly believed that they were honoring them, taking them into their next life. They are appalled to learn otherwise.

The descolada killed many humans, including Novinha's parents. But these plant–animal partnerships were unknown to the human researchers. The piggies hadn't realized that the humans didn't know, or that things were different for them. Doesn't the humans' own Bible speak of people being "born again" and living after death?

The trees are necessary at the beginning of the life-cycle also. The Little Mothers (sexually mature infant piggies) crawl on the fathertrees and are fertilized with their sap. Then the piggies take the pregnant little mothers to the great Mothertree for gestation. The all-powerful piggy Wives tend the Mothertree and the brood. The piggies are endlessly warlike for ample reason: without conquest of another forest and use of the fathertrees and a new Mothertree, a tribe may not have enough children.

There are other areas of mutual misunderstandings. The piggies do have a technology. They can "ask for the gift of an ancient brother"[5] by singing to a tree, persuading it to fall, and tracing on the trunk outlines of cups, thin-bladed wooden knives, bows, and other desired items, which then emerge intact, without any need of metal tools. No human saw this before Ender came. No one asked the right questions.

A treaty is secured for three species. Lusitania will be the new home of the hive queen and her brood. The piggies are eager to have her and all that she can teach them. Among other things, the treaty provides that the humans will mediate all differences between the piggies and the hive queen; the piggies between the hive queen and humans; the hive queen between humans and piggies. In order to seal the treaty in a way that all piggy tribes will recognize, Ender must plant the piggy he knows best, a piggy whose name is Human. Ender writes *The Life of Human*, a third book added to his books of *The Hive Queen* and *The Hegemon* and signed, as were the others "Speaker For The Dead."

The mediation provision of the treaty is implemented a generation later. After Quim's martyrdom, the local piggies who work with humans in mutual respect and trust are truly indignant with Quim's killers. The local piggies plan a punitive expedition against the forest of the distant, renegade piggies.

But Quim's brother Grego feels that humans should avenge a human. He easily creates an enraged mob. Energized by the cry "For Quim and Christ!"[6] started by Grego's young nephew and repeated over and over, the mob mercilessly attack the *local*, totally innocent, piggy forest with fire. They try to burn piggies, fathertrees, the Mothertree with all the infants—everything.

Grego screams to stop this, but the humans continue with their insanity, doing what neither Quim nor Christ could ever want.

The hive queen's workers—the "buggers," the dreaded enemies of the humans' ancestors—keep the treaty. They arrive and position themselves between the humans and the forest, like terrible avenging angels. This ancient horror makes the humans flee, and enough of the forest is saved to begin again. The ages-old nightmare of humanity has delivered others from human madness.

Neither piggies, nor humans, nor the hive queen are perfect beings. All have their mixtures of good and evil, wisdom and folly. Three imperfect species may keep peace better than two.

A piggy named Planter has a martyrdom that is the mirror image of Quim's. Quim had died from being deprived of the anti-descolada medicine, which all humans need to survive. Planter tells Ela to cleanse him of the descolada virus, which piggies need to survive, and allow him to die, closely monitored throughout. This will decide the question: Did the descolada create the piggies' intelligence? Do the piggies have a personhood apart from the descolada? Ela needs this answer if she is to develop medicines to save Lusitania, and to persuade Starways Congress that Lusitanians will not infect the whole galaxy and need not be destroyed. But if Planter dies this way he will never attain his tree-life.

Planter's sacrifice is similar to Ender's planting of Human; not so grisly, but far more fatal. It even makes Quara act cooperatively for a while. It leaves no doubt that piggies are people.

Radically different societies *can* cooperate with each other and learn from each other, and even rise above painful memories. But it isn't easy; it takes sacrifice.

Another book by Card, one entirely outside the Ender Saga, that deals with the interaction of humans and nonhumans, is *The Abyss*.[7] This book was written three years after *Speaker for the Dead* and two years before *Xenocide*. In this case, the aliens are not on another planet but on our own—at the depth of the ocean. This book is based on the screenplay of a motion picture of the same name. Card goes much further into motives and backgrounds of both the humans and the aliens than the movie does. It again stresses the theme that understanding and cooperation may require self-sacrifice.

Conflict, Change, and Cooperation between Religious Traditions

When Ender first arrives on Lusitania he is opposed by the Catholic Bishop. But the Bishop cannot prevent Ender from winning friends. Also, on Lusitania there is a religious order known as Children of the Mind of Christ, a monastery for married couples who live together chastely. The couple who heads the order disagrees with the Bishop and accepts Ender warmly, helping him with his Speaking. Mutual trust becomes strong. A generation later, all parts of the Catholic Church in Lusitania are cooperating with Ender. They sometimes disagree, but it is a disagreement among friends.

The Spiritual Dimension of the Speaker Trilogy

In these books we find a false "religion" on the world of Path. If the chapters dealing with Path were told separately,[8] we might suppose that the author was a skeptic who believed that all religions were neuroses. Anyone who thought that would get a shock from the ending of *Xenocide* and from nearly every chapter of *Children of the Mind*.[9] The events are too complex to summarize, but a reviewer sums up their impact on the reader in a review of *Xenocide*. "[The ending] depend[s] on a . . . mysticism available only to the deeply religious. And that mysticism is . . . at the heart of [these books] . . . the nature of the soul and of God. . . . I still enjoyed the book. If you are more religious than I am, you will *love* it."[10]

The critic is right. If you cannot imagine a reality in which miracles can happen and prayers are granted, if "mysticism" means mythology, if "spiritual" means spiritualistic fakes, if "supernatural" means ghost stories or Halloween, then there will be much in these books that seems contrived, although you might still like the stories.

But if you can imagine a reality in which our cosmos of matter, energy, space, and time is just a tiny fraction of a Greater Reality (or "Outside" as it is called in these stories) and that this Greater Reality might do miracles, grant prayers, send visions or prophecies, then these books will not seem contrived. You may, as the critic says, *love* them.

Card's worldview does not make miracles cheap. There is always a price, a sacrifice. You may have to give your life, or the life of the person you love. You must be prepared to find out things about your innermost self that you never wanted to know. This happens to Ender when he is confronted with creations of his mind: Young Peter and Young

Valentine who represent Ender's worst and best selves. If you call for a miracle, don't tell God where to stop!

Learning From All

When a technological culture meets a culture with less technology (or a different technology) there is usually one of three types of reaction:

1. The Imperialist: "These 'savages' are not people. We will ignore them, enslave them, exploit them, or kill them off—whatever best suits our own interests."
2. The Missionary: "These poor helpless people are lost. We must make them over into a copy of our own society, as far as possible."
3. The Anthropologist: "We want to study these people. We will not share our technology. We will pretend to believe their myths. If they should commit atrocities, we will not hold them accountable. If some of us are killed, we will just be more careful."

These viewpoints, that seem so different, are alike in one respect. All three assume: *These people have nothing to teach us.* They may be worth exploiting, (or converting, or studying), but we know more than they about everything important.

This reflects relationships in our world, especially dealings between whites and Native Americans. If we meet intelligent beings in space, we will probably repeat the same mistakes. The human xenologers on Lusitania are so "respectful" of piggy beliefs that it never occurs to them that these beliefs might be true. Tragic errors would have been prevented if the piggies had been treated as people, not just objects for study.

Is there any prevention, or cure, for these tragedies of misunderstanding? Perhaps. Ender is ready to learn. He teaches, but he learns first. He respects the rights of all people to be what they are, as long as they do not harm others. When Ela wants to try biological experiments to alter the piggies' life-cycle (it appalls her that the grubs eat their way out of the little mother, killing her), Ender talks her out of it. But when he finds that the local tribe is planning war against the other tribes, he teaches peace and mutual cooperation.

It is one thing to change a species' basic biology without consent, but a very different thing to teach that war is not the best answer. Ender tries to be the best of both Missionary and Anthropologist.

Recognizing Truth; Admitting Error

But it is not enough just to have a leader like that. It is vital that the *others* be able to learn. This learning is painful when people are asked to lay down beliefs at the core of their existence. George MacDonald once defined this terrible choice: "Do you so love the truth and the right [that] you welcome, or at least willingly submit to, an exposure [that makes you] ashamed and humble? . . . Are you willing to be made glad that you were wrong when you thought others were wrong?"[11]

This theme is repeated many times. The scientists of Lusitania do submit to the exposure of the truth that they, not the piggies, were deluded. Some of the piggies are able to see the truth about war, even though the contrary belief was bred into their very being.

But on Path deception is necessary. When a virus is released to heal the engineered genetic OCD, the people are persuaded that they have received a gift from the gods. Han Fei-tzu and the Lusitanians see ethical problems in deceiving people. Deception, like war, is sometimes needed, but should not be undertaken lightly. Qing-jao cannot be deceived by the popular persuasion. So she clings desperately to a more fundamental untruth.

Each one must find his or her own response to the humbling exposure of truth.

THE ROOTS OF THESE STORIES[12]

Usually, a notable book is written first; then sequels follow. Here we have the opposite. When Card first got the idea of *Speaker For The Dead* he had no intention of writing about Ender Wiggin, (who at that time existed only in the original novelette of "Ender's Game.") What he planned was to write about an intelligent species that had to have war in order to reproduce. There must be a human in the story who could understand. Ender could understand. He had destroyed a whole species and regretted it. But the story must have Ender as a man. So Card expanded "Ender's Game, " the novelette, to the full-length novel. The narrative now went beyond the victory, giving Ender the hive queen and her pupa. This gave Ender a reason to travel from world to world. The Speaker Trilogy is responsible for the full-length novel of *Ender's Game*, and, indirectly, for the Shadow Books as well.

Speaker for the Dead won both the Hugo and Nebula awards, just as *Ender's Game*, the novel, did. *Speaker* also won the Locus award.

Card cast the humans of Lusitania as Brazilian Catholics because he knew that culture from his missionary days and because it annoyed him that most American science fiction assumed that only American types would ever populate distant planets. In *Xenocide* he puts the Chinese into space. With *Children of the Mind* he includes Japanese and Pacific Island cultures. In an afterword to *Children* he discusses his use of these cultures.

LOOKING BACK

In all these books, from *Ender's Game* through both of its branches, Card has taken us on a long journey. We have seen uprisings, alliances, revolutions, heroism, and betrayals. We have visited peoples of the Far and Middle East and Latin America. We met humans of different cultures and beliefs on our own world and on distant worlds.

We have met intelligent nonhumans who are insectoid with a true hive-mind. We have met intelligent beings who are mammals at one stage of existence and trees at another. We have had a glimpse of a reality—an Outside—infinitely beyond all this.

We also see the close-up portrayal of parent and child, brothers and sisters, teacher and student, and the love of man and woman. We see that there is no limit to how evil humans, or other people, can be. There is also no limit to how good they can be. And whether we are just around the corner or at the opposite end of the galaxy, whether one is dealing with a family member or a totally different kind of being, we hear the same message, whispered softly:

> Keep trying to understand each other. Ask the right questions. Ask respectfully. Give everyone the benefit of the doubt. Stop evil if you can, but forget revenge. Admit it when you are wrong. Heal. Build up. Encourage. Love.

NOTES

1. Orson Scott Card, "Investment Counselor," in *First Meetings, Three Stories from the Enderverse* (Burton, Mich.: Subterranean Press, 2002), 55–94. Originally in *Far Horizons: All New Tales from the Greatest Worlds of Science Fiction*, ed. Robert Silverberg (New York: Avon Books, 1999), 89–117.

2. Orson Scott Card, *Xenocide,* paperback edition (New York: Tom Doherty Associates, Tor, 1991), 269.

3. Card, *Xenocide,* 251. Quim is quoting Matthew 12:46–50.

4. Card, *Xenocide,* 299.

5. Orson Scott Card, *Speaker for the Dead,* paperback edition (New York: Tom Doherty Associates, Tor, 1986), 244.

6. *Xenocide,* 337. This phrase is often repeated.

7. Orson Scott Card, *The Abyss,* a novel based on a screenplay by James Cameron for a motion picture of the same name, starring Ed Harris, Mary Elizabeth Mastrantonio, and Michael Biehn (Twentieth Century Film Corporation, 1989). Out of print.

8. *Analog Science Fiction and Fact* actually *did* print the chapters dealing with the world of Path alone: "Gloriously Bright," *Analog Science Fiction and Fact,* January 1991, 12–108.

9. Orson Scott Card, *Children of the Mind,* paperback edition (New York: Tom Doherty Associates, Tor, 1996).

10. Tom Easton, *Analog Science Fiction and Fact,* mid-December 1991, 159–160.

11. C. S. Lewis, ed., *George MacDonald: An Anthology* (New York: Macmillian, Touchstone, 1947, 1974), 102. Lewis is quoting *Unspoken Sermons, Third Series,* "The Final Unmasking."

12. The data in this section come from the same sources cited in note 9 of chapter 1 and also from the introduction to the paperback edition of *Speaker,* ix–xxii.

Part II

The Other Great Series

The Tales of Alvin Maker,
The Homecoming Series, and the
Beginning of The Mayflower Trilogy, *Lovelock*

4

✢

The Tales of Alvin Maker

Seventh Son, Red Prophet, Prentice Alvin,
Alvin Journeyman, and *Heartfire*

SETTING AND GENRES

We often think of fantasy as having kings, princesses, wizards, and a setting in the Middle Ages, with some of the medieval myths and superstitions, such as dragons, becoming true. Or, sometimes we think of a modern setting: a ghost, for instance, troubling the lives of people in various situations today.

Card can write both medieval and modern fantasy, as we will see in later chapters. But in The Tales of Alvin Maker he is doing something different. He is setting the story in the early days of an alternate North America, similar in many respects to the early North America that we know. There are settlers from Europe and especially from Great Britain, interacting with each other and with Native Americans (called "Reds" in these books). The geography is the same; the mountains and rivers are all where they should be, although they have slightly different names.

But the assumption is made that almost every superstition, every old wives' tale, all folklore of the early North American frontier is actually true. Many characters have magic gifts, known as "knacks."

Alternate history is a favorite genre of writers of speculative fiction. The writer asks himself a question, such as, What if gunpowder were discovered in ancient times? or What if Hitler had won World War II? and constructs a work of fiction around the supposition. Historical characters from our reality may exist in the story, provided that their actions and fortunes are changed consistently with changes in history.

For example, when the Alvin Maker tales begin, in the early 1800s, George Washington is a part of the recent past history of the characters on the frontier. But the American Revolution never happened, so General Washington never became President Washington; instead, in this history, he was beheaded by the British.

Instead of the thirteen colonies becoming the thirteen states, the United States here consists of states and territories stretching from what we call New York State to the Mizzipy (Mississippi) River. New England is a separate nation of states; so, also, is a group of states around the Appalachian Mountains known as Appalachee. These three nations, United States, New England, and Appalachee, *did* all achieve independence from Britain in this alternate history, but not all at once in one war as in our history.

The southeastern slave-holding states are "Crown Colonies" and the king of England lives there in exile; England does not have a king, but has a Lord Protector, a descendant of Cromwell. All of this is revealed gradually, and Card helps the reader with maps on the endpapers.

Alternate history and fantasy are not usually combined in one narrative. However, most reviewers agree that he succeeded in this daring experiment. "Card achieves the near-miracle of bringing something new to fantasy."[1]

Indeed. Card makes it all so believable that it is necessary to give the reader a completely serious warning: *"Do not read these books shortly before taking a history examination!* When you have *passed* your history course, these books can be ideal summertime reading."

ALVIN

Alvin's Beginning and Early Life

The Miller family is moving from New England. The mother, Faith, is in labor with her thirteenth child just as the family is approaching the Hatrack River. They are trying to reach an inn three miles on the other side. When the wagon is in the middle of the river there is a sudden flooding so massive that the Miller family almost loses everything and everybody. They *do* lose the oldest son, Vigor, who jumps from the wagon to deflect an uprooted tree aimed directly at his mother.

Vigor does not die at once; he holds onto life until the baby boy, named Alvin for his father, is born at the inn. When Vigor is buried, and Faith has recovered, the family later moves on to make their own homestead further west. This homestead is eventually known as Vigor Church.

Since Vigor was alive when Alvin was born, Alvin is a seventh son of a seventh son born under a caul (a scrap of flesh covering his head and face.) This makes him powerful. The nature of that power is something that Alvin, and we, slowly discover.

In childhood he is Alvin Miller, Jr. because his father is literally a miller. In the frontier, children take the name of their father's occupation. When Alvin first begins to realize his powers, he does just what a small boy would do: He uses them to tease and embarrass others, especially those who have teased or embarrassed him. But one night when he has sent roaches into his sisters' room (after they had put pins in his nightgown), a revelation comes to him in the form of a mysterious Red man in his room. Since he appears to glow in the dark Alvin calls him the Shining Man. He learns from this revelation that he must never use his unique abilities just for himself; his calling is to "make all things whole."[2]

Alvin Versus the Unmaker and the Unmaker's Tools

Alvin's supernatural adversary appears to him as a shimmering dark cloud of *nothingness* (but a destructive nothingness). The only way to keep the nothingness at bay is to *make* something, even if it is just a tiny basket woven from grass. When Alvin confides this strange perception to the itinerant traveler Taleswapper (the artist and poet William Blake), Taleswapper suggests a name for the nothingness: The Unmaker.

The Unmaker has endless ways to try to undo Alvin, most of them by water at first (a near-drowning, a falling ridgebeam split where water weakened the wood, a millstone falling where the earth is damp, and other incidents). The Unmaker also uses Alvin's own moods; when he is angry the Unmaker draws near.

The Unmaker also appears to others, but not as a shimmering nothingness. To its victims, persons that it wishes to convert to tools against Alvin, the Unmaker takes on some appearance that that person will trust. An intellectually proud clergyman sees a scholarly Visitor who encourages him in all of his hatreds, persuading him that these hatreds are divine; a corrupt and lustful slave owner sees a supreme Overseer who encourages his lusts and greeds; a lonely woman sees a Best Friend who plausibly encourages her to lie.

Alvin's younger brother Calvin is poisonously envious of Alvin. He believes that he, Calvin, should be the true Seventh Son since Vigor is now dead. Calvin refuses to believe in the existence of the Unmaker. This does not make him safe from the Unmaker; it just makes him think that his evil ideas against Alvin were entirely his own. Defense against the Unmaker is not in skepticism; defense is in creativity, and especially in creativity for the benefit of others.

The Unmaker is not all-powerful. In some cases its victim-tools come to awareness of the true situation and stop trying to harm Alvin, or may even be converted to actively helping him. Also, the Unmaker does not really understand goodness. It does not understand, for instance, that when good people hear the cry for help in a child's voice they will rush in that direction even though the Unmaker tries to drive them another way by feelings of fear and horror. The fear and horror make good people run *faster* in the direction of the cry!

Alvin's First Glimpse of His Quest: The Crystal City

In the midst of a terrifying adventure that threatens to bring destruction to many people, Alvin is escorted into the heart of a tornado by the Red who taught him the correct uses of his powers. This Red is known as the Prophet, the brother of the Indian chief Ta-Kumsaw (Tecumseh). The Prophet shows Alvin a vision:

> A city, shining in sunlight. . . . Towers of ice . . . or clear glass . . . Inside . . . there were people. . . . What he felt . . . Not peace, no . . . It was excitement. . . . The people . . . weren't perfect. . . . But nobody was hungry. . . . nobody was ignorant, and nobody had to do anything just because someone . . . made them do it.[3]

From then on, Alvin's goal is to build the Crystal City. He hasn't any idea how this is to be done; his life quest will be to find out.

Alvin's First Making

Later, Alvin is apprenticed to a blacksmith. At this point he has no last name. He is just the blacksmith's apprentice, Alvin. As his skill at blacksmithing becomes apparent, people begin to call him Alvin Smith. But from his birth he has another name not known to everyone: Alvin *Maker*.

A Maker is exceptional. Makers are born about once a century. The creative energy of a Maker is different from that of a gifted creative artist or writer such as Taleswapper or imaginative inventor such as

Benjamin Franklin. The talented artist or the clever inventor can, at the most, be a wizard. A Maker is far more. His powers include healing, mending, and seeing into the structure of solid things. That is only the beginning.

As Alvin is passing from apprenticeship to journeyman status, he perceives the ability to make a plow of gold. He does this by actually putting his hands into the fire of the forge, healing his own burns as they occur (but not blocking the pain), teaching the plow, willing it to be gold, to live. The result is a golden plow that moves by itself and will not permit itself to be owned by anyone. Alvin is its sole custodian.

It is a useless miracle from a practical viewpoint. The implement cannot be used for plowing. It gets Alvin into repeated trouble with his master-blacksmith, who wants the plow for its gold. Later Alvin has to keep hiding it from curious people. Nevertheless, wherever he goes he takes the golden plow. It is a symbol, a promise. If he can make *this,* then just possibly he can find, or make, the Crystal City.

Alvin's Quest for the Crystal City As a Man

This quest takes Alvin through some extraordinary adventures. Twice he is in jail for false reasons. Because of his abilities in magically manipulating matter he never has to stay in a jail, but sometimes it is more practical to stay and get cleared of charges.

He tries to teach the people of Vigor Church to be Makers, but that is a mistake: they cannot learn the important things.

He goes with friends to New England because the Puritans are the ones who have tried to build the City of God on Earth, and they have indeed built a society where there is little crime, much community support of one another, and strong family loyalty. But Alvin comes close to being convicted as a witch in New England, where people believe that all magic knacks come from the Devil no matter how benevolently they are used. "The City of God tried so hard to be pure that it created its own impurity."[4]

In all of these adventures Alvin is never really alone. He has three principal allies in his quest to create the Crystal City.

Alvin's First Ally: Peggy Guester (Also Known As Miss Larner or Peggy Smith)

It is five-year-old Peggy Guester, the daughter of the innkeeper, who prevents the tragedy of the Miller family at the Hatrack River from being even worse. Peggy is a "torch"; that is, she can see things happening at a distance; she can also see the alternative happenings in the future and what can be done to prevent or to encourage them. She sees the desperate plight of the Miller family and alerts others to come and rescue them.

Peggy's mother, Old Peg, is a midwife. Peggy is present at deliveries since she can tell her mother the position of the unborn baby. It is Peggy who removes the caul from baby Alvin's face. Looking into his possible futures she sees that there are forces that hate this child; he will never live to be a man unless someone with a powerful knack is watching over him. So Peggy appoints herself to do this because she knows that this is a Maker, and that his survival will be important to many people.

For eleven years she secretly keeps the caul. The Miller family moves on, but with a little pinch of the caul between her fingers, Peggy can look into Alvin's "heartfire" (mind, soul, personality) wherever he may be and see danger near him. She saves him by splitting the ridgebeam before it strikes, by cracking the millstone, and by similar acts at critical moments. When she is sixteen and knows that Alvin is coming back to his birthplace at Hatrack River to be a blacksmith's apprentice, she sees a subtler danger.

Alvin knows the story of his birth; he realizes that he is going to be a Maker. He will seek out the innkeeper's daughter, the torch who stood by at his birth, and beg her to teach him how to be a Maker. Peggy foresees that if she does teach him:

> [W]hen he is a handsome . . . twenty-one and I am a sharp-tongued spinster of twenty-six he'll feel so . . . *obligated* [to] . . . propose. . . . And I, lovesick . . . I'll say yes . . . [but] his eyes will hunger for other women all . . . our lives.[5]

The only way she can avoid a miserable life for them both is for her to be away from Hatrack River when he arrives. She flees to Philadelphia, where she makes friends, becomes acquainted with society, becomes educated, and continues to watch over Alvin from a distance.

When she is twenty-three and Alvin is eighteen, she returns, disguised by magic charms. Instead of using charms to look prettier, she uses them to look plain and older. No one, including her parents, recognizes little Peggy, the torch, who ran away seven years ago. She presents herself as Miss Margaret Larner, who has come to teach school.

Just as she had hoped, a warm and completely sincere relationship develops between herself and Alvin. He loves the spinster-schoolteacher that she seems to be.

But Peggy's torch-knack is not perfect. Like other people, she can let her judgments and actions be swayed by her own desires; she can misinterpret what she foresees, or simply not be paying attention at a critical moment. She fails to prevent her own mother's violent death because her attention is on Alvin. After she has revealed her true self, her guilty feelings about this tragic failure prevent her from marrying him.

Also Alvin has some second thoughts about marriage to a torch. Is he a suitable mate for someone who is nearly always right? Would it be like marrying one's mother? Would he have any freedom left? Their inward misgivings and outward circumstances combine to keep them from marriage for four years. When they do marry, on the wedding night she foresees:

> [H]is grave, and herself and their children . . . weeping. [But] that scene was possible in every wedding night; and at least there would be children; at least there would be a loving widow . . . at least there would be memory . . . instead of regretful loneliness.[6]

Peggy cannot physically be with Alvin every time his quest takes him somewhere. But through their magic knacks they stay in close touch. Alvin cannot read minds at a distance the way a torch can, but he can see material objects. At a mutually agreed upon time and place Peggy writes Alvin a letter that never has to be mailed; he can read the letter as she writes it, and reply to her, as she writes, just by thinking the words.

When Card describes the love of Alvin and Peggy after their marriage his words are lyrical. In some fantasies the story ends when the Poor Boy marries The Princess; in *this* story we get the feeling that their marriage is only the beginning.

Alvin's Second Ally: Arthur Stuart

Just the day before little Peggy leaves her parents for Philadelphia she becomes aware, through her knack as a torch, of someone trying to cross the Hio (Ohio) River near the mouth of the Hatrack. It is a young fugitive slave-girl who had been raped by her master; she has the boy baby in her arms. She has used a dangerous magic. She has literally flown on magically created wings and is weak. But she will not be taken into slavery again. Rather than let that happen she will kill her baby first and then herself.

Peggy alerts her father, innkeeper Horace Guester, who gets help. The girl and her baby are found and carried to the inn, where the girl dies. What will Horace and Old Peg do with a half-black baby boy? Because of the Fugitive Slave Treaty they are criminals if they keep the child. And even if the Slave Finders with their magic arts never come looking for him, there will still be problems with prejudice.

Accepting all dangers and disadvantages, Old Peg adopts the baby and persuades her husband to agree. She gives the child the name of Arthur Stuart, which happens to be the name of the King-In-Exile in the Crown colonies. "And if the King don't like such a namesake . . . His Majesty will have to change his own name first."[7] Peggy is glad that her mother will have a child to raise when Peggy is gone.

It was Peggy who saved Arthur Stuart's life; it is Alvin who turns out to be his brotherly companion. Whenever Alvin is at the forge, Arthur Stuart is there. He knows that Alvin has more knacks than most people realize. Powerful knacks can cause hostility.

Arthur Stuart has knacks also. He remembers what has been said, and he can repeat it in *exactly* the same voice as the speaker. He understands the secret language of a magical redbird and tells it to Alvin: "A Maker is the one who is a part of what he makes."[8] This oracular interpretation by a child who does not even know what it means eventually leads to the Making of the golden plow.

When Arthur Stuart is old enough for school, Old Peg wants him enrolled. This causes problems. The white people of Hatrack River are more or less against slavery, but they do not welcome the idea of a half-black child in the same classes as their children. Some feel that an education would be wasted on this child.

A compromise is worked out. The new teacher, Miss Larner, (actually, little Peggy) is willing to give Arthur Stuart private lessons after regular school hours. At the same time she tutors Alvin. This is how their friendship begins, with Arthur Stuart a part.

The Slave Finders come, and Alvin makes the manacles for Arthur Stuart while plotting his escape. When the boy is rescued, Alvin uses his knack to work changes, at the atomic level, in the "signature" of Arthur Stuart's body so that the Slave Finders' magic charms will not locate him. To do this he must immerse both himself and Arthur Stuart in the river while he concentrates on changing the signature so that it is more like Alvin's own. This happens earlier on the same night that he later makes the golden plow. In a way, the transformation of Arthur Stuart could be considered Alvin's first Making, although the change is invisible to ordinary sight.

That night is also the night that Old Peg Guester is murdered by a Slave Finder. It is a night of great wonders and horrors.

The transformation of Arthur Stuart is effective. The Slave Finders are completely frustrated. The Unmaker no longer tries to kill Alvin with water; it works through other people instead. And there is a price for the transformation: never again is Arthur Stuart able to mimic another person's voice.

When Alvin begins on his quest to fulfill his role as a Maker and build the Crystal City, Arthur Stuart is with him. When Alvin and Peggy are married it is Arthur Stuart who stands beside Alvin. Arthur Stuart is there when Peggy cannot be.

This does not mean that he is meekly obedient to Alvin. He is quite capable of running off in the morning to watch Jean-Jacques Audubon, the naturalist–artist, painting pictures of birds by the river, and thus holding up the departure of Alvin and his friends by a day. A Quaker friend explains Arthur Stuart's behavior to Alvin: "He doesn't obey thee like a boy, but like a man, because he wants to please thee. He'll do nowt because thou commandest, but does it only because he agrees. . . . [H]e doesn't act in fear of thee."[9]

Arthur Stuart is truly free.

Alvin's Third Ally: Verily Cooper

Verily Cooper comes from England, ruled by the Protectorate. He has a knack, carefully concealed, for which he could be executed for witchcraft: he can make things fit together exactly right.

After he becomes a lawyer, he meets a young man, Calvin Miller, traveling overseas in an attempt to find ways for powerful uses of his knacks. Through Calvin, Verily learns of this part of the American frontier where knacks are not necessarily considered evil. Although Calvin hates Alvin, it is not hard for Verily to pump him for information. He crosses the ocean to find Alvin and become his follower.

Twice his skill as a lawyer comes in handy when Alvin is in court. Once Verily successfully opposes Daniel Webster. Another time he delights John Adams, wh is sitting as judge. Verily's skill at putting things together is more than just material.

Alvin has other allies, but these three are the most significant.

THE REDS[10]

The Reds have magic also, but it is unlike the knacks. White knacks are a way of bending, twisting, changing nature. The Red way is to work *with* nature, understand it, cooperate with it, learn to sing its song.

The Reds, through their "land-sense" will ask permission of a tree before cutting it down for a lodge house; if the tree does not want to give itself for that purpose it will not be cut. A Red hunter will call the game to come to him to be eaten but only the willing will come (although it may be fearful as well as willing). A Red can run for miles, faster than a horse, never tiring, by means of "greensong," which tells him where to put a foot so he does not stumble; branches will move out of the way.

All of this, of course, adds to the difficulty of White and Red in understanding each other. To the Whites, the Reds are stupid naked savages. Selfish Whites want to exterminate them, like a native pest. More kindly Whites want to convert them, not just to Christianity, but to all the good and bad of European civilization.

To the Reds (the ones who still live as Reds) the Whites are rapacious invaders who distort and abuse the living land and its rightful inhabitants in every possible way. The only peace is to drive the Whites off forever.

Some Reds do *not* still live as Reds. In the little State of Irrakwa, certain Reds have beaten the Whites at their own game. They run factories and shipping. They are learning of that new invention, the Rail Road. Their Governor is a Red woman. The Irrakwa have forgotten everything related to land-sense and greensong, and become more White than the Whites. But the Irrakwa are only a small portion of all the Reds.

Some Reds have succumbed to alcohol and are known as Whiskey Reds. These pathetic creatures will do anything to get their drinks and thus are considered "tamed" by Whites who exploit them. Officially, it is illegal to sell whiskey to Reds; unofficially, there are some Whites who see such sale as a cheap way to exterminate the savages.

Reds such as Chief Ta-Kumsaw regard the Irrakwa and the Whiskey Reds with the same pity and contempt. To him, true Reds will use nothing that comes from the Whites, unless they are using it to defend their lands against them. And, indeed, when really evil things are done by Reds in these stories, they are generally done by Reds carrying muskets. Rescue by Reds is done with bows and arrows.

Alvin is capable of learning Red magic as well as White. He learns land-sense and greensong. Indeed, for a time, he is rumored to be a renegade. But he learns these things without forgetting White knackery, and without feeling contempt for either one.

At Eight-Faced Mound, a supremely magical place for Reds, Ta-Kumsaw and Taleswapper must cooperate to save Alvin, who is in serious trouble. Each person who climbs the mound sees something different and goes by different paths. There is no way to find Alvin's path unless these friends of Alvin's, the Red and the White, grip each other

> face to face . . . breast to breast . . . if there had been anyone to see them [no one] would know which leg belonged to which man . . . [Ta-Kumsaw explained,] "We are one man with two souls, a Red soul and a White soul, one man."[11]

In this way, they find Alvin in time. But Ta-Kumsaw then learns the news of a dreadful massacre by Whites of his Prophet-brother's peaceful village (because of a false rumor, maliciously and deliberately started by a White). Ta-Kumsaw then quarrels with Alvin and Taleswapper and tries to make his way down Eight-Faced Mound alone.

To his anguish, it is not possible do so. He cannot even live to get revenge on the Whites without a White man's help.

Ta-Kumsaw and his followers eventually ally themselves with the French but are betrayed by them. Across the Mizzipy, the Prophet has established a homeland for Reds who still wish to live as Reds, wrapped in impenetrable fog that will admit no Whites.

Ta-Kumsaw goes to join his brother.

THE BLACKS[12]

The magic used by the Blacks differs from that of the Whites and that of the Reds. The Blacks store parts of their heartfires in objects, such as little dolls, or clusters of knotted cord. In the case of slaves, what they store is anger and rebellion; otherwise slavery would be so unbearable that Blacks would be violently and constantly rebelling—and would lose their lives. The part of the heartfire that contains anger (and also hope) is called the True Name (that is to say, the African name). With the True Name unavailable the slaves are passive, rebelling only in subtle ways, such as being lazy and slow.

But if the power that contains the True Name is broken and the slave remembers his or her True Name, all the stored up rage explodes at once. Only a very good Black can restrain himself, or herself, from trying to kill every White in sight, including little babies. Some *are* heroically good enough to restrain themselves; many are not. Of course the reprisals taken later by the Whites are appalling.

Peggy is a tireless worker for the abolition of slavery. With her ability as a torch she can see the self-crippled heartfires of the slaves and knows exactly what they have done to themselves in order to survive. They are passive, but not content. But she also knows that a general slave rebellion is not the solution. Furthermore, there is an even worse and more probable outcome of slavery—war. Indeed, her torchy knack (confirmed by someone with even more remarkable gifts than hers) tells her that war has become inevitable. Yet she won't stop trying for a better way.

These three different types of magic (the White knacks, the Red land-sense and greensong, the Black storage of the True Name) are not in-born racial traits. They are cultural matters, handed down from parent to child, nurtured in the community. It is not impossible for someone raised in one culture to learn the magic of another.

However, too often, instead of trying to understand another culture (in either its magic or mundane characteristics) people will try to imitate the *worst* traits of the culture they envy. Denmark Vesey, a very bright Black, was illegally taught to read, write, and do math so that he could be more useful to his plantation master (who is also his father). When his master died, Denmark went to the city pretending to be the messenger-slave of a nonexistent White man who does bookkeeping jobs and copywork at home. Denmark himself would do the work and take the money. When he got wealthy enough he bought himself a woman, in the name of his fictitious white master.

The former slave became a slave owner, and a harsh one at that. It is a parallel, of sorts, to the musket-carrying Reds who are more cruel and untrustworthy than the ones with bows and arrows. Greedy imitation is not true learning, and it is no way to get the best of what another culture has to offer. Denmark eventually changes radically for the better, but it takes a catastrophe of giant proportions for him to do that.

THE UNKNOWN PURPOSE OF IT ALL

Is there any supreme purpose behind these events? Again and again there are hints. Here is what Arthur Stuart thinks:

> Somebody is in charge of all this. Somebody gave Alvin the powers that he's got. Somebody led his family to Horace Guester's roadhouse, so Little Peggy would be in place to watch over him. Why did my mother fly so

near to that place, so I'd be there waiting when Alvin came back? And [these other friends]—how did they get to meet up with him? Don't tell me it was chance cause I don't believe in it.[13]

At different times, both Alvin and Peggy separately make such statements. They don't know all the details, but their lives are in the hands of Someone. Not everything is revealed, even to a torch; but a pattern can sometimes be discerned.

The image of *weaving*, of combining different threads into a pattern, occurs often in these books, shown literally and equated with knowing the future. An individual thread has little awareness of the pattern; but the weaver can see it.

A divine purpose will not protect you from tragedy, but it can ensure that the results will (in the long run) be worth it. With confidence in Someone in charge there will always be a note of hope.

FANTASY AS EXAGGERATION

One of the uses of fantasy (aside from entertaining storytelling) is to take something from our real world and exaggerate it so that we can see it better.

It is a fact that the European settlers of North America brought with them many tools and machines and ways of using them that must have seemed like magic to the Native Americans. It is a fact that Native Americans could move through the forest with such speed and silence that it seemed impossible. It is a fact that the enslaved Africans must have had some way of suppressing their normal anger for the sake of survival.

One of the many historical characters in the Tales of Alvin Maker is Napoleon Bonaparte. Details of his life and work are different, but his character is shown as very similar to that of the Napoleon we know. His knack is to win the trust and confidence of anyone whomsoever. *Do* we know *why* it is that dictators and despots are often so much more popular than they deserve? Isn't it somewhat mysterious?

No, Card is not suggesting that it is true that seventh sons have extraordinary powers, or that Native Americans could call the game to them to be killed, or that slaves hid their anger in objects, or that Napoleon's charm was literally a magic charm. But by taking aspects of life and history that are hard to understand, and exaggerating them, he can almost make us believe it.

Card does not believe in magic; but he certainly *does* believe in a God who ultimately rules the world.

THE ROOTS OF THESE STORIES[14]

When Card was a graduate student at the University of Utah, he was required to read *The Faerie Queen* by Edmund Spenser. This is an immense work of epic poetry, longer than most long novels. Few people, including literature professors, have actually read every word all the way through. Card loved the poem and hated it. He hated it for being overly and obviously allegorical, but he was fascinated with the way that Spenser, who was an Elizabethan, reached back to an older tradition that still resonated in Elizabethan Britain: the tradition of knights on a quest, Arthur and The Round Table, all imbued with fantastic adventure. Spenser said that his poem was The Matter of Britain.

Card thought, "Why not The Matter of America? Why not set a quest story on the early American frontier, which had almost as many legends and superstitions as the early Middle Ages?" He first thought of trying it in narrative verse, as Spenser did, and began "Prentice Alvin and the No-Good Plow."[15]

After about twelve pages he realized that narrative poetry was not the means he wished to use to tell this story. However, he did submit the poem, incomplete as it was, to a Utah State Fine Arts Contest and won a prize.

Once he started on the series of Alvin Maker novels (it was originally intended to be four or five books long; now he believes that it will be about seven) he ran into trouble with copyeditors. He wanted his characters to speak in a frontier dialect but he kept getting his manuscripts back with the spelling and grammar "corrected!" Finally, Card convinced the copyeditors of the rightness of what he was doing.

There are those who realize, reading these books, that in many ways the life of Alvin Maker parallels the life of Joseph Smith, the original prophet of the Latter-Day Saints (Mormons). However, in many ways, Alvin's life does *not* parallel Joseph Smith's life. Card says that he took Joseph Smith's life as the "skeleton" of the story, but "all of my stories come out of my own head." And he further says, "I don't care if people get the Mormon allusions or not."[16]

These are the Tales of Alvin Maker, a fictional character. This is The Matter of America, not The Matter of Mormonism. It is not in the least necessary that one know anything about Mormonism, or want to know anything about Mormonism, to enjoy these stories completely.

Indeed, there may even be times when such knowledge is a disadvantage to enjoyment. Sometimes there is an episode that Mormons recognize and think "intrusive" but non-Mormons don't mind it at all.[17]

However, there *are* some beliefs basic to enjoyment of these stories:

- You must believe that good and evil are in conflict in the world, and that each one of us is eventually on one side or the other.
- You must believe that some people have unusual gifts, and that proper use of those gifts is a vital matter.
- You must believe that everyone is important, and that no one, no matter how gifted, will do great things all alone; you must be willing to learn from everybody.
- And finally, no matter what tragedies occur there is always hope that, in the long run, the outcome will be worth it.

If you can believe that—or, at least pretend that you do while reading—you can enjoy The Tales of Alvin Maker.

NOTES

1. Faren Miller, "Locus Looks At Books," review of *Seventh Son, Locus* 20, no. 5 (May 1987), 13.

2. Orson Scott Card, *Seventh Son,* paperback edition (New York: Tom Doherty Associates, Tor, 1987), 65.

3. Orson Scott Card, *Red Prophet,* paperback edition (New York: Tom Doherty Associates, Tor, 1988), 164–165.

4. Orson Scott Card, *Heartfire,* paperback edition (New York: Tom Doherty Associates, Tor, 1998), 244.

5. Orson Scott Card, *Prentice Alvin,* paperback edition (New York: Tom Doherty Associates, Tor, 1989), 14.

6. Orson Scott Card, *Alvin Journeyman,* paperback edition (New York: Tom Doherty Associates, Tor, 1985), 369.

7. Card, *Prentice Alvin,* 46.

8. Card, *Prentice Alvin,* 125.

9. Card, *Heartfire,* 14.

10. Episodes concerning Reds occur throughout these books, but most of the development of this theme occurs in *Red Prophet* (1998). Readers who have read Card's book *Speaker for the Dead* (1986) or the discussion of it in chapter 3 will see some similarities of the themes in *Speaker* and in *Red Prophet.*

11. Card, *Red Prophet*, 255–256.

12. Episodes concerning Blacks (free or slave) occur throughout these books, but most of the development of this theme occurs in *Heartfire*.

13. Card, *Heartfire*, 134.

14. Some of the information in this section can be found in *Maps in a Mirror: The Short Fiction of Orson Scott Card* (New York: Tom Doherty Associates, Tor, 1990), 670–671. Also, from my interview, September 12, 2000.

15. *Maps in a Mirror*, 589–600.

16. The remarks quoted in this paragraph are from the interview mentioned in note 14. For a further discussion on this topic, see Alma Jean Porschet, "Orson Scott Card: Without Joseph Smith and Mormonism There Would Be No Seventh Son, No Red Prophet, No Alvin Maker" (a thesis submitted to the Department of English of the State University of New York, College of Brockport, in partial fulfillment of the degree of Master of Arts, 1994), published online at Hatrack River (www.hatrack.com), the official website for fans of Orson Scott Card. Porschet and I are in agreement that one need not know Mormonism to appreciate these books.

17. Porschet, "Orson Scott Card," 23.

5

The Homecoming
Series and More

The Memory of Earth, The Call of Earth, The Ships of Earth, Earthfall, Earthborn; also, the Beginning of The Mayflower Trilogy, *Lovelock*

The five books of The Homecoming Series are unique in their scope and origin. They have a religious model that will not be obvious to everyone and are developed beyond that model.

Millions of years before these stories begin, a remnant of the human race had departed Earth. Humans had ruined their world with wars and exploitation. Some starships found a livable world less than a hundred light-years away. Because of relativistic time effects, the hundred years were just ten years to the ship. They named their new world "Harmony" and gave it a master computer, known as the Oversoul. They genetically altered the minds of their descendants to be sensitive to its influence.

HOW THE OVERSOUL RULES HARMONY

The Oversoul patrols the planet by satellites. It does not prevent all wickedness. Humans must be free to be human, but not free to destroy their world. The people of Harmony commit violent crimes and even have small wars. But knowledge that would enable anyone to quickly destroy a large number of people is withheld. Any person thinking that way becomes "stupid," unable to concentrate.

For the people of Harmony, the Oversoul is that invisible, mysterious power that spreads art, music, poetry, and learning over their world. It is worshipped. The people don't know that their technology is censored.

Some technology is advanced; for example, a seriously handicapped person uses magnetic floats or a solar-powered chair that can fly. But no one on Harmony has ever thought of using *wheels* except in children's toys or as small gears in machines. People travel on foot or on animals. No farmer puts his produce in a wagon. No general uses wheeled vehicles to rapidly transport troops, munitions, and supplies. There is no means of fast communication except through the Oversoul. There are computers, but no Internet.

This mixture of high technology with no technology produces strange scenes, although they are natural to the characters in the story. We read of a camel caravan stopping in the desert and are told that they make "a corral for the camels, made of piled stones bonded with a gravatic field powered by solar collectors."[1]

With the frequent mention of donkeys, camels, and open-air markets, and the prevalence of desert (studded with oases and fertile valleys), the atmosphere is one of an unevenly technological Arabian Nights—or an unevenly technological *biblical* scene.

The Oversoul allows some personal weapons. The weak must have power against the strong. The people of Harmony have a solar-powered handgun called a pulse, and a charged-wire blade, but nothing explosive.

The body of the Oversoul computer and the original starships are enclosed in a stasis field from which all corrosives (such as oxygen) are excluded. A strong aversion perimeter is established so that people thinking of going in that direction lose interest. There is one blind spot in the Oversoul: It cannot see its physical self, the starships, the stasis field, and the aversion perimeter. Thus, even persons who are expert in understanding the Oversoul cannot use it to find that location.

The humans who settled Harmony planned for this system to last twenty million years. By that time (they believed) humanity could be trusted with technology of potential mass destruction—or humanity would be naturally extinct. Either way, it would not matter if the Oversoul's satellites fell and its powers decayed.

The builders of the Oversoul succeeded beyond their dreams, but they also failed. Their machines have lasted *forty* million years and are just now beginning to deteriorate. But humans are still human. There are people of greediness and ambition as always. There are people of love, generosity, and courage, but, as ever, there are never enough of them.

The wheel is being reinvented. Empire building is starting. Some people realize that their thoughts are controlled. Every year more satellites fall and the Oversoul's power grows weaker. The Oversoul must return to Earth and get help from the Keeper of Earth.

What is this "Keeper of Earth"? We will get many clues, but the answer will remain ambiguous.

To return to Earth the Oversoul needs help. Humans have hands that can wield tools to repair robots that are designed to recondition a starship. Since humans are intuitive, they may help the Oversoul find the starships and find *itself*.

There are many different civilizations on Harmony. The Oversoul chooses to look for the humans it needs in the city–state of Basilica.

BASILICA, THE CITY OF WOMEN

Only women may own property in Basilica. No man even stays overnight in the city unless a woman has invited him. Marriage is at the discretion of the woman. She agrees to a contract with a specific duration; she decides whether or not to renew. Unmarried persons are not expected to be virgins. Indeed, when a boy begins puberty he is assigned an "auntie," an older, experienced woman to instruct him in basic sexuality. Then he can instruct a girl, or even contract for a first marriage.

Basilica has a busy commercial life; markets sell practical items and decadent luxuries. It has a busy entertainment life of poetry, music, drama, and dance. The schools are renowned. There is little violent crime within the walls; but in the slums outside the walls, where men live who never qualified for citizenship, violence can be terrible.

The men speak of the Oversoul as "he," the women speak of it as "she." Even persons who have begun to realize that the Oversoul is an artifact cannot quite say "it."

The city is beautiful, and it is doomed.

In the first book, *The Memory of Earth*, before that doom occurs, the Oversoul begins plans to draw sixteen persons, eight men and eight women, out of Basilica. These are the ones that the Oversoul will guide to return to Earth. The first selections are from the families of Volemak.

THE FAMILIES OF VOLEMAK

A vision of the doom of Basilica comes first to Volemak, a respected citizen who sells exotic plants. He is married to Rasa, who runs a prestigious school. Their marriage is devoted and faithful. Each has been married before.

They have two sons together, Issib and Nafai. Issib, handicapped and dependent upon Basilican technology, has done scholarly studies that are enabling him to discover the Oversoul's censorship and even to penetrate it briefly. Nafai, fourteen, is learning this from Issib. When they realize that their father is correct in his visions of doom, Nafai offers himself to the Oversoul to help save the city and the planet.

Volemak has two other sons from other marriage contracts. Elemak, the eldest, heads the caravans necessary for Volemak's business. He leads with determination, strength of purpose, and general knowledge. However, his discipline of unruly caravan members is rough and cruel. He knows no other way to keep order.

Nafai grew up admiring Elemak, his eldest half-brother. Now, the two clash, sometimes brutally on Elemak's part. Elemak soon wants to kill Nafai, since Nafai is clearly favored by the Oversoul. He tries to kill him on Basilica, and also during the voyage to Earth and again on Earth. The Oversoul can protect Nafai, but not alter Elemak's mind or make him forget his intent; Elemak's mind is too strong. His repeated humiliating failures at murder do not teach him generosity, humility, or even justice; they only teach him subtlety, patience, and long-term planning.

Volemak's second oldest son, Mebbekew, is simply Elemak's jackal. He is not very bright, and he follows Elemak, doing whatever his brother wants.

Rasa has two daughters by her earlier marriage with Gaballufix, a Basilican citizen of unscrupulous ambition. These daughters have married badly and are unfaithful to their husbands. Rasa is closer to many of her students than to her daughters. Among these students is Luet, only twelve. She is a waterseer who understands dreams and visions. She interprets Volemak's vision.

Gaballufix, Rasa's former mate, is working to seize power. He plots against the life of Volemak and deceitfully gets cooperation from Elemak and Mebbekew. The Oversoul tells Luet, the waterseer, and Luet warns Nafai.

Volemak and his four sons all leave the city by night and camp in a green valley in the desert. But Volemak, guided by a dream, sends his sons back to the city to get the Index, a sphere that makes the words of the Oversoul entirely plain. The Index is in Gaballufix's possession, and it is mortally dangerous to try to get it by any means.

Gaballufix has filled the city with identical soldiers who wear holographic-illusion costumes. Nafai comes upon what seems to be one of Gaballufix's soldiers, drunk in the ditch. He tries to steal the costume for a disguise. But this is not a soldier; it is Gaballufix himself. Gaballufix has been celebrating the assassination of another major rival. He plans to have Nafai blamed for that.

The Oversoul speaks in Nafai's mind, telling him to *kill* Gaballufix, to put on the clothes and the holographic costume, go to Gaballufix's house and get the Index.

Nafai feels that this is impossible. Gaballufix deserves it, but Nafai's grudges against him are too personal. This wouldn't be justice, it would be cowardly revenge taken on a helpless man. The Oversoul charges him: "You are going to *save* lives. . . . Should the billions of souls . . . die so that you can keep your hands clean?"[2]

The only weapon available is Gaballufix's own charged-wire blade. It doesn't stab. Nafai must take off Gaballufix's head. Nafai never completely recovers from this. For the rest of his life that scene haunts him. Elemak and Mebbekew taunt him with it when they feel that he pretends to be better than they are.

But he does bring back the Index. When they return to Volemak, the Oversoul, speaking through the Index, tells them of the quest that they are to fulfill.

The second book, *The Call of Earth*,[3] shows us how Basilica is in anarchy from the death of Gaballufix. In this uproar, a military general arrives from outside to "help restore order." He is the sort of person that The City of Women was organized to *prevent* having any authority. The general's nickname is Moozh, which means "husband." The city accepts him as leader, "marries" him. General Moozh brings his bride, Basilica, security and prosperity in the near future, but total ruin eventually.

Another dream, this time sent to Elemak, sends the sons of Volemak back into Basilica one last time, to get women for their quest.

The confusions following the death of Gaballufix and Moozh's coup give rise to various circumstances in which certain citizens are encouraged to leave Basilica. These are Rasa, her daughters and their current husbands, and some young women who are present or former students of Rasa. Luet is one the students; she marries Nafai. One former student is Shedemei, a biologist who had not intended to marry or leave

Basilica. However, she has received a dream of a whole planet for her laboratory.

THE QUEST FOR THE OVERSOUL AND THE STARSHIPS

Now, in the third book, *The Ships of Earth*,[4] most traditions of Basilica are reversed. In the trek across the desert, women count for nothing outside their reproductive functions. Men are the strong ones who load camels and do other heavy work. Marriages are permanent. Infidelity can be punished. Old grudges flare, and Luet's skill as a seer prevents a double murder.

After three years of travel, the eight men and eight women and the children born in that time settle on a fertile and uninhabited peninsula. They build houses, plant, hunt, and raise families for six years. By then, there are thirty-five children for whom stories of a city called Basilica sound as mythological as stories of Planet Earth.

They are only a day's journey from the Oversoul and the starships. The aversion perimeter keeps their hunters away. By adroit questions through the Index, Nafai deduces the aversion perimeter. He goes alone, overcomes the aversion and at great risk punctures the invisible fence and penetrates the stasis field. The Oversoul recovers the blanked-out part of its memory, realizes that Nafai belongs here, and abolishes the fence.

In the great building that *is* the Oversoul, Nafai becomes Starmaster, the one who will have authority on the space voyage. He wears a transparent cloak next to his skin that makes him luminescent, vastly increases his knowledge and powers, and makes him almost invulnerable.

A STARSHIP CALLED *BASILICA* AND THE
EARTH TO WHICH IT RETURNS

In the fourth book, *Earthfall*,[5] the community works together to repair a starship. They name it *Basilica*. The Oversoul duplicates itself, putting one version of itself on board. En route, in his antagonism to Nafai, Elemak comes close to causing the death of everyone. The colony begins to divide between "Elemaki" and "Nafari."

In four million years, two intelligent species have evolved on Earth. Images of them have been appearing in the dreams of the colonists.

These dreams are not from the Oversoul. The colonists refer to the two species as "angels" and "diggers."

Angels are batlike, but with both hands and wings. They create sculptures. At the time that the humans enter the *Basilica,* an angel sculpts a face that he is sure is a face of an Old One, a member of the intelligent species that lived on Earth long ago. No one knows what the Old Ones looked like.

The diggers, who are giant rodents, take the sculptures underground and worship them. But this strange sculpture is set apart and worshipped differently.

Soon after the humans from Harmony arrive, Elemak tears an angel's wings in fury. He believes that it has stolen his baby daughter. It was actually the diggers who had taken the child, and it is Nafai who arranges to have her returned unharmed. Shedemei, the biologist, succeeds in repairing the torn wing. Humans and angels begin to communicate and share technology. Angels call individual humans "aunt" and "father."

As a gesture of peace, the diggers show how they have preserved the strange sculpture. It is a portrait of Nafai!

Elemak, shamed by his error, becomes a broken man who will make no decisions. Volemak, to restore his son, appoints him liaison with the diggers. Elemak recovers too well and uses his position to build an army of diggers loyal to the Elemaki.

It isn't easy for all three species to live together in peace. Diggers have had a habit of seizing and eating angel babies. Humans do not always set a good example. Two killings occur in the human colony, and a digger witnesses this.

After humans have been back on Earth for about twenty years, Volemak is dying. It was Volemak who had kept some peace between Elemaki and Nafari. Now, an Elemaki coup, backed by his loyal diggers, seems inevitable. The Nafari wish to seek a homeland far from the Elemaki, but Elemak has forbidden them to leave.

Nafai gives the cloak of the Starmaster to Shedemei who uses the power of the cloak to cover their retreat and help the Elemaki get safely away. Then she goes back up into orbit to live in the *Basilica.* The cloak prolongs her life, and she uses the hibernation chambers to sleep and to wake up in later centuries.

The human nations of Elemaki and Nafari develop separately, dividing again and again. Gradually the terms "sky people" and "earth people" are used as often as "angels" and "diggers." Humans are "middle people." After about 400 years the number of humans on planet Earth is in the hundreds of thousands. Shedemei, known in folklore as The-One-Who-Was-Never-Buried, returns to Earth again, in the last book, *Earthborn*.[6]

AKMA: A SLAVE WHO BECOMES A PERSECUTOR

Akmaro, of the Nafari, used to be a priest. He taught heretical doctrines: that everyone, not just priests, should learn to read and write; that the Keeper of Earth wants all people, (earth, sky, and middle) to be friends; that women's minds are as good as men's; and that the Wives of the Heroes of Old (such as Rasa or Luet) are Heroes too. Now, this Nafari kingdom has been conquered by Elemaki. An Elemaki named Pabulog forces Akmaro's family to work in the fields, driven by the whips of digger overseerers.

Pabulog's four nasty sons connive in the persecution of the family, but Akmaro makes friends of these tormentors of his family. He teaches them the heretical doctrines and converts them. The sons of Pabulog cease their torments, repudiate their father, and help the Akmaro's family, and all the other Nafari slaves, to escape

But Akma, son of Akmaro, cannot accept this. Akma feels that his family, and the other Nafari, should not be allied with the sons of Pabulog even if they are repentant. "Father forgave them before they asked" he bitterly exclaims.[7] Nor can Akma accept his father's beliefs about equality. To Akma, the only good digger is a dead one.

Darakemba

Akmaro, his family, and the other escaped Nafari, together with the regenerate sons of Pabulog, come to the free Nafari land of Darakemba. King Motiak of Darakemba appoints Akmaro as High Priest. It is proclaimed that, in Darakemba, all people, male and female, earth, sky or middle, have equal rights. All are the "Kept" of the Keeper. Diggers, and others who have had second-class citizenship, rejoice. Others conform.

Akma is quietly angry with his priestly father and also with the King. He has a long-range plan. He will be the chief advisor to the *next* king. He will wage war, exterminating diggers and crushing Elemaki. Akma makes friends with all four of Motiak's sons and is persuasive. He teaches disbelief in the Keeper. After thirteen years, Akma has the princes plotting against their father, the King.

Shedemei and Her School

Shedemei comes down from the *Basilica* and founds a school for girls—middle girls, sky girls, and earth girls, all together. This is a scandal for many sky people and middle people. Angels and humans going to school with former *slaves*? Shedemei is brought to trial. The judge rules that Shedemei has not broken the law, but that the accusers have. They are heretics, and are liable to Akmaro, the High Priest, for heresy.

Akmaro has the authority to impose severe penalties for heresy, but the only penalty he imposes on Shedemei's accusers is excommunication from the faith of the Kept. This is well-intentioned. But people who have always hated the Kept, and the doctrines of equality, now feel that the Kept can be attacked without any serious risk.

Persecution and the Prayer of Desperation

It begins as vandalism, then escalates to violence. Akma, claiming that he never wanted violence, eloquently proposes a boycott. Don't hire diggers. Don't buy crops or merchandise grown or produced by diggers. Drive diggers out of Darakemba by a peaceful boycott, and there will be no more problem. Many earth people start sad treks to leave the only homes they have known.

High Priest Akmaro, agonized, prays a prayer of desperation. He puts his beloved son Akma into the hands of the Keeper for justice. He prays that the Keeper will save the *victims* of his son. He hopes with all his soul that the Keeper can save them without striking Akma dead. But if that is the only solution he will accept it.

Shedemei's Dream

Shedemei hears of Akmaro's new prayer. She goes back up to the *Basilica* and demands that the Keeper send her a True Dream. Her Dream reveals the Keeper as a power that controls all of Earth, including earthquake, the magma flow, and continental drift. Also, the Keeper watches over all the forty worlds colonized from Earth millions of years ago, and over all the Oversouls of those worlds.

As Volemak had once done, Shedemei dreams of a tree with perfect white fruit with exquisite taste. When she wakes, she knows what she must do.

Confrontation and Descent into Hell

Akma and the King's sons are walking, planning their next speaking stop. The ground shakes, there is a roar, and a huge gray object (the *Basilica*'s lander) plummets toward them with fire. A humanlike figure emerges. It is so radiant that it cannot be clearly seen. Its voice is unendurable. (Shedemei has ignited the light of the Starmaster's cloak to the maximum and she is using a distorting microphone set to five painful pitches.)

The shining one condemns Akma for being the same kind of oppressor that once oppressed him. Electricity leaps towards Akma. He collapses. The four deeply shaken and wildly repentant sons of King Motiak carry Akma back to the city.

Akma, in his coma, is experiencing torments of the damned. He realizes that he had always known that there was a Keeper. His anger had been at the Keeper for not letting him, Akma, be the one who heroically freed the slaves and giving that honor to his father and to the repentant sons of Pabulog instead.

Akma, in his coma, experiences the suffering that he has caused. He is in the body and mind of an old earth woman being beaten by huge humans, and in the body and mind of a child crying with hunger whose father lost his income in the boycott. He experiences not just the victims, but also the perpetrators, and the influential people that the perpetrators were trying to impress, everyone affected by his speeches.

Akma's crimes are endless. He wants to die. But he remembers the words of his father, High Priest Akmaro: "When you are at the point of despair, my son . . . then remember this: The Keeper loves us . . . all."[8]

Is it true? Can he be given another chance? As he asks this, he remembers all the people who love him. He tastes a perfect white fruit. He opens his eyes and sees his parents who had already forgiven him before he asked. Akma begins his lifetime of undoing the harm he has done.

Shedemei does not go back up to the *Basilica*. She is finished with sleeping centuries away. She stays in Darakemba to teach and to live out her life on Earth.

SOME MEANINGS OF THESE STORIES

Feminine and Masculine: Basilica Versus the Nomadic Life

Card invented the city of Basilica as an exaggeration of a common theory that "civilization exists to serve the needs of women."[9]

The female-dominated city of Basilica (not typical of most of Harmony) is in decay; its mating habits are a symptom of that. Basilica has much that is good, but it is fragile. It can be symbolized by the women's worship: a priestess floating on water to receive her visions. That can be appealing, but she must be floating on calm water. What would she do if she came to rapids? What can The City of Women do when it drifts into anarchy, civil war breaks out? The city embraces what she feared: The Dominant Male.

The male-dominated society is also doomed. Elemak, typical of male domination at its worst, has a discipline adapted from his days of leading camel caravans. He ties a misbehaving person up in an unnatural position, wrists tied to ankles. This is an image of over-domination, strangling the nourishing flow of the blood in an "uncivilized" way. Over-dominant males will warp society into something unnatural before they yield.

Does Elemak have any excuse for his enmity towards Nafai? It must be galling to see a younger brother succeed where oneself has failed. But the Oversoul tries to make Elemak see that he need not be inferior. It is Elemak, not Volemak or Nafai, who receives the dream of the need for wives. The Oversoul speaks in Elemak's mind to remind him of this at a moment of jealousy. But Elemak would rather believe that the voice in his mind was his own delusion than believe that Nafai really received all those inspirations.[10]

It is obvious (*except* to men and women who want to dominate) that no society can flourish without the partnership of masculine and feminine thinking. Volemak and Rasa can accomplish more than either can alone. Nafai and Luet learn from each other. In Genesis 1:27 we read, "In the image of God . . . male and female."

When the colony has that six-year rest on the peninsula, the habits of masculine domination persist. Even men who should know better, such as Volemak and even Nafai, fall into the habit of treating their intelligent, kindly wives as servants. After Nafai receives the Starmaster's cloak, this is the first thing that he changes in himself.

The Command to Murder

In all the religions and ethical codes of humanity the one most constant is Thou Shalt Not Murder. The deliberate killing of fellow humans is to be reserved for wars in a just cause and properly legalized death penalties (and perhaps not even then). If a life must be taken for the public good, execution should be done by those who do their duty and have no personal bias against the one executed.

Possibly, once in a million years, there may be an exception. If so, then the command must be given to someone who obeys it with horror. Neither Elemak or Mebbekew would have had trouble killing Gaballufix, helpless or not. Either one would have bragged about it. Therefore, neither one must be allowed to do it. The one who is sickened, distressed to his soul, will not become something as evil as the one he kills.

Dreams

On the trek on Harmony to find the Oversoul, the original colonists and their children have dreams of angels and diggers sent to them by the Keeper of Earth. Volemak is the first to dream of the perfect white fruit; he dreams of people climbing the tree while others mock them. Four hundred years later Shedemei, in her own dream, will identify that fruit as the symbol of the love of the Keeper.

Nafai has a dream of the angels and diggers, and also the white fruit. At the end he almost sees the Keeper of Earth, but the light is too dazzling "as if the Keeper were a small star, a sun too bright to look into."[11] This dream is our first evidence of the nature of the Keeper.

When Nafai wakes, he is looking into the face of a friendly baboon!

Symbolism of the Baboons

It is a descent from the sublime to the ridiculous for Nafai to wake from his transcendental dream in that way. The baboons are symbols in Book 3, *The Ships of Earth*. Mebbekew wants to hunt and kill them. When humans abandon a garden to move on, Luet teaches the baboons how to find good fruit.

Card, in his Acknowledgments,[12] mentions Shirley Strum, the author of a book on baboons titled *Almost Human*. These creatures, near the border of rational thought, show us the nature of humanity by comparison. These humans, as their dreams show, will encounter "animals" that have crossed that border on Earth. It is appropriate that they should get preparation for relating to them by first relating to the "almost human."

Freedom is the Best, but Freedom is Risky

Was it wrong for Volemak to try to rehabilitate Elemak when Elemak was despondent after his mistake in attacking the angel? It might have been better if Elemak had stayed lethargic. Some people have preferred that Elemak turn suicidal.

But Volemak could not have left Elemak despondent and still be Volemak. There was an error of judgment: Volemak underestimated Elemak's ingenuity. But Volemak would never agree that there was an error of principle. Elemak, like everyone else, deserved freedom to make amends, to have his own work, to shape his own life—even at a risk to the community.

Was it wrong for High Priest Akmaro to impose no sentence upon Shedemei's heretical accusers except excommunication? In the end, there is little middle ground between total freedom of speech and religion on one hand, or merciless, corrupted despotism on the other. If you don't want the despotism, you have to risk the freedom.

But that freedom *is* risky! In our day, freedom of religion has led to suicide cults, such as Jonestown Village and Heaven's Gate. True, the followers made their own choice, but the little children did not choose. Akma was "only speaking" but his speech was a wildfire. "Eternal vigilance is the price of liberty."[13]

Forgiveness is Essential

Akma complained that it was not justice for his father to forgive the sons of Pabulog for their cruelties "before they asked." He was right; his father was going *beyond* justice, not falling short of it. Justice by itself is never enough. It is better to "destroy" an enemy by making a friend of him, if possible. We should learn to be quick with forgiveness because we all need it, sometimes before we ask.

People who cry for justice will get it, as Akma certainly does. Happily, Akma was not Elemak; there was a limit to his self-righteousness and self-deception.

The Intellectual Dishonesty of Some Religious Skeptics

There is honest doubt. There is doubt that is not honest at all.

Elemak has evidence, over and over again, of the Oversoul (and later of the Keeper of Earth) working through Nafai, but he will not accept it. Mon, one of the sons of Motiak that Akma corrupts, has a gift of "truthsense"; he can tell when something is wrong. But in order to belong to the group, Mon will deny his gift. Akma sees miracles for which the existence of the Keeper is the most straightforward explanation. He prefers to explain them away.

The irony is that the dishonest skeptic does precisely what he accuses believers of doing. Skeptics tell believers: You just *want* to believe that. You won't look at the evidence. You are going along with others; trust your gut instinct instead. You are inconsistent in what you believe, and won't accept straightforward explanations. You explain things away. And so the dishonest skeptic describes himself.

The Keeper of Earth

Who is this Keeper of Earth? Who is this One who sends dreams, images, and messages over a hundred light years in an instant, who controls the Earth's magma flow, who is clearly *at least* as much beyond the Oversoul as the Oversoul is beyond human thought? If this is not "God the Father, Creator of . . . all that is, seen and unseen"[14] then this must be an archangelic power (not a sky-person, but a power of Heaven).

Even if the Keeper is less than God Almighty, The Keeper speaks for God Almighty, just as Shedemei, in her Starmaster cloak, spoke for the Keeper. Whatever the Keeper may be is beyond human analysis.

Symbolism of Cloaks and Disguises

Throughout, but especially in the first book, we encounter masks, cloaks, costumes, and other disguises.

The cloak of the Starmaster is the opposite of the holographic costumes worn by the soldiers of Gaballufix and that made all the soldiers look alike. The Starmaster's cloak, on the other hand, enhances the individual self, unless it is necessary to use it otherwise. Other cloaks can be stolen. The Starmaster's cloak cannot be stolen from the Starmaster (which is frustrating to Elemak) but it can be freely given. Power from a higher source does not conceal as often as it reveals. It cannot be stolen; it can always be shared.

So pervasive are these symbols of cloaks, masks, and the like that the reader may wonder whether Card is telling us that this whole story is a mask.

ROOTS OF THE HOMECOMING SERIES[15]

Some years before 1992, Card conceived the idea of turning the stories in certain parts of The Book of Mormon into a science fiction narrative; a voyage across the sea would become a voyage across space. It would have embellishments of Card's own. The plot structure for the first four volumes would come from the Book of Mormon, First and Second Nephi, and the fifth and last from the Book of Alma.

His publishers agreed that nothing anywhere in the book would say, "Based on the Book of Mormon." Mormons would recognize it; others wouldn't be deterred from a good story that they might enjoy. (Similarly, when Isaac Asimov wrote The Foundation Trilogy the books did not say "based on Gibbon's *Decline and Fall of the Roman Empire*.")

Most reviewers were not familiar with the Book of Mormon (including this writer). *The Memory of Earth, The Call of Earth,* and *The Ships of Earth* were usually reviewed as straight science fiction. The religious overtones were instantly detected: "[A] Biblical parable and a thoroughly enjoyable piece of storytelling;"[16] "An allegorical retelling of Exodus."[17] Sometimes the response was more on the ethical dilemmas than on the religious dimension: "As always, Mr. Card writes with energy and conviction about agonizing moral problems."[18]

A discordant note came from Tom Easton, the book reviewer at *Analog Science Fact and Fiction*. Easton usually likes Card, but in this case he felt that the "mimicry of scripture" was overdone. Easton objected to what he saw as an anti-rational message, that is, sometimes the Oversoul is more accurate than a person's reasoning. "[W]e must hope the series is . . . a temporary aberration."[19]

Mormon commentators were generally favorable: "Card's commitment to belief echoes through his characters' commitments [not so much by] theological assertion [as by] elemental truthfulness of human motivation—love, faith, greed, ambition, fear, revenge—that underlies the true Story."[20] But there were Mormon readers disturbed by this series. What Card was doing seemed like plagiarism, or at least disrespect. Some wrote or telephoned Card, which he appreciated because he could then discuss the matter directly.

There were other complaints, behind his back, that he did not appreciate. Some "revealing" Card's "offense" wrote to the publisher. Others wrote to the general authorities of the Mormon Church expecting some sort of discipline.

Finally, Card posted an eleven-page document online at his Hatrack River website, "An Open Letter From Orson Scott Card to those who are concerned about "plagiarism" in *The Memory of Earth*." In this letter he made the following points: One cannot plagiarize history. There is a distinguished tradition of fiction writers retelling stories from history, legend, myth, and sacred writings. There is no obligation to inform the reader that a retelling is going on. Even if the Book of

Mormon *were* fiction, retelling it in completely different words is not plagiarism, and even if he *had* used the exact words of the Book of Mormon, the copyright expired long ago.

Does this mean that Card feels that he can do what he wants with anything not copyrighted? No! He feels that there are ethical limits. When borrowing from a respected source (historical, legendary, mythological, or sacred) the writer must keep the theme of the original—not make villains into heroes, heroes into villains, or reverse the meaning (as Card feels that *Jesus Christ Superstar* did, by glorifying Judas). He kept this rule in the Homecoming Series; he added much to his model (especially by adding women, including gifted ones). But he did not distort or reverse anything that was there.

Is it disrespectful to use science fiction to discuss the relationship of humans to God? Card emphatically thinks that it is one of the *best* genres for that purpose. His words on that subject, from "An Open Letter . . ." appear at the beginning of this book, under the heading "In The Hands of the Savior."

The Homecoming Series has fans. Some feel that it is Card's best. Card, himself, thought that it might rival *Ender's Game* in popularity.[21] But it does not. It sells, but not as well as the Ender books, or as well as the Tales of Alvin Maker. It provokes fewer questions when Card has public interviews. It has won no awards.

It contains magnificent writing, but the sheer *scope* of the story— forty million years of time, a Keeper who monitors the Oversouls of forty worlds—is staggering. The reader feels as though a marathon has been run, or a mountain climbed. If you *are* in the mood to run a marathon of ideas, or climb a mountain of imagination, try these books.

WHAT CARD ACCOMPLISHES IN HIS SERIES BOOKS

The central message of the Homecoming Series is similar to that in the Ender Saga and in The Tales of Alvin Maker. The Other Person (whether a being of another race, the other gender, or another species) is someone we need to understand. Wrongs will be committed, but some people can change, and conversion, not revenge, is best whenever possible. Since series books are good in showing development over time, they can sometimes make this message clearer than a single volume might.

A Series Long Unfinished

In collaboration with Kathryn H. Kidd, a longtime family friend and writer of mostly mainstream fiction that Card admires, Card began what was intended to be The Mayflower Trilogy, a series completely different from those we have discussed, but with similar themes.

The first book, *Lovelock*,[22] came out in 1994. The original intended theme was "small towns in space," but as Card and Kidd worked on it, the theme developed into something more.

In this book, humans have learned how to enhance the intelligence of certain species of animals, known as "witnesses" because they have total recall. To keep them under control, the witnesses are conditioned to go into agonizing convulsions if the owner utters the pain word. Humans have created slavery without shame.

Lovelock, an enhanced capuchin monkey, really likes his owner, the scientist Carole Jeanne Cocciolone. Yet he knows that she would turn him in for euthanasia if she knew his real thoughts. There is a potential slave revolt in this little subcommunity on a large starship, but in this first book we see just the potential, not the actual rumblings.

This is definitely a story of "How should we relate to the Other People?" just like the Ender Saga, The Tales of Alvin Maker, and The Homecoming Series. It holds some implications for the rights of the "dumb" animals of today, especially the brighter ones, such as chimpanzees and dolphins. *Library Journal* calls it "a penetrating exploration of inalienable rights in a story that gives 'humanistic' beliefs a new twist."[23]

Book 2 of the Mayflower Trilogy, *Rasputin*, has been listed as "in progress" since 1994. This series should be finished.

Taking Off the Mask

In Card's books there is not only the question of how mortal beings relate to each other. There is also the question of how we relate to the Immortal and Eternal.

Anyone who has read *only* the series of Card discussed at length in these first five chapters might be a bit impatient at this point. Perhaps the reader might say: "But Mr. Card, if you want to write about the relationship of people to God, why not say 'God' instead of 'Outside,' or 'Someone in charge,' or 'The Keeper'? If you want to write stories from Scripture, why not write about *Bible* characters? If you want to write about Mormons, why not write about Mormons, past, present, or future? Take off the mask, Mr. Card!"

In fact, he *has* been doing this, almost from the time he began writing. In part III we will see Card as the explicit Christian and as the explicit Mormon.

NOTES

1. Orson Scott Card, *The Memory of Earth,* paperback edition (New York: Tom Doherty Associates, Tor, 1992).

2. Card, *The Memory of Earth,* 307.

3. Orson Scott Card, *The Call of Earth,* paperback edition (New York: Tom Doherty Associates Tor, 1993).

4. Orson Scott Card, *The Ships of Earth*, paperback edition (New York: Tom Doherty Associates, Tor, 1994).

5. Orson Scott Card, *Earthfall,* paperback edition (New York: Tom Doherty Associates, Tor, 1995).

6. Card, Orson Scott, *Earthborn,* paperback edition (New York: Tom Doherty Associates, Tor, 1995).

7. Card, *Earthborn,* 265.

8. Card, *Earthborn,* 398. Akma is remembering words spoken at p. 326.

9. Orson Scott Card, the reply to a question by Chris Riding, Hatrack River website (www.hatrack.com), Student Research Area, "OSC Answers Questions," September 4, 2000.

10. Card, *The Call of Earth,* 312.

11. Card, *The Ships of Earth,* 157. Michael Collings finds it significant that this vision of the Keeper of Earth occurs almost in the exact center of *Ships,* the third of five books, and thus in almost the exact center of the whole series. Michael R. Collings, *Storyteller: The Official Orson Scott Card Bibliography and Guide* (Woodstock, Ga: Overlook Connection Press, 2001), 228.

12. Card, *The Ships of Earth,* vii.

13. Wendell Phillips, in a speech to the Massachusetts Anti-Slavery Society (1852), in *The New International Webster's Pocket Quotation Dictionary of The English Language,* revised ed., (Naples, Fla.: Trident Press, International, 2000), 209.

14. The Nicene Creed.

15. Information in this section comes from Collings, *Storyteller* (note 11) and from Orson Scott Card, "An Open Letter from Orson Scott Card to Those Who Are Concerned about 'Plagiarism' in *The Memory of Earth*" (Hatrack River Enterprises, 2000), Hatrack River website (www.hatrack.com). Also used is material from my interview with Card on September 12, 2000.

16. David E. Jones, a review of *The Memory of Earth, Chicago Tribune Books,* March 1, 1992.

17. Gerald Jonas, "Science Fiction," review of *The Ships of Earth, New York Times Book Review,* May 8, 1994, 25.

18. Gerald Jonas, "Science Fiction," review of *The Memory of Earth, New York Times Book Review,* March 15, 1992, 15.

19. Tom Easton, review of *The Memory of Earth, Analog Science Fact and Fiction,* August 1992, 166–167.

20. Collings, *Storyteller,* 203.

21. Panel discussion at Massachusetts Institute of Technology, Orson Scott Card and Allen Steele, November 20, 1997, online at www.hatrack.com.

22. Orson Scott Card, with Kathryn Kidd, *Lovelock,* paperback edition (New York: Tom Doherty Associates, Tor, 1994).

23. *Library Journal,* June 15, 1994, 99.

Part III

Card the Explicit Christian, and Card the Explicit Mormon

6

✝

Stories from the Bible

WOMEN OF GENESIS: BOOK ONE, *SARAH*

Sarai, ten years old, is drawing water for a visiting traveler at her father's house. He has "the face of a god, his eyes so bright, his smile
so warm, his cheek so golden with sunlight."[1] He is Abram, uncle of
Lot, come to negotiate the marriage of Lot with Sarai's sister, Qira. (Uncle
and nephew are both about twenty.) Abram promises that before Sarai
is twenty he will return to ask for her for himself.

Sarai and Qira's father is an exiled former king of Ur. Abram's people are wealthy desert nomads, of the lineage of Noah. Qira is not impressed. She must never live in a tent. Lot is required to maintain a city
house for her.

Sarai waits for Abram. He comes, two years early, and Sarai is joyful.
Eleven years go by, and apparently Sarai is barren. But a severe
drought is a more immediate problem. Abram, after consulting God,
says that they must sojourn in Egypt although that has dangers too.
Approaching Egypt, Abram learns from God that Pharaoh will kill him
if he knows that Sarai is his wife. He introduces Sarai as his sister. They
are separated, and Pharaoh tries to court Sarai.

This goes on for a year, and during this time Pharaoh's wives have
no children. Evidently, the household is under a curse. Finally Pharaoh
confesses his duplicity to Abram and his "sister." He had hoped to
marry her so that Abram's wife would come to the wedding. Then he

would poison Abram, marry his widow, and through that marriage so-
lidify his own shaky position as Pharaoh of Egypt.

When Pharaoh realizes the true situation, he is eager to get them out
of Egypt! Sarai asks for the slave that has waited on her, a girl named
Hagar.

Back in Cannan, Lot welcomes Abram but hard times continue.
Quarrels develop between their herdsmen. Lot goes to the plains,
which puts him nearer the cities, while Abram goes to the hills, which
he likes better anyway.

The years go by. Abram and Sarai still have no child. Sarai insists that
Abram take Hagar as his concubine. Hagar conceives, and she no
longer calls Sarai "Mistress." She expects Sarai to wait on *her* when she
is unwell. Sarai is willing, but Hagar orders her about in pathetic tones,
exciting the sympathy of the camp. If Sarai leaves the tent, Hagar com-
plains about being neglected. If Sarai appoints another servant girl to
attend to Hagar, then Hagar says Sarai hates her. Whatever Sarai does
Hagar puts her in the wrong.

Temporarily, Hagar can deceive everyone. They had all assumed that
Sarai *would* be jealous if Hagar conceived. But Abram eavesdrops on an
exchange between Sarai and Hagar, and he is no longer deceived. Hagar screams and runs into the desert. When she returns, she has had a
divine encounter in the wilderness.

The boy Ishmael is born, and grows. Peace and justice continue in
the camp for thirteen years. Then Abraham (as his name is now, by
God's word) has a visit from the great priest Melchizedek, who brings
two strangers, one of whom is mysterious and stays hooded. It is revealed that Sarah (God has also changed *her* name) will be a mother.
Sarah laughs silently in disbelief. Melchizedek reproves her.

The visitors have other news: the cities of the plain, where Lot and
Qira live, are going to be destroyed. Abraham appeals to the hooded
stranger, asking him to spare the cities if fifty, or even ten, righteous
souls can be found.

When the strangers visit Sodom they are at risk of gang rape. Lot
gives them shelter and tries to pacify the enraged crowd by offering his
daughters in marriage if they will leave the strangers alone. The
strangers themselves settle the matter by rendering everyone in the
crowd blind. Then they advise Lot to save his family.

Qira packs a trunk of clothes and jewels. On the way, Lot smashes
the trunk so that they can go faster. The jewels scatter. Qira turns back
to get her jewels and is caught in the meteor shower and earthquake.

Her last thought is that this is Lot's fault: he should have tried harder to hold on to her!

On the night that the cities of the plain are destroyed, Sarah conceives a son. She breastfeeds for the usual three years, then there is the customary feast to celebrate little Isaac's weaning. Sarah retires to her tent and is aroused by the sound of muffled baby screams. Ishmael has tied a scarf around Isaac's mouth and is laughing at little Isaac's terrified attempts to reach his mother. The scarf is so wet that Sarah has to cut it.

Sarah tells Abraham that Hagar and Ishmael must go. Abraham loves both his sons and wants to believe that Sarah exaggerates. He asks God how he should deal with his fearful, suspicious wife. God tells him that Sarah is right. Abraham sends Hagar and Ishmael off with flocks and herds, a tent, and his trusted steward, Eliezer, to guide them. But Hagar is convinced that Eliezer has secret orders to murder them. She and Ishmael leave the caravan and escape into the desert, with only such bread and water as they can carry. Abraham is confident that God will protect them and keeps Ishmael's share of the herds separate. In later years it is delivered to Ishmael.

More years pass. Isaac is a young man, startlingly good looking as his father was. "If God himself had a son," thought Sarah, "surely he would be like Isaac."[2] Abraham and Isaac are going out to inspect the distant herds and to offer a sacrifice at Mount Moriah. Abraham seems reluctant to go on this journey. Does he have a premonition of death? Sarah asks if she will see him again. Abraham replies that she will—*if* she wants to.[3] She watches them out of sight, meditating on the blessings of her life. The book ends there.

WOMEN OF GENESIS: BOOK TWO, *REBEKAH*

Rebekah grows up without a mother. While Rebekah and her brother Laban are still children their father, Bethuel, is rendered deaf by an accident. Rebekah and Laban scratch images in the sand signifying that their father could teach them to write.

This is unusual. Reading and writing are for sacred matters. No girls are taught to write. Boys are taught if they are in the line of the holy birthright; that is, the custody of the ancient writings going back to ancestor Noah. Bethuel was once considered a possible heir. That was before the great and distant Uncle Abraham had a son.

Bethuel remembers enough writing to teach his children. The household servants learn by watching. Then, a servant boy is expelled from the camp, because the boy wrote obscene and insulting remarks about Rebekah. Rebekah is shaken with the thought that her beauty caused this. From then on, she usually wears a veil. She prays that she may find a husband who will not want her just for her appearance. She wants a husband much like what she imagines Uncle Abraham to be.

Later, Rebekah and Laban discover that their mother was not dead, as they had been told, but had been sent away by Bethuel for exposing the children to the worship of false gods. Rebekah's feelings are painfully divided. Her father was right to raise his children in the worship of the God of Abraham. But he should not have lied to them.

When Rebekah goes to the city well to draw water one day, there is a man seated there, with camels and attendants nearby. He asks her for a drink, which she gives. Then she empties her filled water jug into the trough around the well and invites him to bring his camels to drink. This man inquires of her father's name, then drops to his knees to give a prayer of thanks, and takes out gifts of golden jewelry for Rebekah. He is Eliezer, the steward of the great Abraham. He has come for a wife for Abraham's son Isaac. The gift of the water and the offer to draw for the camels was the test he had set the Lord to show him who the chosen bride would be.

Rebekah takes him home, but she and Eliezer insist on leaving the next day, rather than waiting the customary month. At the end of the journey Eliezer sees Isaac coming towards them. Rebekah hastily puts on her veil.

Isaac is everything that Rebekah had hoped and prayed for, in character and kindness. However, he lacks self-confidence. He has always suspected that his father preferred his half-brother Ishmael. That moment of near-sacrifice on Mount Moriah, when his father stood over him with the knife, has stayed with Isaac. Isaac's mind agreed that the Lord's will should be done. As Isaac puts it, "I consented but as I lay there, I couldn't help but think. . . . I'll be dead and he can have Ishmael back."[4]

When, after an interval, Rebekah gives birth to twin boys, Abraham is openly favoring to the first-born, Esau, giving Jacob, the second-born, no more than a polite nod.

Isaac favors Esau also. The fact that Jacob is in many ways like Isaac (he would rather hug an animal than throw stones at it) lowers him in Isaac's eyes. Isaac would rather have a son who resembles the "manly" Ishmael, than one that reminds him of himself.

Esau is not interested in the holy birthright, the custody of the sacred writings, and is barely able to learn to read. He would rather hunt. Jacob takes to reading and writing quickly, although he has only his mother to teach him.

Jacob gets Esau to sign away his birthright in exchange for a bowl of pottage, on a day when Esau comes in hungry from hunting. Jacob arranges for his parents to overhear, so that his father will know that Esau does not value the writings. But this leaves Isaac convinced that Jacob is a lying trickster taking advantage of a hungry man to make him say things that he does not mean.

Before the elderly Abraham dies he exacts an oath from both boys not to marry Cannannites. Esau keeps the letter of the oath, but not the spirit. He marries two Hittites, who, like the Cannanites, worship false gods. This causes trouble. But Isaac remains convinced that Esau is the heir since God had him born first.

Rebekah thinks that God was giving Esau the *chance* to be worthy of the birthright. She says, "If the birthright goes to Esau, the way he is right now, then it will be lost to the whole world, because he will never care for it."[5]

Isaac, feeble and going blind, announces that he will give the birthright blessing after Esau has hunted and prepared game for him. Rebecca tells Jacob to take a kid and Rebecca will season it so that it tastes like venison. Jacob is to dress in Esau's clothes and put the skins of the kid on his wrists and arms to simulate Esau's hairiness.

Jacob prefers to leave the matter in the hands of God. Nevertheless, he does it all, and brings the savory dish to his father, claiming to be Esau, and asking for the blessing. Isaac is briefly suspicious, but after feeling Jacob's arms and meditating, he gives the blessing. When Jacob leaves, and the true Esau comes, Esau wails in fury.

Isaac does not revoke the blessing that he gave Jacob. He gives Esau a different one. Isaac tells Jacob and Rebecca that in that hesitation before the blessing, the Lord spoke in his heart telling him that "This is the right son. Bless him."[6] Isaac had assumed that this was indeed Esau. Later, Isaac realized that the Lord was telling him that Esau, through his Hittite marriages and other law breaking, had forfeited his birthright.

Rebekah perceives that her trickery was not necessary. She should have trusted the Lord, as Jacob suggested. The Lord would have stopped Isaac from blessing Esau. When Isaac takes the chest of the holy writings and gives them to Jacob, Rebekah knows that the writings are safe now, but she feels too guilty to hold or to look at them.

Esau is now an implacable enemy of his brother. Jacob's life will be in danger. Rebekah tells him to flee to her brother Laban. Then she and Isaac put their arms around each other, and Isaac gives thanks to the Lord for Rebekah's wisdom.

SOME MEANINGS OF THE STORIES OF WOMEN OF GENESIS

Women of Understanding

The accounts in Genesis[7] of Sarah and Rebekah make them both look somewhat capricious. Sarah is shown as asking Abraham to use Hagar to have descendants. But then when Hagar does get pregnant, and haughty, Sarah is shown as blaming Abraham.

In Genesis, Rebekah is shown as having Jacob as her favorite son, while Isaac has Esau as his. Rebekah appears to be taking mean advantage of a blind man to promote *her* favorite. Esau's Hittite wives are mentioned, together with the statement that they "made life bitter for Isaac and Rebekah" (Genesis 26:34–35), but no cause and effect is stated between the wives and the blessing of the birthright.

Indeed, the very nature of the birthright as shown in Card's account (care of the ancestral writings) is not stated in Genesis. The "birthright," as far as we can tell from the Bible text, might simply mean getting more sheep and goats than the other children do.

Card makes his own modifications of all this and feels he is being essentially faithful to Genesis.[8] Sarah is shown, in the Bible text, as a woman whom kings fall in love with, who is beloved by God, who is sometimes correct when her inspired husband is mistaken. Card feels that her harshness with Hagar makes sense only if we assume that Hagar began it. The final expulsion of Hagar and Ishmael is understandable if "Ishmael . . . playing with . . . Isaac" (Genesis 21:9) was something alarmingly dangerous.

Similarly, Rebekah, a woman with a heart kind enough to water a stranger's camels, and modesty enough to veil herself when her husband-to-be approaches (all in the Bible text) hardly seems to be someone to deceive her blind husband *just* to promote her favorite child. She must have had a more powerful motive. Card supplies her with one. To her, the guardianship of the sacred writings is paramount. She will not see it go to one who does not respect that trust.

Divine Inspiration

Abraham receives messages from God in a clear and direct manner, sometimes contradicting what Abraham himself had assumed. Sarah has no such direct relationship with God. She has, however, a subtler form of inspiration. At a difficult moment in Pharaoh's house she finds herself saying things that she had never planned to say. She "was on fire with those words."[9]

She may have made matters more dangerous by speaking, but that is not the point. The point is that God recognized *her*, knew her. Knowing and doing God's will does not always mean being safer. Sarah has to learn that "Faith doesn't mean that you never doubt. It means that you never act upon your doubts"[10] and that "[T]o behave as if you were certain when you had no certainty was to throw yourself into the hands of God."[11]

A direct and clear relationship with God does not automatically keep Abraham from error. In the matter of the expulsion of Hagar and Ishmael, Abraham is mistaken and Sarah is correct—not by divine revelation, but by common sense. After speaking to God, Abraham admits that separation is the only way to save Isaac's life and Ishmael's soul. But he had to have humility to let God tell him that.

It is difficult for Isaac to trust inspiration, because of his self-doubts. But Rebekah, right from her childhood, seems to have some version of the same trusting faith that Sarah had to learn. The knowledge that a prayer is answered by God does not just mean that things happen as one wishes. That could be coincidence, as is used in worshipping idols. There is more to it than that. "These ideas from God entered her mind with such surety that she simply knew them to be true. . . . Her own ideas came with doubt . . . she had to wrestle with them. . . . It was completely different—and impossible to explain."[12]

Ironies

Again and again human sacrifice is mentioned in *Sarah*, and always as detestable, especially to Abraham. Then, at the end of *Sarah*, the sacrifice of Isaac is indicated. In *Rebekah*, a lie told by a father to his children is devastating. Rebekah declares that *she* will never deceive anyone who loves her. She can't imagine anything worse, except brothers fighting each other. But she does deceive, and in so doing causes enmity between her sons. It is risky to predict what one will never do.

Christian Prefiguring

At the beginning of the first book, little Sarah sees Abraham as having the face of a god. At the ending, the elderly Sarah sees Isaac as God's son. The reader may well reflect thus: A descendant of Abraham (and of Sarah) *will* be God's Son, and he *will* be sacrificed. God will not be as merciful to Himself as he was to Abraham. Indeed, many Christian theologians have made that comparison.

But a patriarch or prophet is not the same as an Incarnation. While Card understands those who insist that Isaac must have been willing in mind and heart for this sacrifice, Card feels that there is room to suppose that "Isaac would come away . . . with . . . pain . . . that when his father was commanded to kill him, the old man did *not* love his son [enough to disobey God]."[13]

Card sees a better prefiguring of the Christ (although still not a perfect one) in his book on Moses and the Exodus.

STONE TABLES

Jochabed has given birth to a baby boy, and like all boys born to Israelite slaves in Egypt at this time, the child is to be thrown into the Nile. If anyone puts him into the river, Jochabed will do it. She floats him in a basket lined with pitch and sets her young daughter Miriam to watch.

The Egyptians despise the Israelites. In the days of Joseph, when the families of Jacob originally came to Egypt, the Pharaoh rulers were Hyksos—hated foreign invaders. Under the Hyksos, the Israelites prospered. The Egyptians rebelled against the Hyksos and threw them out; the Israelites were considered guilty by association. Now the Israelites are slaves, with their population controlled by infanticide.

Meanwhile, Pharaoh Tuthmose I, because of palace intrigues and poisonings, has no surviving son. He has a daughter, Hatshepsut, who is wise and capable of governing. Tuthmose wants to put a false beard on her, declare her to be his son, and have her be Pharaoh after him. Hatshepsut will consider it.

While she bathes in the Nile she finds the basket with the baby. This is the Holy River's answer: A son! She names him Moses, the Egyptian word for "son." She accepts her father's plan and names Moses to be Pharaoh after her. Jochabed, the birth mother, is brought to court as the baby's nurse.

Moses grows up bilingual—speaking Egyptian with Hatshepsut and the court, speaking Hebrew with Jochabed, Miriam, and his older brother Aaron. Hatshepsut forbids him to speak Hebrew where Egyptians can hear. This gives young Moses a stammer since he must be careful always to use the correct language for the setting.

Moses is a victorious general for his adoptive mother, Pharaoh Hatshepsut. His Israelite family is embarrassing. He cares little for the slaves. Aaron sneers, "Moses wouldn't last two minutes in [an Israelite] village . . . without . . . soldiers."[14]

Moses accepts the challenge. One evening he goes into the Israelite neighborhood incognito. He has enlightening experiences. He beds down in straw behind a stable and wakes to the sound of an old Israelite slave being savagely cudgeled by the Egyptian innkeeper. Moses seizes the cudgel, the innkeeper draws a knife, and Moses' trained soldier reflexes take over. He kills. Although he buries the body in the desert, the matter is known. Hatshepsut has no choice but to exile him.

In exile, Moses encounters Jethro, a Midianite shepherd and priest. Moses had rescued Jethro's daughters from ruffians at the well. Jethro completes Moses' knowledge of the One True God, the God of Abraham, Isaac, and Jacob. He shows Moses written records of those Patriarchs. These are not in the pictographs of Egypt, but in a kind of writing that Moses has never seen.

While learning to herd sheep, and to read alphabetic writing, Moses falls in love with the eldest daughter, Zeforah. She is amazing. Although a woman, she can read her father's books! Moses knows that he can never be a true son to Jethro, or a husband to Zeforah, unless he knows their God.

Out on the hills he tries to pray but stammers helplessly when he begins to utter the name of "God." After many false starts, and after seeing and hearing Zeforah give a prayer of thanks for the beauty of the evening, he finally asks God to give him *speech*. The prayer is granted, and he can pray without stammering.

He begins with thanks for his life with Jethro's family. But, surprising himself, his prayer turns to anger. "There is peace here. But I am not at peace. . . . You're . . . the mill and I'm the barleycorn. . . . While you're grinding me, you might give me a hint of what I am being ground up *for!*"[15] His prayer moves from rage to pleas for a gift of patience, from there to thanks for the miracle of speech. He closes the prayer as he has heard Zeforah do.

Moses becomes Zeforah's husband, and a father of children. Eventually, he becomes Jethro's ordained successor as priest. Right after this, he takes the sheep to the Holy Mountain. There, he is confronted with a burning bush, a voice, and evidence that the Lord can work miracles through him. Moses is commanded to bring the Israelite slaves out of Egypt, and back to their own land. Pharaoh Tuthmose III (Hatshepsut is now dead) will resist this, but he will be broken. Moses will have the help of his brother Aaron.

When Moses and Aaron first confront Pharaoh Tuthmose III, Pharaoh gives orders that make slavery even worse. Plagues and disasters follow: the Nile turns bloody; frogs, lice, flies and locusts multiply; cattle die; people get boils; there is hail with lightening and darkness in the day. More than once Tuthmose agrees to release the slaves. Each time he goes back on his word.

Now the first-born of every household will die. Moses gives the Israelites a word from the Lord. Each family is to slaughter a lamb to eat, and put its blood on the doorpost. The angel of death will then pass over that household. This "Passover" feast will be a ritual forever. They are to prepare to leave quickly.

Tuthmose is furious to discover his wife is planning lamb for supper. He disowns her and orders the cooks to burn the lamb, uneaten. When his son dies, along with many other Egyptians that night, he even disowns his dead little boy.

The Israelites depart, carrying spoils of Egyptian gold and jewelry, guided by the Lord who appears as a pillar of cloud by day, and a pillar of fire by night. Tuthmose pursues, with his army, and the Lord parts the Red Sea. Then the waters return, drowning hundreds of Egyptians. Tuthmose announces a *victory!* It is sad, he says, that so many brave soldiers were lost while deliberately driving the runaway slaves into the sea to drown them, but, says Tuthmose, it is a victory nonetheless.

For the next forty years Tuthmose looks for the Israelites. He assumes that they perished in the desert. They are in the desert, but not perishing. They receive manna, a breadlike substance found on the ground. They receive water from newly cleft rocks. Quails settle in the camp for meat. Still the cloud, which is fire by night, goes before them.

When the people reach Mount Sinai, Moses climbs up to receive the word of God on stone tables. Instead of asking Aaron to come up the mountain with him, he takes Joshua, a young man who has done an excellent job in organizing the tribes for security. Aaron is left to oversee the people until Moses returns. He feels slighted and cannot overcome his envy. Why should Moses be chosen to see God's face, instead of Aaron, who had been a faithful Israelite all along?

Aaron's envy makes him vulnerable to flattery and deception. Moses and Joshua are gone for so long that some chant "Moses is dead and God has forgotten us."[16] The pillar of cloud, or fire, is there and the manna appears, but *because* these miracles are so dependable they don't excite wonder, joy, and love of God any longer.

A leader of the troublemakers, Harubel, pretends to be helpful. He suggests compromise. "Let's put it in the Lord's hands . . . a form with a hollow place. . . . Gather the gold . . . melt it down and pour it in . . . ask the Lord to make [the] shape. . . . *We* aren't making a graven image, God is."[17] Aaron's instincts tell him that Harubel is a liar. But perhaps God can work miracles through Aaron. He proceeds with the plan.

At the last minute Aaron forbids Harubel to break the form, but too late. The image that emerges is the old Hyksos image of the Bullcalf. This is worshipped with naked dancing and worse obscenities. Aaron shouts that this is wrong. He is not heard.

Moses returns. Those who danced naked around the Bullcalf are put to death. Moses finds Aaron guilty of pride, envy, and stupidity, but *not* of willful obscenity or blasphemy. Since his repentance is genuine, he is spared.

There are more trials ahead over those next forty years. The day comes when the people cross over the Jordan into the land that has been promised. Moses entrusts to his son Gershom the writings he received from Jethro. Then, he has a blessed death.

SOME MEANINGS OF THIS STORY

The Sin of Pride

Towering sinful pride is found in Tuthmose III. When he disowns his innocent son rather than admit that Moses' God conquered him, his wife says he is "beyond madness" and "has given his heart to evil."[18] This extremity of pride is easy to see. But there are other cases, some more subtle.

When Moses reproves Aaron it hurts worse to have Moses call him "stupid" than it would to be sentenced to death.[19] To be a great sinner is to be a great *something*. To be stupid is to be nothing. Aaron can learn humility, but it is a most painful lesson.

Tuthmose I and Hatshepsut each have pride: Tuthmose I believes that he can make a woman into a man by saying so. Hatshepsut tries to make an Israelite into an Egyptian by forbidding him to speak Hebrew in public.

Moses must contend with pride. At first, he is the prince who acknowledges no kinship with the slaves. Then, humbled and in exile, he is willing to learn from Jethro and Zeforah. When he stands before Pharaoh, or when he lifts his hand over the Red Sea, he is a mixture of humility and daring. He makes every demand, gives every warning, every promise, in the name of God, not in the name of Moses.

But in the desert he tries to govern the whole Israelite people by himself, settling every dispute personally. His father-in-law, Jethro, corrects him in this. He should be training others to share the burden. Moses wonders why he didn't see this himself. "[I] couldn't . . . let go of the responsibility for fear the people would stop needing [me]. . . . And yet . . . the most important work . . . is to get Israel to a point where I am *not* needed."[20]

Humility with Daring

Jochabed, Jethro, Zeforah, and Joshua are examples of the virtue of humility at its best. They would rather get results than get credit. Like Moses, they can combine humility with daring, as Jochabed did when she put baby Moses on the water. Jethro waits for Moses to ask before teaching him the writing of the Patriarchs. Zeforah teaches Moses how to pray by example, not by instruction.

When Joshua organizes the tribes for defense, he knows nothing of warfare, but "neither did Adam. Somebody had to be the first soldier."[21] Pharaoh Hatshepsut had depended on highly trained advisors, but advisors did not prevent her stepson from poisoning her. Moses, in the desert, must depend on faithful men who can learn on the job. With God, (until Aaron's pride disrupts it) it is enough.

Divine Inspiration

Long before Moses comes to the Holy Mountain to meet with God, even when he is still embarrassed by his Israelite heritage, he experiences the phenomenon of speaking God's words without intention. When Tuthmose III, as a nasty little boy not yet Pharaoh, taunts Moses saying, "I have the blood of Pharaohs in my veins." Moses responds, "My . . . blood is the blood of prophets."[22] He is astonished to hear himself say that.

When Hatshepsut exiles Moses, he counsels her to free the Israelite slaves. Hatshepsut had ended the infanticide, but she contends that Egypt needs the cheap labor. Moses responds that Egypt will be far more injured by keeping the Israelites than by releasing them.[23] He doesn't know why—he just had to say it. Moses is not Jochabed's prophet, or Miriam's or Aaron's. He is the prophet of God.

The Son of God and Moses As His Foreshadowing

In her father's writings of the Patriarchs, Zeforah finds a prophecy of someone to be known as the Son. "The power of God would be in him, and he would deliver the people of God from their most awful enemy. . . . The Son stood between man and God, protecting men from God's wrath and trying to teach men to be worthy of God's love."[24] Ever since Zeforah found this passage she has ended her prayers with "In the name of the Son" or "Let the Son carry these words" or in some similar way.

When Moses (whose name means "son") begins to pray, he imitates Zeforah's practice, and eventually reads the passage himself. Later, on Mt. Sinai, when he is confronted by God he is told: "Moses . . . Your life has been shaped to be a harbinger of the life of my Only Begotten Son." And God continues to tell of the parallels between the life of Moses, as God has shaped it, and that of the Son to come.

His coming will be foretold. He will be born under sentence of death. He will be both king and servant. When he grows to manhood he will go out in the wilderness to meet his God. He will return to his people and deliver them from their enemy by the power of God . He will save them from death by the blood of the lamb. He will be lawgiver, judge, priest, a prophet. At his command water and bread will be given. "Because of your work, there will be a people ready to recognize my Only Begotten of the Father when he comes, and obedient enough to receive the higher law that he will bring. For my Only Begotten is and shall be the Savior, full of grace and truth."[25]

Later, on the mountain Moses sees the enemy of God who appears beautiful and tries to lure him away. Moses is not deceived. "I can judge between you and God. You blind me with your light, but God enlightened me."[26]

These passages contain Card's reason for the book.

THE HISTORICAL BASIS OF *STONE TABLES*

Hatshepsut, the only woman ever to be a Pharaoh, is historical. So are the relatives of hers mentioned in the narrative. Not all ancient history scholars agree that the "daughter of Pharaoh" who took baby Moses from the Nile was Hatshepsut, or that her father, Tuthmose I was the Pharaoh who ordered the Israelite babies killed, or that her stepson Tuthmose III was the Pharaoh at the time of the plagues and the Exodus. Most scholars concede that there *were* plagues, and a departure of the Israelites from Egypt, but most opinions put this at different times than that of Hatshepsut.

There is, however, a minority opinion,[27] and that is the one that Card is using in this book. This is not a "belief" of his in the sense that one "believes" in a creed. He sees it as a useful theory that fits many of the facts. For example, what other daughter of a Pharaoh would have the power to adopt an Israelite baby boy?

DEVELOPMENT OF *STONE TABLES* AND WOMEN OF GENESIS[28]

When Card was a Mormon missionary in Brazil, in 1972 at the age of twenty-one, he found it frustrating to go day after day without hearing or speaking English. He began writing a free-verse play called *Stone Tables*, based on Moses. He sent two acts to a favorite professor, Dr. Charles Whitman of Brigham Young University's Department of Theater. He hoped for a critique that would tell him how to make it better.

Dr. Whitman wrote asking for the rest of the play so he could add it to the BYU winter theater schedule. He also told Card that music was being written for the *songs*. Card had not thought of his play as a musical, or his unrhymed blank verse as songs. But now he did, and the musical was successful in Utah.

Card revised the musical several times.[29] In 1996 Card rewrote it as a long novel. This book, which began with Card as a young missionary, is now a work by an established writer. Michael Collings says, "*Stone Tables* . . . in Card's hands, strengthened by . . . decades of artistic development, emerges as a powerful novel."[30]

When Card wrote *Sarah* he did something that he does not usually do. He wrote two books at one time, going back and forth between *Sarah* and *Shadow of the Hegemon*.

These books seem to have little in common, but both deal with "history during times of chaos and transformation, like the one the world is embarking upon [now]."[31] The same thing could be said of anyone's version of the story of the Exodus.

CARD'S APPROACH TO BIBLICAL FICTION[32]

There are two opposite extremes that Card tries to avoid.

One is the view of many "higher critics" and many archeologists who start from the assumption that Abraham, Sarah, Isaac, and Rebekah never actually existed, and *if* Moses and the Exodus occurred, the story is exaggerated. These, Card calls the "Rejectionists."

At the opposite pole are those who feel that it is blasphemous to modify the literal words of the King James Version, no matter what common sense may imply, or what historians or archeologists have discovered. These, Card calls the "Apologists."

Card seeks a middle way: The Bible is a collection of stories of God's dealings with people. Card believes that Abraham, Sarah, Isaac, Rebekah, and Moses existed, and did most of the things that they are recorded as doing. But also, as with any writing done and preserved by human beings, there will be inaccuracies, duplications, and omissions.

For example, Genesis tells three stories of a man telling a king that his wife is actually his sister. Twice it is Abraham and Sarah, once Isaac and Rebekah. Card finds it more believable to assume that this only happened once.

Card also apparently finds it more believable that Lot would try to protect his holy guests by offering his daughters in marriage, rather than to be raped. Also, Lot's wife turning into salt seems unnecessary. Why should God send a meteor shower to remove whole cities, and then have a separate miracle for one woman?

When Aaron pleads to Moses, "They gave the gold to me, I put it in the fire and out came this bull-calf" (Exodus 33:24, revised English version), his apology doesn't make sense. But, if one assumes that Aaron actually didn't know what the image would be, then his words are more reasonable.

Since Card is writing books labeled as fiction, he feels free to make modifications of this sort. But he keeps to his own standards for the use of respected sources.[33] The heroes and heroines retain their heroic nature. The villains are still evil. Sins and stupidities are shown, and greatness and goodness shine like beacons.

Card never modifies anything *just* because it is miraculous. He stands by a traditional belief in a God who works both through nature and beyond it. As for divine inspiration, Card insists upon it! But even divine guidance needs common sense. Good advice can come from intelligent, less inspired, people.

Card is well aware that some religious liberals ("Rejectionists") and some religious conservatives ("Apologists") object to his handling of biblical stories. To both these groups Card has one answer. "[The Bible] is still there. I have done it no harm. If you feel that I have got it wrong, don't punish me. Write your own book."[34]

Most reviews of the Women of Genesis series have been favorable. "Card takes the tantalizingly rich references . . . in the book of Genesis and brings them to life."[35] The *Jerusalem Post* says, "A lively novel that enlarges our appreciation for this complicated matriarch."[36]

Card will continue with biblical fiction. The third book in the Women of Genesis series will be *Leah and Rachel*, one book on these two wives of Jacob. Card sees Rachel as "a bit of a brat."[37] She was the one who stole and sat on her father's household gods.

This is Card, writing openly in the Christian tradition. As he accurately says, "If you really don't believe in God, you won't feel at home in these books, but they're not tied to any denomination."[38]

What is Card like when writing openly in the tradition of his own denomination?

NOTES

1. Orson Scott Card, *Sarah*, Women of Genesis (Salt Lake City, Utah: Shadow Mountain Press, 2000), 6.

2. Card, *Sarah*, 372.

3. For what Abraham is planning at Mount Moriah, see Genesis 22:1–18. Obviously, Sarah has no idea of this.

4. Orson Scott Card, *Rebekah*, Women of Genesis (Salt Lake City, Utah: Shadow Mountain Press, 2001), 229.

5. Card, *Rebekah*, 347.

6. Card, *Rebekah*, 409–410.

7. The story of Abraham and Sarah is in Genesis, chapters 12 through 22. The story of Isaac and Rebekah is in Genesis, chapters 24 through 25:6. All direct quotations from the Bible text are from the revised standard version unless otherwise stated.

8. Card's views on his work are taken from the afterword to *Sarah*, 379–390, and the preface to *Rebekah*, ix–xxi.

9. Card, *Sarah*, 158.

10. Card, *Sarah*, 208.

11. Card, *Sarah*, 247.

12. Card, *Rebekah*, 166.

13. Card, *Rebekah*, x–xi.

14. Orson Scott Card, *Stone Tables* (Salt Lake City, Utah: Shadow Mountain Press, 1997), 73.

15. Card, *Stone Tables*, 205–206.

16. Card, *Stone Tables*, 403.

17. Card, *Stone Tables*, 408.

18. Card, *Stone Tables*, 327.

19. Card, *Stone Tables*, 423.

20. Card, *Stone Tables*, 376.

21. Card, *Stone Tables*, 349.

22. Card, *Stone Tables*, 79.

23. Card, *Stone Tables*, 105.

24. Card, *Stone Tables*, 178.

25. Card, *Stone Tables*, 378–388. The last five words are from the Gospel of John 1:14.

26. Card, *Stone Tables*, 393.

27. Card, *Stone Tables*, xiv. This minority opinion is attributed to Charles Pellegrino, *Return to Sodom and Gommorah*.

28. Information on the development of *Stone Tables* not otherwise attributed is from the preface to *Stone Tables*, ix–xvi.

29. The latest version is available on compact disc from Rosewood Recording Company of Provo, Utah. It can be ordered through the website for fans of Card, www.hatrack.com.

30. Michael Collings, *Storyteller: Orson Scott Card* (Woodstock, Ga.: Overlook Connection Press, 2001), 270.

31. Orson Scott Card, afterword to *Shadow of the Hegemon* (New York: Tom Doherty Associates, Tor, 2000), 364.

32. Card's views on his own handling of biblical fiction are from his afterword to *Sarah*, his preface to *Rebekah*, and his preface to *Stone Tables*.

33. See the section titled "Roots of the Homecoming Series" in chapter 5 of this book.

34. Online interview with DeseretBook.com, September 10, 2000.

35. *Publisher's Weekly*, review of *Sarah*, September 11, 2000.

36. Morton I. Teicher, "A Strong Woman Married to a Patriarch," *Jerusalem Post*, March 22, 2001. Text available online at www.hatrack.com.

37. Personal interview, September 12, 2000.

38. Orson Scott Card, "Casting Shadows," interview, *Locus* 49, no. 6 (December 2002): 7, 71–72.

7

Stories from Mormon Life

A STORY OF MORMON LIFE FROM THE 1800s: *SAINTS*[1]

In 1829, in Manchester England, John Kirkham abandons his family to appalling poverty. Daughter Dinah loses her factory position for reasons that are not her fault and is forced into a loveless marriage.

In 1840, Dinah's younger brother Charlie meets a missionary from America, Heber Kimball of the Church of Jesus Christ of the Latter-Day Saints. Heber's fervor makes such an impression on the family that Charlie, Dinah, and their mother Anna are converted and baptized by him. The eldest brother, Robert, believes that his family is insane. Dinah's husband, Matthew, believes that Dinah had an affair with the missionary and reacts with violence.

Many of the new Saints of England, including Dinah, Charlie, and Anna, resolve to travel to America to help the Prophet, Joseph Smith, build the new City of God: Nauvoo, in Illinois on the Mississippi River. Matthew and Robert have Dinah declared insane and they seize her children. Dinah's heart breaks, but she is true to her new faith.

In Nauvoo, "Sister Dinah" gains a reputation for wise and compassionate counsel and scripture interpretation, a "Prophetess." She is also a schoolteacher, a writer, and a poet, whose works are published in the newspaper. Eventually, Dinah becomes a "plural wife" of Joseph

Smith, according to the "Principle of Celestial Marriage" that requires more than one wife. Joseph feels that he received this Principle as a revelation in the tradition of Abraham and Jacob.

It was supposed to be a practice in which co-wives live like sisters, giving each other emotional support. However, the Principle is still a secret from most of the membership, including Joseph's first wife, Emma. Most of the Saints would consider Joseph and Dinah's relationship to be adultery, if they knew about it.

The Saints at Nauvoo, most of whom are genuinely trying to be righteous, see their reputation suffer from the behavior of hypocritical Mormons and lapsed Mormons. The mayor of the town, John C. Bennett, is nominally a Mormon. He is also a physician, who, unknown to anyone of influence in Navoo, performs abortions for the whores in a neighboring town.

When Bennett first hears of the Principle, he delightedly distorts it into debauchery and attempts to seduce other men's wives. These women tell Sister Dinah. She goes to tell Joseph and arrives just as Joseph is beginning his first open ceremony of plural marriage.

Emma has, with reluctance, come to accept the Principle. But when Emma realizes that Dinah, whom she trusted, has been her husband's other wife for over a year, she strikes Dinah in fury. Dinah falls down a flight of stairs and miscarries. Dr. Bennett is called. When he is finished with Dinah she is infertile.

Bennett leaves the community and gives profitable lectures throughout Illinois on the evil practices of the Mormons. Events lead to Joseph Smith's arrest and later to his arranged murder in jail in Carthage, Illinois, in 1844. Under the leadership of Brigham Young, the Saints migrate westward.

Eventually, Dinah becomes a plural wife of Brigham Young. In Utah, she continues her teaching, public speaking, writing for publication, and counseling of young women. She lives to see Utah become a state, with polygamy outlawed by the Utah constitution and disallowed by the Mormon Church. She outlives her younger brother, Charlie, and, in her seventies, she adopts Charlie's youngest child. At her death, in 1919 at age 100, there are thousands of mourners.

Historical Background and Card's Method of Telling This Story

Dinah Kirkham Handy Smith Young is a fictional character. So are her parents, her brothers, her English husband Matthew, and her children. Card has woven together incidents from the lives of several different women, chiefly Eliza Snow. More than one early Mormon woman was declared insane and/or lost custody of her children. More than one made speeches or published poetry. The only invented incident is the one where Dinah is knocked down the stairs by Emma Smith.[2]

Joseph Smith, his brothers and other family members, Emma Smith, Brigham Young, and other prominent early Mormons are all historical persons. So is the infamous John C. Bennett. When episodes of their lives are shown, they are presented accurately.

Card has chosen a special method to tell this blend of fact and fiction. Only Card's name is on the cover. But, inside the book, he pretends that this book is being written by "O. Kirkham," a descendant of Dinah's brother Charlie, living in Salt Lake City. O. Kirkham tells of how he researched the church archives for data about his "great aunt" Dinah. There are footnotes and acknowledgments citing nonexistent sources such as the "Charles Banks Kirkham Family Organization."

This is the same method of telling fiction that Conan Doyle used in The Sherlock Holmes stories, and that Mark Twain used in *Personal Recollections of Joan of Arc.* One book that made an impression on Card when he was seventeen was *The Wall* by John Hersey. This novel pretends to be an original diary written by someone involved in the Warsaw Ghetto Uprising in World War II. Card spent days in the library trying to "research" fictional persons in the book until he realized what Hersey was doing. Card remembered this when he wrote *Saints.*[3]

Card is just as realistic as Hersey was and has also confused readers, including one experienced reviewer for a metropolitan newspaper.[4] The book is convincing because Card did, in fact, do a great deal of research on the nineteenth century and on matters of everyday life in both England and America.

It is also convincing because the vividness of Card's writing can often suggest more than Card actually portrays. His agent and his editor objected that Card had never described Dinah. Card asked them how *they* saw her. Each woman described herself.[5]

The first edition (titled *A Woman of Destiny* against Card's wishes) has a cover that suggests a bodice-ripper historical romance. The Tor version, titled *Saints* (Card's title), shows a woman standing against a background of mountains and covered wagons.

A STORY OF MORMON LIFE FROM THE 1980s: *LOST BOYS*

Many works of fiction can be read more than one way. A writer may chose a background that is as interesting as the events that take place against that background. For example, Margaret Truman writes murder mysteries against a background of places in Washington, D.C. Some people who read her mysteries remember details of the background after they have forgotten who murdered whom. *Lost Boys* is a fantasy/suspense story of the recent past about a serial murderer. As such, it will be discussed again in this book in chapter 9.

The background of this story is that of a Mormon family newly arrived in North Carolina, who are facing problems: They have little money, their older boy is having difficulties, the father's job is disappointing, and their new baby is born with cerebral palsy. This background closely parallels what actually occurred in the life of Orson Scott Card his wife and children, at the time this story takes place. (But the Cards did *not* have any problems with a serial killer in their new location.)

The religious faith of the parents, Step and DeAnne Fletcher, is shown throughout as relevant to all of their problems. This book will now be considered from that viewpoint.

Why Does God Permit Misfortune and Evil to Happen?

Step and DeAnne have to stop the car on the shoulder of the superhighway because baby Betsy has thrown up. A policeman stops to see if they need help, coming up so quietly and suddenly that Step doesn't hear him. Four-year-old Robbie is impressed that a man with a gun could appear out of nowhere. What if it had been a bad guy?

DeAnne wants to reassure Robbie by telling him that God would not allow them to come to harm. But Step will not say that even to quiet a child's fears. "God doesn't work that way . . . if someone is truly, deeply evil, sometimes good people can't stop him until he has done a lot of bad things."[6] Step assures Robbie that he is reasonably safe. Step quietly apologizes to DeAnne for contradicting her. She says that he was right.

A similar question surfaces when Step Fletcher is aware that a young male coworker, Gallowglass, who volunteers to babysit, is taking an unhealthy interest in the diapering and cleaning of baby girls. Gallowglass volunteers to babysit everywhere, and has not yet done anything legally wrong that can be proved.

Step silently muses (only theoretically, for Step Fletcher is decidedly *not* a violent type): If he were to kill Gallowglass, to protect children, would God see it as murder? Yes, it would be murder, because Gallowglass would then lose the chance to repent. "God lets the guilty live right along with the good . . . he lets the tares grow with the corn."[7]

How Should We Pray? What Should We Expect from Prayer?

Step gives his family quick goodbye kisses as he rushes to catch an airplane. He is miserable at his job at Eight Bits, Inc. His bosses are demanding, capricious, and undercutting each other, with Step in the middle. Also, his bosses are trying to steal a program, Hacker Snack, that Step developed before coming to this job.

At this conference he might be able to sell someone else the rights for Hacker Snack. Then, perhaps, he could afford to quit his job with Eight Bits, and work freelance at home with his family, which he dearly wishes to do. As he settles breathlessly into his airplane seat he doubts if he should be praying at all, just now, "because his mood was so angry and vindictive, but still he had to say it, silently: God, make this go, please. Make this work. Set me free. Send me home."[8]

Many Christians have noticed that prayer is often followed by temptation. Step, at the conference, does meet with a competitor to Eight Bits who is interested in buying Hacker Snack. But this competitor wants Step to spy on Eight Bits for him. While Step draws a salary from Eight Bits, this is clearly wrong. Step refuses and secures a promise for the contract anyway. But before the contract actually comes, the Fletchers must go through more financial ordeals.

Step turns to prayer in times of trial as a reflex. Step and DeAnne reach a crisis in their marriage: DeAnne feels that Stevie's adjustment problems are serious, and that he should see a psychiatrist. Step is opposed to this. DeAnne works to see that Step begins his home teaching in the new ward (congregation) with a young partner whose mother is a child psychiatrist; Step may get to know the mother and have a more favorable view of psychiatry. Step detects what she has done and he hates being manipulated.

His first reaction is inner rage. (He keeps it in. He does not tell DeAnne that he knows. She is tired and in the last weeks of pregnancy.) His second thoughts are that he must be a bad husband if his wife feels that she has to deceive him for her child's sake. Sitting alone in the kitchen, he gets up for a glass of water, asking himself if this is how marriages break up. "No, I forbid it. . . . Lord, help me to be whatever . . . she needs me to be so that we can hold this thing together . . . through this summer . . . Through this year."[9]

He turns around. DeAnne is there, red-eyed, confessing her duplicity. Step holds her and tells her that he knew and was mad, but didn't say anything. He got a glass of water instead. DeAnne responds with laughter and tears. Step doesn't mention his silent resolve ("I forbid [divorce]!") or his prayer (for the Lord to change *him*).

This isn't the last time that the Fletchers hurt each other, but they come back like a pair of gyroscopic balances, sometimes with each one arguing the other one's viewpoint. When it becomes clear that Step was right about the psychiatrist, he never says *I told you so*. His prayer (to be sustained to meet his wife's needs) was granted.

Divine Inspirations and Blessings

In the Mormon Church, nearly all adult males are "priests" and a father is the priest of his family. It is traditional for a father to baptize his child. After Step baptizes his son Stevie, Step then must confirm the baptism. This is done with ritual words, but also with a particular individual blessing. Step is poised with his hands on Stevie's head. He prays the ritual part, but then cannot remember what he had planned to say.

Then something happens that had happened to Step before, when he served in the mission field in Brazil. Words rush into his mind. Step speaks of how the Lord knows Stevie, and of Stevie's purpose in the world to perform works of love, to listen to the Holy Ghost so as to make choices that will bring joy and peace to his family and friends. It is not a typical confirmation blessing, but later events show that it was right.[10]

Some weeks later, DeAnne gives birth to a baby boy who has unexplained seizures, and must go into Infant Intensive Care. Step comes in with another Mormon man who is also a priest, and with the doctor's permission they open the incubator to put a drop of oil on baby Jeremy's forehead and gently touch him. Step prays that the doctors will make no mistakes and that Jeremy will soon be home.

Later, DeAnne asks Step why he hadn't asked that Jeremy be healed. Step replies that he had wanted to ask for "a perfectly normal healthy body [for Jeremy] . . . Maybe it's a lack of faith on my part, or maybe I was being told not to bless him that way. . . . I just couldn't say it."[11] Later, Jeremy is diagnosed with cerebral palsy. There is much that can be done to help him, but no cure.

Some people see every claim for divine inspiration as insanity. Step's young home teaching partner, Lee, is one who gives inspiration a bad name. He is a Mormon convert who was attracted by *anti*-Mormon books and films that distorted Mormon doctrines. Lee goes all the way into a full-blown psychosis in which he believes that he is God.

The Church As a Career for Laypeople

When Step blesses baby Jeremy, the doctor asks if Step is a minister. He is impressed to find out that Step is a computer programmer and his friend an accountant. "It . . . felt good to see a father do that for his own child. Never seen that before."[12]

All adult Mormons are expected to have a "calling" in the Church. For DeAnne Fletcher, motherhood is her life but the Church is her career.[13] In North Carolina, DeAnne is asked to be the spiritual living teacher for the Relief Society of the ward. It is her most responsible calling yet, and she earnestly wants to do a good job.

However, there is another woman in the ward, Dolores LeSeur, self-appointed to everything, who skillfully undercuts both Step and DeAnne. DeAnne's problems in the ward are a parallel, up to a point, with Step's problems at Eight Bits—but this is bitterness and infighting between people who profess to love God. That makes it worse.

The Church As a Family

Dolores LeSeur and her cohorts are a blight on the ward, but the ward as a whole is otherwise quiet. Whenever Step and DeAnne need help, the help is there. When DeAnne goes to the hospital to have Jeremy and someone is needed to stay with the children, or to pick up DeAnne's mother at the airport, a "brother" or "sister" of the ward is there. When a ward family leaves for another state, they give one of their cars to the Fletchers telling them to send payment when they can. They saw how much the Fletchers needed two cars. When the Fletchers can no longer live in their house because of a catastrophe, it takes one telephone call for them to find a place to stay.

The Family As a Church

Step's role as "priest of the family" includes teaching. Advice to the children is often accompanied by a reference to a Bible story, or to something from the book of Mormon (and the children often give disconcerting responses). This teaching, generally done in concert with DeAnne, is not always explicitly scriptural, yet it is always the teaching of a man of faith. For instance, Step is preparing Stevie and Robbie for what they might expect when the cerebral-palsied baby Jeremy is brought home. Step had a retarded aunt. He tells how his mother, their Grandma, was so embarrassed that she would walk on the other side of the street when children would tease her retarded sister.

> DeAnne [asked] "Why are you telling this story?" . . . Step was confused . . . so . . . he pretended that he had intended . . . a "teaching moment." "Why do *you* think I told this story, Robbie?" asked Step. "Cause we don't *care* if [the other kids are mean] we're going to walk to school with [Jeremy] anyway! And we're going to walk right with him and not cross the street without him because then he'd be scared!" Robbie had found the right lesson in the story even if Step had forgotten what it was supposed to be.[14]

"Step Fletcher . . . is me" says Orson Scott Card.[15]

The roots of *Lost Boys* will be discussed in chapter 10, where the rest of the story is discussed.

STORIES OF MORMON LIFE FROM THE FUTURE

The Folk of the Fringe[16]

This book is a collection of five works of less-than-novel length (three short stories, one novelette, and one novella), all written with the same background.

In this future time, there has been a limited nuclear war. There is sufficient climate disruption to reverse some weather patterns. Formerly arid areas of the United States Southwest now get floods. There is a breakdown of law and order. When a civilization collapses, some people look for scapegoats. In parts of the eastern United States, Mormons are scapegoats. As their ancestors did, persecuted Mormons find ways to trek westward.

In Utah and surrounding areas, the Mormon Church has asserted some civil authority. The part of land that is neither desert nor floodplain—known as The Fringe—is planted, cultivated, and expanded so that agriculture and cities can exist there. Outriders on horseback scour the plains for groups on foot and escort them in.

"West"[17]

In the East, Jamie Teague sees adults and children, black and white, walking along a highway, *singing*. This is reckless; they are practically inviting outlaws! Jamie is a loner, but he joins them and teaches them safer behavior. They are survivors of persecuted Mormons who are trying to travel to Utah. Circumstances make Teague the leader.

Teague is concealing a sin that, to him, is worse than murder. Eventually, after getting to know the Mormons, and watching their worship, he tells his sad, terrible story.

Teague saves the lives of these Mormons. They, in turn, save his spirit. He is assured of God's forgiveness and is baptized. Later, he rescues a little boy whose family has been killed. Teague would like to keep the child, but he is an outrider now, and still a bachelor. The child (named Deaver Teague for the two men who found him) is put up for adoption.

"Salvage"[18]

A generation later, Deaver Teague is now a young man in the salvage business, finding everything salvageable from trucks to personal computers—things no longer being manufactured. Deaver is not a Mormon. Mormons are the annoying government.

The rains have raised Lake Bonneville to flood stage and the Salt Lake Temple is submerged. Just a few towers can be seen breaking the surface. There are rumors that gold can be found in the drowned temple. Deaver gets diving equipment. He has two companions in this venture, both Mormon. They do their best to talk him out of this.

Below, Deaver finds some metal pieces, and triumphantly surfaces. They are flattened tin cans with a prayer scratched on each, prayers for healing, forgiveness, and safety of loved ones. Deaver is moved and annoyed with his companions for not having told him. They feared that he would laugh. Deaver protests that he would *not* laugh. He knows now that he can have no true close friends here. It is time to move on.

"The Fringe"[19]

Timothy Carpenter of the town of Reefrock, just beyond The Fringe, is a schoolteacher, trying desperately to instill learning into uncaring teenaged sixth graders. Carpenter is a spastic. His legs are useless; his fingers do not grip. His natural voice is an animal howl. With a specially designed wheelchair and computer, he can key in a synthesized, powerful voice, using hands as fists.

It is now thirty years since the Six Missile War. The ecology of the area is delicate. For at least eighteen more years, farmers must plant as they are told, and sacrifices must be made by all, to preserve civilization. Some citizens are in the black market. They make money to buy luxuries, such as wristwatches or new jeans, at the expense of honest neighbors. To Carpenter's horror, the Bishop himself is a part of this thievery.

Carpenter notifies the authorities. Helicopters arrive. Men are arrested, wives weep, and children must shoulder adult burdens.

Three of Carpenter's students kidnap him, and deposit him, his chair, and his computer in the bottom of a dry wash that will soon fill with rain. He tries to climb out, using his weak arms. On this tortuous journey, he faces self-knowledge. However justified his actions were, his motives were mixed. He had wanted revenge against the able-bodied and the clear-spoken, who misused their gifts.

He hears a vehicle, and cries for help in his natural, bestial voice. The vehicle is a pageant wagon. When the pageant-gypsies see that the cries come from a man, a cripple, they get out and rescue Carpenter, his chair, and his computer. Carpenter had once had a low opinion of traveling entertainers. Now, he turns his house over to them, so they don't need to pitch tents in the rain.

The next day Carpenter declines to identify his tormentors. The fathers went to jail on Carpenter's information; the sons will not. And Carpenter knows that the boys will never forget that they almost committed murder.

"Pageant Wagon"[20]

Deaver Teague is working as a range rider (a job much less prestigious than that of an outrider) and his horse has just died. He hitches a ride with a pageant wagon, and finds himself involved with the multigenerational family of actors and stage technicians. Deaver spent his childhood shuttled from one foster home to another, in part because he never became a Mormon.

The pageant wagon is very nearly the only source of public entertainment in the area. Electricity is not "wasted" on such things as motion pictures or television. The town turns out excitedly to see the pageant. Deaver, who is helping with flag raising, finds it almost as interesting to watch the audience as to watch the pageant. But the pageant itself, a combined presentation of general American history and of Mormon-American history, is more stirring to Deaver than it is to some of the actors. The actors have done it so often that some no longer hear the words they recite.

The most exciting drama of all is behind the scenes, as the family deals with its internal and external problems. Deaver has a chance to apply for the outriders, but his ambitions have changed. He transfers his right to apply to the misfit son of the pageant family, Ollie, who has reasons to want to get away. Deaver learns Ollie's job of managing the lights. Deaver finally has a family, which like most families, is sometimes obnoxious. However, they are people to love and who love him.

"America"[21]

"America" extends over forty years. The events begin before the events of "West" and conclude after the events of "Pageant Wagon."

Anamari Boagente, a South American Indian woman in her forties, is the only source of health care for her Brazilian jungle village, although she has had no professional medical training. She can do nursing care, and knows the correct use of the medicines, but it isn't always possible to get the medicines.

Sam Monson, a fifteen-year-old Mormon boy from the United States, is in Brazil in the summer custody of his divorced father who is a member of an oil-drilling team. Sam is contemptuous of his father, an inactive Mormon that drinks and chases women. Sam is determined to be as unlike his father as he can. Following a strange dream of the night before, he comes into the jungle looking for Anamari. He asks if he can help. She gives him the most unpleasant jobs. He does them.

As they become friends, Sam learns something of how people like Anamari see the world. Sam and Anamari are both true dreamers. He interprets her dreams and recognizes the ancient Mexican myth of Quetzalcoatl. He sees in her dreams the possibility of uniting all the native peoples of North and South America by one name: "We are all Indians" or, better yet, "We are all Americans."

Anamari is quite willing to be the virgin-mother of a reborn America, but she makes it clear to Sam that she will need a father for Quetzalcoatl. Sam flees back to the oil-digging camp (all the more horrified because he *is* tempted). He dreams of making love to Anamari "Virgin America" for in his dream, the land has married them, made them one.

And when he wakes, it is not a dream. He is lying beside Anamari. He has sleepwalked from his father's tent to her village. In distress, he leaves South America.

It is forty years later. The Americans, the native people who follow Quetzalcoatl, son of Virgin America, control nearly all North and South America, having taken over in the chaos after the Six Missile War. An exception is Deseret, the Mormon state developed from what had been the state of Utah and surrounding territory.

Virgin America, now in her eighties, arrives with authority to speak for her son and graciously allows the State of Deseret status as a federated state in America. The treaty is signed by Governor Sam Monson, a man in his fifties with authority to speak for Deseret. It is recorded by Timothy Carpenter, a wheelchair-bound spastic whose research at the University of Deseret made it possible to use the rains to expand the forests.

Virgin America advises Governor Monson that he and Quetzalcoatl never meet. It would not do for them to be seen standing side by side. The legend is that Quetzalcoatl was conceived by a virgin, from an angel. But he looks very much like the angel.

The Meanings of These Stories

Card sees the stories of *Folk of the Fringe* as being stories of community.[22] In each one, people are aware of belonging—or, more often, poignantly aware of *not* belonging—to some family, faith, race, nationality, or the community of the able-bodied. These are indeed stories of community, belonging and exclusion, as Card says.

But they are also stories of *civilization*, or of the lack of civilization. Timothy Carpenter, the spastic teacher, defines civilization not as technology but as "[Living] in peace and [knowing] that today's work brings tomorrow's bread."[23] In each story, people are trying to understand this meaning, and to live it as best they can.

They are also stories of *understanding, acceptance,* and *forgiveness* (including forgiveness of oneself). The episode in which Carpenter is trying to climb out of the wash, is the pivotal point of the book. By degrees, Carpenter faces his own self-righteousness and sees the element of evil in himself; this makes it possible for him to forgive the boys, who haven't even asked for forgiveness.

Carpenter in the wash can be compared to Jamie Teague in his baptism. Teague knows his own evil, certainly, he knows it too well. What he didn't know was the possibility of a clean new beginning.

Carpenter and Teague come to the same point from opposite directions, each one rising out of water. Deaver also rose out of water with engraved prayers in his hand. This taught him his need of acceptance and prepared him to realize that an imperfect family is a great deal better than none.

The Roots of These Stories

There is a long author's note at the end of the book titled "On Sycamore Hill."[24] It is a nonfiction narrative of a workshop of writers who share recently written short stories. It is full of self-deprecating humor: Card hopelessly trying to stay on his reducing diet, sharing the room with a cat, the writers critiques of each other, "He withered me with a forgiving look."[25]

Card didn't come with a story written. Since his novels were beginning to be successful he had written fewer shorter works. He had stories in his mind. At the workshop he wrote "The Fringe" and "Salvage" and was pleasantly surprised that the others, none Mormon except himself, were not put off by Mormon content.

After the workshop he wrote "America." It is not science fiction; it is fantasy, or even mythology. But Card felt that it shows "a purpose behind the loss and suffering . . . it revises the meaning of . . . the other stories."[26]

Elizabeth Mitchell of Baen Books asked Card to write a story about a mercenary soldier for an anthology she was doing. Card felt that he had said all he wanted to say about military subjects in *Ender's Game*. But he imagined a woodsman leading a mixed group of Mormons, trekking westward, and the result was "West." The terrible secret of Jamie Teague was based on a true story from a newspaper.

"Pageant Wagon" was the first one of these stories imagined, and the last one written. Right after he had signed the contract for *Folk of the Fringe*, which would include "Pageant Wagon," Card was asked to write the new script for the Mormon Church's Hill Cumorah Pageant. He was pleased to do this, and proud of the result. However, when he got to his third Sycamore Hill Writer's Workshop, once again, he didn't bring a story. Again, he wrote a story *at* the workshop; it was the first draft of "Pageant Wagon." It was critiqued, and the ending drastically revised.

Combined in one book, the five stories of community, civilization, understanding, and forgiveness in a Mormon future add up to more than the sum of the parts.

WHAT KIND OF A MORMON IS ORSON SCOTT CARD?

Saints, Lost Boys, and *Folk of the Fringe* have been praised and de-
nounced by liberal and conservative Mormons.

In *Saints,* Joseph Smith and other leaders, however divinely inspired,
are capable of being fools on the worldly level. Card shows just one example of plural marriage working relatively well (the wives are literally sisters) and many cases where it does not.

Also in *Saints,* the fictitious researcher, O. Kirkham, says that authorities in Salt Lake City tried to restrict his access to certain docu-
ments that would show that Dinah Kirkham had a greater influence on
Mormon doctrine than women are generally believed to have had. In
Lost Boys, a mystically minded convert to Mormonism goes insane. Sister LeSeur, an officious busybody, makes perverted use of Mormon
doctrine to get her way. In *Folk of the Fringe,* the Mormon bishop is at
the heart of the black market network.

What kind of a Mormon could write such things?

An *honest* one. Every denomination has something in its history it
might prefer to have the world forget. Almost every congregation
knows of The Indispensable Woman (with whom many would be
happy to dispense). Many believers of different kinds have encoun-
tered The Embarrassing Convert who comes to this church for all the
wrong reasons. (He may be a mad materialist instead of a mad mystic.)
No faith tradition, anywhere, has shown itself to be divinely protected
from either fools or rascals.

Card loves his Church too much to pretend that Mormons are not
human. Saint Paul said it, almost 2,000 years ago: "But we have this
treasure in earthen vessels, to show that the transcendent power belongs to God and not to us."[27] Card's honesty makes goodness and wisdom, which is clear in all his works, shine out all the more believably
and brightly against the dark or mundane background.

Secondly, Card believes that his Church is based on divine revelation—
an *expanding and changing* revelation. He spells this out in one of his nonfiction essays:

> [T]here has been a great deal of doctrinal change . . . over time. . . . We sing
> it dozens of times a year—"The Lord is extending the Saints' understand-
> ing." Line upon line, precept upon precept, we change our doctrines as we
> become better able to cope with greater light.[28]

The Mormon scandal of the nineteenth century was polygamy. That
was changed. The Mormon scandal of the twentieth century was

racism; black men were once not considered eligible for the priesthood. That changed too, in 1978. Mormons have become one of the most interracial of the Christian denominations.[29]

Where will the Lord *next* extend the Saints' understanding? What might be the great change of the *twenty-first* century? Card won't guess; he does not see himself as divinely inspired. "I have never seen the face of God. But I believe that I have seen the *hands* of God—that's a metaphor, of course."[30]

NOTES

1. Orson Scott Card, *Saints* (New York: Tom Doherty Associates, Tor, 1988). Originally published as *A Woman of Destiny* (New York: Berkley, 1984). The Tor version restores Card's original title and has a different cover, but it is otherwise essentially identical.

2. Michael R. Collings (quoting Orson Scott Card), *Storyteller: Orson Scott Card* (Woodstock, Ga.: Overlook Connection Press, 2001), 83.

3. Orson Scott Card, *Characters & Viewpoint* (Cincinnati, Ohio: Writer's Digest Books, 1988), 135.

4. Kristiana Gregory, "Soft Cover," *Los Angeles Times Book Review,* July 22, 1984, 8, cited in Collings, *Storyteller,* 84.

5. Card, *Characters & Viewpoints,* 80.

6. Orson Scott Card, *Lost Boys* (New York: HarperCollins, HarperPaperbacks, 1992), 14.

7. Card, *Lost Boys,* 450. Step is remembering Jesus' parable of the tares in Matthew 13:24–30.

8. Card, *Lost Boys,* 104.

9. Card, *Lost Boys,* 186.

10. Card, *Lost Boys,* 297.

11. Card, *Lost Boys,* 408–409.

12. Card, *Lost Boys,* 407.

13. Card, *Lost Boys,* 140–142.

14. Card, *Lost Boys,* 456.

15. In my interview with Card, September 12, 2000, I asked him: "If one of your characters should walk in right now and join the discussion, who would you like it to be?" Card declined to name one. He said that he would be ashamed to meet the ones better than he, and afraid to meet the ones worse than he. "And how could I ever want to meet Step Fletcher? He *is* me."

16. Orson Scott Card, *The Folk of the Fringe,* paperback edition (New York: Tom Doherty Associates, Tor, 1989).

17. Orson Scott Card, "West," in *Folk of the Fringe,* 1–84. "West" first published in *Free Lancers: Alien Stars IV,* ed. E. Mitchell (New York: Baen Books, 1987).

18. Orson Scott Card, "Salvage," in *Folk of the Fringe*, 84–137. First published in *Isaac Asimov's Science Fiction Magazine*, February 1986, 56–75. Also published in *Nebula Awards 22: 1986*, ed. George Zebrowski (New York: Harcourt Brace Jovanovich, 1988), 250–273.

19. Orson Scott Card, "The Fringe," in *Folk of the Fringe*, 109–137. First published in *The Magazine of Fantasy and Science Fiction*, 140–160. Also published in *Nebula Awards 21: 1985*, ed. George Zebrowski (New York: Harcourt Brace Jovanovich, 1987), 44–65. Also published in *Future on Ice*, ed. Orson Scott Card (New York: St. Martin's Press, 1998), 400–432.

20. Orson Scott Card, "Pageant Wagon," in *Folk of the Fringe*, 138–239. First published in the first edition of *Folk of the Fringe* (West Bloomfield, Mich: Phantasia, 1989). Also published in *Isaac Asimov's Science Fiction Magazine*, August 1989, 116.

21. Orson Scott Card, "America," in *Folk of the Fringe*, 240–273. First published in *Isaac Asimov's Science Fiction Magazine*, January 1987, 22–53. Also published in *The Year's Best Science Fiction: Fifth Annual Collection*, ed. Gardner Dozois (New York: St. Martin's Press, 1988) and in *The 1988 Annual World's Best SF*, ed. Donald A. Wolheim (New York: DAW, 1988). "America" was again published in *The Norton Book of Science Fiction*, ed. Ursula LeGuin and Brian Attebery (New York: Norton, 1993).

22. Card, "Author's Note: On Sycamore Hill" in *Folk of the Fringe*, 293.

23. Card, *Folk of the Fringe*, 116.

24. Card, *Folk of the Fringe*, 274–300.

25. Card, *Folk of the Fringe*, 282.

26. Card, *Folk of the Fringe*, 293.

27. Second Corinthians 4:7. For more about the role of honesty in the fictional treatment of one's own faith, see the appendix of this book, which discusses a motion picture novelization by Orson Scott Card's son, Geoffrey Card.

28. Orson Scott Card, *A Storyteller in Zion* (Salt Lake City, Utah: Bookcraft, 1993). A collection of essays by Card written at different times. This selection is from "The Problem of Evil in Fiction" (1980), 83.

29. For some of Card's opinions on the most effective methods of correcting overt or covert racism, see his online article, "The Press Isn't Helping the Church Wipe Out Racism," at www.belief.net, February 20, 2000.

30. Card, author interview, September 12, 2000.

Part IV

Novels That Stand Alone (Not in a Series), and Shorter Works and Poems

8

Four Early Novels

A PLANET CALLED TREASON (1979)
AND ITS REVISION, *TREASON* (1988)[1]

On the world known as "Treason" certain people have the freakish talent of regeneration: they can grow back extra body parts that are injured or lost. Some are radical regeneratives ("rads") and spontaneously grow extra body parts without being injured. Sometimes these body parts are those of the opposite sex. Spare parts are harvested for the offworld oppressors, in exchange for iron. Treason is very poor in hard metals.

The story is told in first person by Lanik Mueller, a rad, who is determined to escape his fate of being imprisoned and harvested. In the adventures that ensue, Lanik discovers that radical regeneration can be taken to extremes never imagined. He also discovers the true history and nature of his world and its great variety of societies. Much of this book foreshadows Card's later writings.

Most of us, as we go through our developing teen years, have some mixed feelings of delight and bewilderment about our changing bodies. There may even be doubts about sexual identification ("Am I *really* a true man? A true woman? Do the others feel like this?") This book is an extension of those bewilderments on a larger scale.

Also, such societal horrors as slavery, prostitution, and child labor have been called "the sale of human flesh" by would-be reformers.

Here, Card takes that metaphor literally and shows us the implications. The reviewer Tom Easton recommended *A Planet Called Treason* for the Nebula Award.[2]

Card himself believed in the book enough to revise it. Yet, it has never had the success of his other works. Lanik is brave, persistent, and tries to be honorable, but, for many readers, he is simply not as likable as most of Card's young protagonists.

SONGMASTER[3]

Mikal the Terrible wants a Songbird. Mikal is the ruthless Emperor of all humanity in many star systems. But not even the Emperor can simply command the Songhouse.

The Songhouse on the planet Tew takes in children as young as three years who have signs of musical ability. They are trained until they are ready to be Singers on planets, usually at about age ten. They serve as Singers until fifteen. Drugs are taken to postpone the breaking of the voice. After age fifteen they may return to the Songhouse as teachers, or make lives for themselves elsewhere, if they prefer. Some of those who return will rise to the highest level: Songmaster of the High Room.

But about once a decade a Singer is found who is not just a singer, but a *Songbird*. A Songbird has a very special gift. He (or she) can sense the innermost feelings of an audience. The Songbird can then create a song, with or without words, that is an acknowledgment of, and an answer to, the "song in the heart" of the listener. This power can have an overwhelming effect.

The beautiful boy Ansett is the most powerful Songbird that the Songhouse has produced. The Songhouse sends Ansett to the court of Emperor Mikal the Terrible on Planet Earth. To Ansett, his employer is not the Emperor, but "Father Mikal." Ansett can sense that Mikal's fearsome ruthlessness overlies a true desire to do good through peace, order, and justice.

Mikal has clever enemies. Ansett is kidnapped, brainwashed with drugs, and trained in vicious unarmed combat to kill Mikal upon a verbal signal, then forced to forget it all consciously, and turned loose to return to Mikal. The plot is foiled by chance. Then Mikal, who is by now extremely elderly, abdicates in favor of his chief minister, Riktors Ashen, whom he knows to be the mastermind behind the plot to kill him.

Mikal does this because he is convinced that Riktors will succeed at keeping the Empire together far better than any of Mikal's sons could. Ansett becomes Riktors' Songbird, and even becomes a friend.

But Riktors jealously punishes Ansett for looking forward to returning to the Songhouse. He forces Ansett to stay on Earth by deceiving both Ansett and the Songhouse. As a consolation prize, Ansett is made Manager of Earth, at first a nominal post, as a mouthpiece for others. But soon it is clear that Ansett's talents as a former Songbird make him an excellent negotiator. He can "hear the song in the heart" of the rival ambassadors and distinguish between what they say and what they mean.

Ansett has kept his virginity. Neither Emperor wanted a catamite, and it would have been impolitic to accept a sexual invitation from either man or woman. But now Ansett wants to satisfy the desires of his bisexual friend Josif. When he tries to do this, the side effects of the Songhouse drugs give Ansett near-fatal convulsions.

Josif, who had intended no harm at all, is arrested. Ansett, when he recovers, flies to Emperor Riktors to plead for Josif. At court, Ansett discovers two things: the lies that kept him from returning to the Songhouse, and the horrifying fact that Josif has been castrated.

Filled with fury, Ansett uses his fighting tricks to force himself into Riktors presence. But Riktors is guarded by Ferret, the very person who taught the fighting tricks to Ansett. So, for the first time, Ansett uses his voice to destroy. His song expresses everything evil and treacherous that Riktors is, and that Ferret is, and turns it all against *them*. Before Ansett is finished, Ferret has disemboweled himself with his own hands and Emperor Riktors is in a catatonic state.

Riktor's catatonia is eventually healed by the Songmaster of the High Room. In three years Riktors dies and names Ansett as his heir. Ansett is Emperor for sixty years, and he is a good one.

Then he designates Josif's son as his heir, abdicates, and returns to the planet Tew and the Songhouse. There, he does something extraordinary. For six days, in his cracked, weak, old-man voice, Ansett sings to the students. Somehow, he can do it so that the students can sense the music that he *means* to sing. He sings of his life, all the tragedy and triumph of it. Over time, every student's singing is improved in its emotional depth. It is almost as if they had all become Songbirds.

And Ansett, former Songbird, former Emperor, has just one further request: he asks to die in the High Room of the Songhouse. His wish is granted.

Some Meanings of *Songmaster*

It has long been known that music can capture people's minds, can transform them into something else. In our present day, music therapy is used to reach out to the mentally disturbed, the autistic and the retarded. Music has been used in the rehabilitation of criminals. It can also be used for evil purposes: to whip up a mob into violent frenzy, for instance. What might be the power of a supreme singing talent combined with a totally empathetic mind? Would there be limits to what it could do?

Songmaster contrasts the power of music with two other kinds of power: brute force and the power of law. When Ansett is kidnapped and conditioned to be an assassin the plot fails; indeed, the power of brute force can be used for the opposite side. When Ansett himself tries to use brute force against Riktors and Ferret he cannot do it, for Ferret is as skilled as he. But the blows of Ansett's singing do far more damage than the blows of hands and feet.

This power remains even when Ansett is not singing. His empathy as a Songbird is what makes him a good ruler of Earth and of the Empire. "If I write the songs of a nation I care not who writes its laws."[4] Card has imagined a universe in which the same person, at different times, has power to make music and to make law. Ansett knows very well where his true power is. He dies in the High Room of the Songhouse on Tew, not in the Palace on Earth. The title of the book is *Songmaster*—not *Emperor of the Universe*.

The Roots of *Songmaster*[5]

When Card had sold "Ender's Game" (the novelette, not the full-length book) in 1977, he quickly sold two more stories, and then wrote five more that did not sell. He thought of trying another story about a child genius who can save the world.

Music has always been a part of the life of Orson Scott Card. He does not consider himself to be a "good" musician, but he has been a boy soprano, played French horn and tuba, and can sing folk songs while he accompanies himself on the guitar. He sings in, and sometimes conducts, his church choir. He has music playing while he writes. Why not a hero who is an unsurpassable genius in music?

A novelette, "Mikal's Songbird," was published in *Analog*.[6] It appeared on the final ballot for the Nebula Award for 1978 and received second place. It was also a finalist for the Hugo award. It begins with

Ansett's captivity by the plotters against Mikal and ends with Riktor's succession to the Empire. At first, Card did not want to try to expand "Mikal's Songbird" although his agent urged him to. He wrote a prequel, a novella called "Songhouse" published in *Analog* the next year.[7] This novella eventually became, word for word, the opening chapters of *Songmaster*.

When Card finally combined "Songhouse" and a rewriting of "Mikal's Songbird," adding much more material as well, the finished product had required many changes. "Events had new meanings; characters had different things to think and say."[8] The original "Mikal's Songbird" had to be discarded. (Card found this "wrenching.")

Reviews tended to be cautious, such as: "Compelling . . . fairy-tale quality . . . broad appeal . . . would be even better if Card were not so obvious in his efforts to tug at our heartstrings"[9] and "If the book has a . . . flaw, it is a certain sense of coldness and austerity . . . perhaps the . . . starkness of the background is intended to make the story's . . . drama and emotional intensity stand out."[10] One review is summed up in its title: "Mythical, Musical Science Fiction."[11]

Fairy-tale, mythical—these are words that suggest fantasy. Indeed, Card so conditions us with his lyrical prose that we accept that a song can drive a strong man to a gruesome suicide. This fits the definition of fantasy in chapter 4: Fantasy as the exaggeration of something real that we do not fully understand. Card says, "I could have written *Songmaster* as a fantasy and set it in Europe in 1312. . . . I wouldn't have to change anything but the word spaceship."[12] But Card didn't do the story as a medievaloid fantasy because of the publishing practices of the time.[13] For most editors "fantasy" had to have magic creatures—gnomes, elves, and so forth—and that was not what Card wanted here.

Songmaster received the Edmond Hamilton/Leigh Brackett Memorial Award in 1981. Card feels that the story has flaws but in his overall assessment "Songmaster is my earliest novel that I am willing to stand by in its original form."[14]

THE CREATION OF *HART'S HOPE*[15]

This is one of the few cases in which Card has actually given us a specific description of his creative process at work in making a novel.[16]

Card was relaxing from writing *Saints*. He was doodling with pencil and paper while watching television. He drew a medieval-style walled city, with temples, palaces, and poverty-stricken areas, naming as he went. One small shrine he whimsically named "Hart's Hope." As with all fortified cities, there were different gates, but he saw that he had made a mistake. He had drawn the gateposts of one entrance, but with no opening between them. Could there be a story here? Why is this gate closed? Perhaps there had been some dreadful prophecy: The one who would come in by that gate would kill the ruler.

News at that time concerned Siamese twins joined at the tops of their heads. Could anything be worse? Well, yes. Suppose they were joined at the face!

He had been reading books by Mary Renault, such as *The King Must Die*. This book suggested the idea of different "gods," different religions, for men and for women. An idea began to take shape in his mind: A city–state where the men worship a deer, (or a *hart*, to use an older term) and the women worship the Sweet Sisters, joined at the face. There was also a third god for this city. His name was God.

Then he began teaching a class at the University of Utah in the writing of fantasy and science fiction. He asked his students to come up with "the price of magic." Magic must have some limit, or there is no story. One idea was this: Power is in blood. "You could kill a fly and . . . keep the soup from boiling over. You kill a rabbit and make an enemy sick or heal a child. You could kill a . . . What if you kill your own child? . . . I had . . . the city of Hart's Hope . . . ruled by a mortal . . . so cruel she killed her own child."[17]

So, how could this monstrous person be defeated? Not by killing another child, but by powers of antimagic. There should be a person in the story who was a "magic sink," someone in whose presence magic could never work.

However, it was not until Card was actually writing the first draft that he realized that the god named God should appear to be a feeble old man polishing the woodwork in the Queen's palace.

As with other books by Card, *Hart's Hope* appeared in a shorter form first.[18]

Some Meanings of *Hart's Hope*

There is no doubt of genre here. This is a fantasy in the "high" or medieval tradition. But it is not a fairy tale for little children. The story is strong and harsh.

Nearly everything in *Hart's Hope* is the opposite of what it appears to be. A "helpless" little girl becomes the source of terrible power. A "weak" country boy can negate that power. Evil wears a face of beauty.

A truth-filled woman becomes ugly. Criminals can be loyal comrades, while men sworn to uphold law are stupidly brutal.

An old, blind (or all-seeing?) servant is God. This recalls Jesus' parable of the sheep and the goats, in which the saved and the damned discover that "the least of these" is the Ultimate Judge.[19]

The reactions of readers to this book are varied. Some think that it is Card's best; some just can't bear it. Michael Collings calls it, "Rich in suggestivity and characterization, replete with mythic, epic, heroic, Christian, folkloric and fantastic elements."[20]

Card himself seems ambivalent. "When . . . somebody . . . tells me that *Hart's Hope* is their favorite novel of mine . . . I just think, 'Well, what kind of a sick person are you?'"[21] On the other hand, he has also said, "If people can get through the boredom of the first sixty pages or so they will find one of my best books hidden in there."[22]

WYRMS[23]

One standard form of the type of speculative literature that we call *myth* or *allegory* is the quest story. The hero must take a complicated journey with many adventures, with a goal at the end. He may travel to slay a dragon (or "wyrm" in the Germanic tradition), or to find some magical object, or to rescue a beautiful woman who may be imprisoned in a tower or asleep in a circle of fire on a mountain, or some such hazard. The quest may involve some combination of these things, but one way or another the hero wins either a beautiful woman or a kingdom, or both.

Although *Wyrms*, like *Songmaster*, disguises itself as a science fiction novel, in truth it is a quest myth, or allegory. But it is different from other quest myths in the one startling respect: the one doing the quest is not a young man but a young woman.

Her name is Patience, daughter of Lord Peace, who should be Heptarch (ruler) of the land of Imakulata. But Lord Peace is politely enslaved by the usurping Heptarch. Patience will be in danger after her father dies. There are prophecies about a "Christos."

When Peace is dead Patience flees, gathering allies, male and female, human and otherwise. She is following the Cranning Call, driving her to the mountain where so many of the wise are drawn, believed to be the lair of the Unwyrm.

Patience is as much a hero as is any of Card's male heroes. She makes mistakes, but no more often than the male heroes do. She needs allies, but so do they. Card has turned the tables on the quest myth: The beautiful woman is not the prize, she is the questor. She does not wait to be rescued; she can do the rescuing.

Wyrms began as a novella, titled "Unwyrm." That shorter version was apparently never published, due to the failure of the publishing house.[24]

Wyrms was acclaimed by critics: "A romantic, comic and nightmarish . . . rite of passage in a world of noble goblins and idiot savants, where the dead guide the living, and human and alien have intermingled in bizarre and inseparable ways."[25]

THE USE, AND THE RISKS, OF THE GROTESQUE

In his works before the novel *Ender's Game*, or soon after that, Card often writes of the grotesque. This is not shock for shock's sake; he always has a point. But for some readers the shock can get in the way of the point.

Compare, for instance, the disembowelment scene in *Songmaster*, an early work, with the deception of the blind Isaac in *Rebekah*, one of Card's mature works. *Songmaster* is about the power of music. *Rebekah* is about the power of the written word. Ansett, revenging terrible wrongs done to him and to Josif, uses the power of his singing to cause the gruesome self-destruction of his enemy. Rebekah, in order to preserve the gift of literacy for future generations, deceives her blind husband into thinking that he is giving the birthright blessing to one son when he is actually blessing another one.

Ansett and Rebekah are each driven to do something that this person would ordinarily never do: to use a powerful voice to destroy, or to mislead a helpless husband. In each case, the scene is distressing. We want to say, "Don't. This is unworthy of you." Yet it is hard to see what else he, or she, could have done.

But in *Rebekah* we have none of the sickening reaction present in the *Songmaster* scene of a man tearing his own guts out. That reaction confuses the issue of whether Ansett had a right to do this. In *Rebekah* we are forced to face her terrible choice with no distraction. Instead of saying "Ugh!" we are compelled to say, "What *should* she do?" This is still painful, but it is a different kind of pain.

Card himself expresses it this way: "[In my early work] without knowing it, I was using violence and cruelty as a way of showing that what was going on was really important. Once I understood that . . . I could stop doing it to such a degree."[26]

We will meet Card as fantasy writer again in the next chapter. He will not be disguising fantasy as science fiction, nor will he be creating medieval worlds of walled cities or quests. He will be writing modern ghost stories, bringing fantasy into our everyday lives.

NOTES

1. Orson Scott Card, *A Planet Called Treason*, hardcover (New York: St. Martin's Press, 1979). Revised as *Treason*, again published by St. Martin's, both hardcover and paperback, 1988. Both versions now out of print.

2. Tom Easton, "The Reference Library," *Analog Science Fiction and Fact*, December 1979, 167–169.

3. Orson Scott Card, *Songmaster*, paperback edition (New York: Tom Doherty Associates, Tor, 1980).

4. The original text of this common quotation appears to be: "A very wise man once said to me, 'If a man were permitted to make all the ballads he need not care who should make the laws of a nation.'" Andrew Fletcher of Saltoun, in "Letter to the Marquis of Montrose, 1704," in Burton Stevenson, *Home Book of Quotations*, (New York: Dodd, Mead, 1956), 123:2.

5. Except for statements otherwise attributed, the information in this section is from *Maps in a Mirror: The Short Fiction of Orson Scott Card* (New York: Tom Doherty Associates, Tor, 1990), 663–666, and from an online interview with Barnes and Noble (bn.com, Live: Chat Transcripts, Friday, March 20, 1998, 8:00 P.M.) in response to a question from Aaron Plikt of Temple, Texas, as to whether Card is a musician. The question was provoked by an admiration of the treatment of musical matters in *Songmaster*.

6. Easton, *Analog Science Fiction and Fact*, May 1978, 72–99.

7. Easton, *Analog Science Fiction and Fact*, September 1979, 12–76.

8. Card, *Maps in a Mirror*, 664.

9. *Publisher's Weekly*, May 23, 1980, 72.

10. Richard A. Lupoff, "Beasts, Songbirds and Wizards," *Washington Post Book World*, August 24, 1990, 6.

11. Ray Boven, *Deseret News*, August 9, 1980, 83. As cited in Michael R. Collings, *Storyteller: Orson Scott Card* (Hiram, Ga.: Overlook Connection Press, 2001), 57.

12. Howard Mittelmark, "Orson Scott Card Interview," online, Research Area of Hatrack River, the official website of Orson Scott Card (www.hatrack.com), reprinted from *Inside Books*, January 1989.

13. Personal interview, September 12, 2000.

14. Card, *Maps in a Mirror*, 664.

15. Orson Scott Card, *Hart's Hope*, paperback edition (New York: Tom Doherty Associates, 1983).

16. Orson Scott Card, *How to Write Science Fiction and Fantasy*, Genre Writing Series, (Cincinnati, Ohio: Writer's Digest Books, 1990), 28–33.

17. Card, *How to Write Science Fiction*, 32.

18. Roy Torgeson, ed., *Chrysalis 8*, hardcover (Garden City, N.Y.: Doubleday, n.d.), as cited in Michael Collings, *Storyteller* (Woodstock, Ga.: 2001), 299.

19. Matthew 25:31–46.

20. Collings, *Storyteller*, 75–76.

21. *Asimov's Science Fiction*, Orson Scott Card and Allen Steele conversation, posted online at www.asimovs.com, August 29, 1998.

22. Scott Nicholson, "Card's Game: An Interview with Orson Scott Card," online Research Area of Hatrack River, the official website of Orson Scott Card (www.hatrack.com).

23. Orson Scott Card, *Wyrms*, hardcover (New York: Arbor House, 1987). The inclusion of *Wyrms* in this chapter is stretching the definition of early novels, since by the time *Wyrms* appeared, Card had published *Ender's Game*, the novel, and *Seventh Son*. But *Wyrms* has similarities to the other books covered in this chapter.

24. "Unwyrm" was intended for an anthology of original works by writers nominated for the Campbell award, edited by George R. R. Martin. But Blue Jay Books ceased publishing before the collection could be published. Card, *Maps in a Mirror*, 666–667. Michael Collings believes it possible that the Italian translation of *Wyrms* is actually a translation of the original novella, "Unwyrm." If so, Collings says, this is the only copy of this shorter version published anywhere. Collings, *Storyteller*, 127.

25. *Publishers Weekly*, May 29, 1987, 68.

26. Orson Scott Card, "Casting Shadows," *Locus* 49, no. 6 (December 2002), 7, 71–72.

9

Fantasy/Mysteries in the Present Age

LOST BOYS[1]

This book was discussed in chapter 7 as a vehicle for presenting Card's perception of the Mormon church in recent times. Here, the book will be discussed again as a fantasy/mystery.

Step and DeAnne Fletcher have problems adjusting to their new home in Steuben, North Carolina. Step's new job is proving unsatisfactory. DeAnne, who is expecting a fourth child soon, is finding the new surroundings unfamiliar. On the first day, DeAnne gets a shock when the landlord's father casually walks in; she had carelessly left the door open. Their new Mormon ward is dominated by a manipulating woman. The area has no sidewalks; hedges come down to the curb; and balls disappear down the storm drains.

Houses are built southern style, off the ground without a basement. *Anything* could get in that crawl-space. During that first summer they have crickets, June bugs, gnats, and spiders. There are financial problems, which will be worse if Step cannot stay at his miserable job and keep the health benefit until the baby comes. The baby boy is born with cerebral palsy. There will be years of therapy ahead.

The worst problem concerns their oldest son, Stevie. He makes no friends. His teacher is a sadist who has picked Stevie as the target of her persecution. Stevie is beginning to have imaginary friends, and he keeps adding more. He won't admit that his new friends are "pretend."

The psychiatrist they send him to believes that religious faith is a neurosis and Stevie's problems are caused by his Mormon upbringing. The psychiatric sessions stop, but Stevie's preoccupation with his "friends" continues. He plays computer games compulsively, as if his invisible friends were part of the game.

In Steuben, boys have been disappearing. The police suspect a serial kidnapper or killer. The names and pictures of the missing boys are published *and every single name is the name of one of Stevie's imaginary friends.*

The crisis of the book is catastrophically tragic, and yet, horror is not the primary emotion that the reader has at the end. For the survivors everything is changed and deep painful loss will always be with them, but love and strong positive memories will always be there also, along with the poignant hope of someday rejoining the loved and the lost.

As Michael Collings writes: "What might have been a conventional ghost story concludes with an evocation of mystical enlightenment."[2]

The Roots of *Lost Boys*[3]

Lost Boys had its beginning as a short story at the Sycamore Hills Writers Workshop in 1985. Card thought that it might be interesting to share a ghost story. He used an accepted convention in ghost story-telling: He pretended that it had all really happened to him. Card wrote it in the first person, used his wife's name for the mother, used the actual names of his own children, (adding a fictitious eldest child). He included the birth of his baby boy with cerebral palsy. He used the name of his town, and the real name of the company for which he had worked.

At the end, he acknowledged that this story was fiction, and that he and Kristine had never faced the catastrophe of this story. The reaction of the other workshop participants "ranged from annoyance to fury."[4] They said that he had claimed a grief to which he was not entitled.

Card accepted their rebukes. Later he realized that there was more in the story than he had known. He was not mourning a nonexistent oldest child. He was mourning his youngest, Charlie Ben, born with cerebral palsy who could not speak or walk, "a child who is not dead and yet can barely taste life despite all our love. . . . I had worn a mask of . . . acceptance so convincing that I had believed it. . . . But the lies we live will . . . be confessed in the stories we tell."[5]

When Card admitted to this to himself he was then able to make changes. He gave different names to the characters and places and expanded the short story into this book.

The book has meaningful developments, including the background of his Mormon faith. All authors of fiction wear masks. But they probably do better work when they know what they are masking.

TREASURE BOX

Quentin Fears is a thirty-four-year-old bachelor. He has never stopped mourning his sister, Lizzy, who died in an auto accident when Quentin was eleven and she was in her teens. Although she was brain dead, Quentin vehemently objected when his parents gave permission for Lizzy to be taken off the respirator.

He has never told anyone that Lizzy spoke to him there in the hospital room. It wasn't the artificially breathing body that spoke. It was Lizzy's voice, speaking from somewhere else, using characteristic phrases. She ordered Quentin to stop "keeping me tied down like this."[6] Over time, Quentin has persuaded himself that he hallucinated.

Quentin is the picture of a successful young man. By lucky choices he ventured early into the computer-software business and became a multimillionaire. He assists ventures of other entrepreneurs. But whenever he meets an agreeable young woman, he compares her to his dead sister.

Now, he has met Madeleine. She is beautiful, and has just enough brains and money to be a suitable partner. She is as inexperienced with sex as he is, which is a relief. She gets along with his parents almost *too* well. Against his lawyer's advice, Quentin rushes into marriage after a few weeks' acquaintance.

There are two dubious matters. First, Madeleine (he calls her "Mad") won't take Quentin to see *her* family. She insists on waiting until after the marriage. Also, Mad sometimes reveals, when off her guard, a hunger for power: Not power to accomplish some purpose, just *power*. Quentin is too much in love to let these matters bother him.

After they have been married a few months he sees her family. In the winter, they go to a pre-Victorian mansion on the Hudson river. It has uniformed servants and a private family graveyard. Her family is eccentric, and Mad seems to hate them. The strangest one is an elderly grandmother. She never speaks but as Mad says, "She makes her wishes known."[7] Mad's Uncle Paul is almost as strange.

In this house there is a mahogany box that contains Mad's inheritance: She calls it her Treasure Box. She cannot open it until her husband stands by her. It disturbs Quentin that she had never told him about this. When the household gathers for the opening of the Treasure Box, Mad asks Quentin to open the box for her.

Grandmother's eyes forbid this. Her hands rest on the sides. Uncle Paul is sarcastic. Quentin feels a strange distaste of the box. Mad goes into a wild childish tantrum, beating the air, weeping, insisting, wailing, "All this work, all these months, I'm so *tired*. All for *nothing!*"[8] Is she saying that she only married him so that he would open this box?

Mad flees. Quentin follows her into the graveyard but cannot find her. Among the tombstones, he finds names that match those of the "family" in the house. The house is empty and dirty. The only footprints in the snow are Quentin's.

By this evidence, and other signs, Quentin comes to realize that Mad never existed. He loved a phantasm, a succubus, created out of his own mind. Whatever *he* believed was beautiful and good, that is what Mad would be. But whatever created the illusion of Mad could not keep its power-hungry nature disguised completely.

What is in the Treasure Box? And most puzzling, who is the power-hungry person who created the illusion of Mad? Quentin refers to this unknown person as the "User."

The powers of evil have their limits. Quentin has his own resources and gets allies. The most shocking revelation is the true nature and identity of the User. Terrible things happen in this book. Dreadful choices have to be made. Goodness triumphs, but at a cost.

Quentin meets Sally. She is quite different from what Madeleine had seemed to be. He learns the difference between loving one's own dream and loving a true other.

Appearance Versus Reality

"Am I am truly in love?" "Is he or she truly what he or she seems to be?" "Is this the right job for me, or the place I should live?" "Is this someone I can trust?" "Pinch me, I'm dreaming, this seems too good to be true." These are questions and statements that people constantly ask.

Reality can be better or worse than what we have imagined, but it is usually different. Surprise ("I never imagined *that*!") is a good test of reality. When Quentin investigates, he finds that the marriage license is forged. His own name, in his own handwriting, appears on both lines. Quentin married himself.

When he finds Sally the experience is so different. "Instead of being exactly what he wished for . . . she was completely herself. . . . He might not understand [Sally] but . . . she . . . was real. He wanted to . . . shout . . . I'm real, too. . . . But . . . maybe he wasn't. Maybe you had to be as pure to stay in the company of good people as to survive among wild beasts."[9]

"Purity" is sometimes used as meaning simply sexually innocent. That is often a part of it. But sexual innocence had been abused by the succubus to seduce Quentin into marriage with himself. What Sally has is *reality*. The real, or pure, person may sometimes be mistaken, or exasperating, or hard to understand. But the inward self is just as good and strong as the outward appearance. That is pure reality.

HOMEBODY[10]

The House

In 1874, Dr. Calhoun Bellamy of Greensboro, North Carolina, wanted an elegant home with a ballroom, parlors, large bedrooms, and an art gallery, built strongly to last for centuries. An old Quaker house had to be demolished first. During the demolition a tunnel under the house was discovered, leading out to a distant gully, probably used for escaping slaves. Bellamy was neither Quaker nor abolitionist, yet he disliked destroying a piece of history. He instructed the builders to leave the tunnel, building the foundation around it. It might be a wine or root cellar someday.

The house was a social center of Greensboro with parties and balls. But by World War I, families with money were building homes in the suburbs. The neighborhood declined. Houses were bought by landlords who divided up beautiful big rooms into small spaces for rent. The Bellamy house had a brief career as a Prohibition speakeasy with rum-running in the tunnel and an upstairs whorehouse with a choice of white or black girls.

By the 1960s, rooms were being rented to female students at the university. There were more dividing walls added. Nobody took care of the yard. Then in the 1980s, the landlord moved and listed the house for sale. No one bought. The house became the neighborhood eyesore, appearance decaying although the structure was sound.

The little house next door had originally been the carriage house and servants' quarters for the Bellamy mansion. It was bought by two women who had escaped from the upstairs whorehouse, and a third woman who had rescued them. All three are now elderly. As the mansion declined, the carriage house continued to be well tended.

Don Lark

Don Lark built new houses when he was married and had a little daughter. His wife left him and took the child. Don could not prove that his wife was drug-addicted and alcoholic. He tried every legal means to get custody. His ex-wife wrecked the car, killing herself and their daughter. Don blames himself, for not kidnapping his child.

Now Don renovates *old* houses. It eases his despairing heart to take some wreck and make it beautiful again. He does the work himself, living in the house while he works. He discovers the old Bellamy mansion in 1997. It should be a magnificent restoration, he thinks.

The old lock, which he pries off the door, leaves holes that the temporary new lock does not quite cover. Those holes disappear, as if the house was healing itself. Don assumes that he remembered wrongly what he did. The friendly old ladies next door talk about the house as if it were a living being capable of holding a person captive. They want to see it torn down. Don thinks of the ladies as the Weird Sisters.

Sylvie

In the upstairs tub Don finds a "squatter," a homeless woman using the house without paying rent. She is Sylvie Delaney, and owns only the faded blue dress that she wears. The last thing Don needs is a crazy housemate, but he won't use force to evict her. He adjusts to Sylvie. She watches him work, asks intelligent questions, and when he brings in pizza or hamburgers, she eats very little. She is a former university student who used to pay rent here, an orphan with no relatives. She has a feeling for the house, as do the Weird Sisters, although *she* wants the house to survive.

Sylvie knows why Don's tools disappear, and why his toolbench was moved close to his cot so that he hit his head in the dark. Don assumes that Sylvie is playing tricks on him. But she knows the house is like a child at the dentist: Everything is being done for its good, but it hurts. Sylvie tries to soothe the house.

Her awareness of the house stops Don from a bad mistake. He was beginning to take out a bearing wall that appeared to be just another added partition. Don begins to take Sylvie more seriously.

Sylvie's Secret

He finds out why she won't go near the tunnel in the basement. She had a roommate, Lissy, who had become an outrageous parasite. She had stolen Sylvie's thesis without even paraphrasing it. This could get them *both* expelled.

Sylvie went down the tunnel where Lissy kept her drug stash. She told Lissy: "Withdraw the paper or I go to the dean." Lissy replied with horrible insults, even blaming Sylvie for Sylvie's parents' deaths. Frantic, Sylvie picked up a loose rock and hit Lissy on the head. Then she tried, unsuccessfully, to find pulse and breath. She fled the tunnel. Her guilt kept her in the house. She has nightmares of Lissy coming back and strangling her.

The Discovery

Don thinks that Lissy survived. Head wounds can be misleadingly bloody. Lissy must have recovered and left the tunnel by the other exit. Don insists that they go down the tunnel. They do not find Lissy's body. They find something *more* terrifying!

The story builds powerfully from that point. It seems, for a time, that everyone concerned (including the Weird Sisters) may lose everything. Eventually, goodness triumphs in a spectacular climax.

Michael Collings calls the book a "richly tailored foray into the unknown and the kinds of relationships that are . . . tested and established by that unknown."[11]

Imagery and Theme in *Homebody*

Homebody can be read simply as a suspense thriller. It is not, in the usual sense, a religious story. But if the reader looks for it, there are images that are strongly evocative of death and resurrection. The last chapter even has crucifixion images.

The book can be seen as an extended metaphor for the renovation of ruined lives. Is a "homebody" someone who never leaves home, or does it refer to the house itself that has a personality along with its body? There are many examples of this extended metaphor. Don Lark is a person to whom others confess (Sylvie is not the first). He doesn't like this, but he treats secrets respectfully. A chapter headed "Hot Water" deals with the repair to the plumbing, but it also describes how Don's consideration for other's secrets makes him liable to blackmail. Similarly, chapters headed "Tearing Up, Tearing Down" and "Wrecking Bar" show how old habits of thought have to be cleared away for new ones. "The Tunnel" deals with buried fears and guilts. This extended metaphor—rebuilding a house representing the rebuilding of a life—appears in Don's dream of himself as a house, with his daughter as the heart. Then the heart is gone and it is winter. He wakes, and Sylvie sits in the alcove.[12]

The first version of *Homebody* was a screenplay. Card turned it into a novel. The intent was to combine the idea of a "haunted house" with the viewpoint of someone who renovates houses.[13]

FANTASY OF TODAY IN CARD'S SHORTER FICTION

Card's short story, "In the Dragon's House" uses an entirely different perspective on the "haunted house theme, and also an unusual perspective on dragons."[14] In the short story, "Inventing Lovers on the Phone," Card gives us a haunted cell phone, and a suggestion of what it is like for pretenses to become true.[15]

CARD'S APPROACH TO "HORROR" FICTION

In Card's book, *How to Write Science Fiction and Fantasy,* he says: "New ideas [are] variations on old themes."[16] Card uses some of the oldest themes in the world: the serial killer; missing children; the "demon lover," or succubus, born of one's need; the mysterious treasure, available only under certain conditions; the haunted house; weird old women.

But Card does a reverse twist on each one. A tale of every parent's worst fear becomes a narration of religious vision. A succubus uses her sexual *innocence* as one of the methods of her seduction. Does a spirit haunt the house, or does a house haunt the spirits of the living and the dead?

These are among Card's most popular books on audiotape. They are shorter, have more direct action, and are more "to the point" than some of his other novels.

Horror Stories or Tales of Dread?

Card himself makes distinction between dread, terror, and horror in the introduction to *Maps In A Mirror*, as follows:

> *Dread* is that tension that comes when you know there is something to fear but you have not identified it. A window you closed is open [and] you're alone in the house. . . . *Terror* comes when you see the thing [you fear]. The intruder is coming toward you with a knife. There is frenzy, but bad as it is, now at least you know. . . . *Horror* is the weakest. The fearful thing has happened, you see the grisly, hacked-up corpse. Pity is tinged with revulsion. You reject the scene and deny its humanity. . . . Horror ultimately dehumanizes you.[17]

Card would prefer that his fiction that uses fear be considered as *dread*, rather than *horror*. The subtitle of the full-length book of *Lost Boys* is "A Tale of Dread." There are many places in all three of these books where he could have been gruesome, but he did not. Michael Collings says in his comments on *Treasure Box*, "[Card's] underlying purposes are humane and healing."[18]

These adventures all take place in recent times. Suppose we went to the past (by magic or by time machine). What kind of adventures might we have then?

NOTES

1. Orson Scott Card, *Lost Boys,* paperback edition (New York: HarperCollins, 1992).

2. Michael Collings, *Storyteller: Official Guide to the Works of Orson Scott Card* (Woodstock, Ga.: Overlook Connection Press, 2001), 209.

3. The material in this section, except where otherwise stated, is from the short story "Lost Boys" in *Maps in a Mirror: The Short Fiction of Orson Scott Card* (New York: Tom Doherty Associates, Tor 1990), 108–118, the afterword to the story, 119–120, and the afterword to the whole section where the story, "The Hanged Man" appears, 130–131. The short story was first published in *The Magazine of Fantasy and Science Fiction,* October 1989. The story is also available on audiotape, *The Elephants of Posnam and Other Stories* (San Bruno, Calif.: Fantastic Audio, 2001).

4. Card, *Maps in a Mirror,* 119

5. Card, *Maps in a Mirror,* 119.

6. Orson Scott Card, *Treasure Box* (New York: HarperCollins, 1982), 9.

7. Card, *Treasure,* 108.

8. Card, *Treasure,* 129.

9. Card, *Treasure*, 272.

10. Orson Scott Card, *Homebody* (New York: HarperCollins, 1999).

11. Collings, *Storyteller*, 274.

12. Card, *Homebody*, 311–312.

13. Online discussion of *Homebody*, bn.com, Live Chat Transcripts, Friday, March 20, 1988, pages 4, 7, and 10.

14. Orson Scott Card, "In the Dragon's House," in *The Dragon Quintet*, ed. M. M. Kaye (New York: Science Fiction Book Club, 2003).

15. Orson Scott Card, "Inventing Lovers on the Phone" in a forthcoming anthology, not yet titled, of stories inspired by Janis Ian's music.

16. Orson Scott Card, *How to Write Science Fiction and Fantasy* (Cincinnati, Ohio: Writer's Digest Books, 1990), 15–16.

17. Card, *Maps in a Mirror*, introduction, 3.

18. Collings, *Storyteller*, 267.

10

Moving in Time

ENCHANTMENT: THE STORY AND SOME OF ITS MEANINGS

Ivan Smetski, a young American graduate student of early Slavic languages, formerly of the Soviet Union, has returned to his roots in the Ukraine, after the collapse of Communism in 1989. Ivan is researching the origins of folklore. He has never told anyone that, as a boy, he once glimpsed a mysterious sleeping woman in this area.

By means of magic, Ivan goes back to the ninth century. There, he encounters the historic original of Sleeping Beauty, Princess Katerina of the land of Taina. In order to save his life and hers from a powerful Bear, he must propose marriage to her, and she must accept. Then, after she takes him home, he discovers that he must save her little kingdom from the evil witch, Baba Yaga.

Every Age Has Its Own Standards of Excellence

A time travel theme, aptly demonstrated in Mark Twain's *A Connecticut Yankee In King Arthur's Court*[1] and many other stories involves a time traveler who goes back to a less technological era and, by using his native wit, cleverness, and know-how, finally rules the country. Card's version of a technological man going back in time is different.

Ivan ruefully remembers *Connecticut Yankee* as he is jeered at for his inability to learn to use a broadsword, or even to lift it. To Katerina's father, King Matfei, he is a "pile of twigs."[2] Almost no one really admires Ivan for anything. He is a *runner*? Runners are despised as people who flee from battle. He can read and write? That is a cleric's work, not the work of a king.

In the ninth century, Ivan has the status of an idiot. Card does not assume that people of our age could easily dominate early eras. "In our education, today, we learn nothing useful," says Card. "We become socialized to our [present day] and that is all. The people in the Middle Ages had to learn complicated technical skills just to survive."[3]

What Perishes and What Lasts through Time

No material object can cross the magic time bridges. But *knowledge* can cross. This is symbolic of what becomes of all things, in time. Even as Ivan works to save his wife's kingdom, he knows that it is eventually doomed. Yet he also knows that the story of the Sleeping Beauty will live and will be passed on, even though people do not remember the name of the land from where it first came. No nation lives forever. Some stories do.

Ivan comes upon a manuscript of St. Kirill, who converted the Slavs. When he wishes to record the folktales that he hears, he uses the reverse side of Kirll's translation of the Gospels. This is another symbol. Folktales are not the same as Holy Writ, but they can be seen as the "other side" of what people remember. Holy Writ is what God tells His people. Folktales are what people tell each other, and, as Ivan ponders, since people are God's creation, their stories are the creations of God's creation.

Ivan tries to preserve these tales because the people of the Ukraine of his time need this folklore. The false religion of Soviet Communism has fallen. What calls itself a Church in the Ukraine has been first the tool of Tsars, then "a whimpering dog kicked around by the Communists."[4] The new imitation of the American worship of profit has its own kind of brutality.

Ivan hopes that the Ukrainians can use these tales to recover the soul that they had "before . . . Saint Kirill gave you your state religion, before the Scandinavian Rus' put their name on your nation and your language, before the Tartars got you used to the yoke . . . before envy of the West led you to remake yourselves . . . in their image."[5]

The Role of Magic and the Limits of Evil

There is a notable saying of the science fiction writer Arthur C. Clarke: *Any sufficiently advanced technology is indistinguishable from magic.*[6] Katerina crosses over into our world to help her new husband get the knowledge to save her kingdom. The technology that we take for granted is "magic" to her.

However, the converse is also true. It could be expressed thus: *Magic, in a believable story, must have rules, exceptions, and limitations similar to those of technology.* Baba Yaga has immense power, but when she goes to war she can't do it all herself. She needs soldiers, and they can be defeated by technology. A great part of her power comes from her enslavement of Bear; but every slave longs for freedom. When Ivan delivers a means of liberation, he no longer has to fear Bear's wrath.

Baba Yaga's greatest weakness is the same as that of all evil persons: she underestimates the power of goodness. She does not understand true love, unselfishness, self-sacrifice, gratitude, love of freedom, or dedication to a cause higher than oneself. This ignorance is important in her undoing.

Belief Systems and What Lies beyond Them

There are at least three named belief systems in *Enchantment*: Judaism, ninth-century Eastern Orthodox Christianity, and Magic. Judaism, for the Smetki family, is more a family tradition or ethnic sentiment than a belief.

Overarching all these belief conflicts, or potential conflicts, is something else. Ivan had trained himself as a runner and discus thrower before he ever came to Taina. He studied an ancient Slavic language. There are many other fortunate "coincidences" in the book, which are not coincidence at all. Increasingly, Ivan and Katerina feel that "Somebody planned all this"[7] or "Some force, some fate, wanted you to find me. . . . Whatever that power is."[8] "That power" has never been adequately explained to them by any priest or wizard. Instinctively, they know that "that power" is beyond all creeds or charms, and certainly beyond their understanding.

Materialism As a Belief

Ivan's father, at first, is skeptical about Ivan and Katerina's story. He believes that Katerina is a modern woman putting on an act. He declares his "faith in a rational universe." Ivan protests:

No, Father. You don't have faith in a rational universe. This is a universe [with] the utterly arbitrary speed [limit] of 186,000 miles per second, where feathers and rocks fall at the same speed in a vacuum, where a measurable but unexplainable force called gravity pins people to planets and planets to stars. . . . But you have faith in all this . . . which you don't *begin* to understand, solely because . . . the priests of the established church of the intellectuals have declared [them] and you don't even think to question them.[9]

No matter how much different faiths (or magics) may disagree with each other, their differences are far less than the difference that they all have with materialism. Materialism is the belief that the cosmos that we know with our senses is the whole story, not just a part of it, and needs no explanation for its existence. Materialism requires as much faith as any other belief. Materialism has parts that are mysterious, data that must be taken on authority, and assumptions that can never be proven. Materialism may be comforting, or consoling, to some. But it is not particularly rational.

The Roots of *Enchantment*[10]

Card's motion picture company bought the rights to a script that another studio had decided not to use. In the original script an American graduate student, after various circumstances and adventures, discovers the original of Sleeping Beauty in Russia and kisses her awake. In the original script, that is the end of the story.

Card felt that the discovery of such a phenomenon should be the *beginning*, or very near the beginning of the story. Also, he wanted to develop the question: What was the background of this student? Why should he care? From this, came the idea that the student's first glimpse of Sleeping Beauty should be as a child, when he could do nothing. This was followed by a plan to have the student be an assimilated Jew of the Soviet Union who comes from the Ukraine before 1989, and returns afterward.

This required a tremendous amount of research. Card had to teach himself not only about medieval folklore, but also much about the daily life and social structure of the early Slavs. Further, he had to learn about Jewish lore and tradition and the traditions of the Eastern Orthodox Church. Then he had to learn about life in what used to be the Soviet Union in the present day—both the Christian and the Jewish life. Card's acknowledgments of his sources take up more than two full pages.[11]

Enchantment received generally favorable reviews, such as: "Richly detailed and engagingly peopled."[12] One review, by a high school student, is particularly notable:

> *Enchantment* is not only intriguing, but it is also one of the most realistic fantasy books I have read. The hero has his faults, the heroine has personal conflicts. . . . It's complex enough to be worth your while . . . but nothing that will put you to sleep. Even if you normally despise the fantasy genre, you'll enjoy the . . . characters.[13]

PASTWATCH: THE REDEMPTION OF CHRISTOPHER COLUMBUS

About two hundred years in our future, it is possible to build a machine to view the past. Then it is discovered that it may be possible to build a machine to project people and objects into the past, and thus change the past.

Indeed, there is strong evidence that this has already been done, and that the reality that we take for granted is actually the result of a Time Intervention in the life of Columbus. In that first reality, Columbus never sailed West to find a route to the Indies; instead, he used his personal magnetism and powers of persuasion to launch a European crusade against the Turks. Europe is devastated by this crusade, and the European voyage to America never occurred.

Instead, the Native Americans, specifically the Tlaxcalans, developed metallurgy and ship building, and discovered Europe. This was catastrophic. The Tlaxcalans had many disagreeable practices, such as human sacrifice by torture. Exactly how the devastation of European civilization proceeded cannot be discovered now, but one thing is clear.

Some people in that first reality discovered time-viewing and time travel. They were so desperate that they would do anything to turn Columbus from his crusade. Europe *must* reach the Americas before metallurgy is discovered there.

So these First Interveners sent back a vision to Columbus, when he was a young sea captain, at the moment he barely made it to shore after being shipwrecked by pirates. At that point, he saw a vision of what looked like Father, Son, and Holy Spirit. They command him to sail West, to discover a people who do not know Christ.

In our reality, at the end of the twenty-second century, the earth is despoiled and polluted beyond recovery. Oil and other resources are depleted, and war and famine have killed nine-tenths of humankind. The worst is yet to come. Polar ice caps are melting from greenhouse gases. Floods and other disasters will either make humanity extinct, or at least doom civilization for about 10,000 years.

All this, too, can be traced back to the time of Columbus. When he returned with tales of gold, slaves, and nations to be converted, pillaging of America and other places began, with the efficient machines that Europeans developed.

This is the choice facing humanity. Either watch your children die of hunger (unless they fight wars to survive in "ice, caves, and ignorance") or wipe out seven centuries of human history through the Columbus Project.

Ethical Dilemmas

There is an old saying: "You cannot change just one thing."

Early in the Columbus Project, Tagiri, the woman who originated it, is asked if she wants to kill Columbus, or put an abortive medicine in his mother's food. Tagiri rejects such homicidal ideas in horror.

But, ironically, she is actually working for something far more deadly: the elimination of seven centuries of humanity. She cannot realize this until her daughter, Diko, discovers the evidence of the First Intervention. Tagiri begins to realize what will happen to *this* reality.

Tagiri had, at first, assumed that the people of the First Intervention had gone on existing, somehow. Or they died, but they *had* existed before they died. But the Project mathematicians tell her that, once the Intervention was done, they had never existed. After Tagiri's own Columbus Project succeeds, our own reality will have never existed. Tagiri is shocked. She retreats to a place outdoors, in the dark, heedless of danger from crocodiles.

Her daughter Diko comes to her carrying a flashlight. Diko reminds her mother of all the things parents give up for their children, including life itself, if necessary: "'The people who sent that vision to Columbus . . . were the parents of our age; we are their children. And now we will be the parents of another age." And Tagiri replies that this is just a case of using language to make "terrible things sound noble and beautiful."[14]

This scene of two women under the starry African sky, debating whether or not to destroy seven centuries, is one of the most evocative scenes that Card ever wrote. In its way, it is more terrifying than the climactic scenes of planet destruction in *Ender's Game* and *Ender's Shadow*; yet, at the same time, it has a poignant beauty.

At the end of this exchange, Diko simply drops the flashlight at her mother's feet and walks away. This is symbolic. We can only walk by the light that we have. We can only do our best. We know that what we do will always have more than one effect for you can't change just one thing.

When Tagiri is convinced that humanity is doomed without the Second Intervention, she nonetheless insists that the people of the world must choose. Of course, the people do not make that choice until famine, disease, and war are already upon them. If the time travelers had simply climbed into their vehicles and Tagiri reached for the switch, without asking anyone outside the project, then much of that famine, disease, and war would not have happened. But that is not the way that Tagiri acts.

There was the possibility that the world might decide the other way. Tagiri was willing to condemn future generations of our reality to extinction, rather than deprive the people now alive of their choice.

There are ethical dilemmas in *Enchantment* also, although they do not occupy center stage, as they do in *Pastwatch*. Ivan studies the making of gunpowder crackers to free his wife's kingdom in the Past, but he takes care that this "magic" will not be learned by the next generation. He could save lives by bringing methods of making antibiotics to the Past, but if he did the microorganisms would develop resistance all the sooner and cause plagues in later ages.

Hope Versus Despair

Dilemmas like these can be found in many of life's decisions. Medicine that saves lives has grim side effects. New highways deteriorate the landscape. More liberty means less security, and more security means less liberty. There is that appalling statement attributed to an officer in the Vietnam War: "We destroyed the village in order to save it."

We, here and now, are not time travelers. We can do nothing to change the past. But our choices now will affect the future. Often we must base our choices on limited knowledge.

Is Card an optimist or a pessimist about our choices? That is a question similar to: Was Christopher Columbus a hero or a villain? When critics reviewed *Ender's Game* some saw Card as an extreme patriotic militarist while some saw him as an extreme pacifist. Similarly, *Past-watch* has been considered as unrealistically optimistic by some, and un-realistically pessimistic by others.

A student, Jonathan Deber,[15] contrasts this book with *Lest Darkness Fall* by Sprague de Camp,[16] on one hand, and with *Making History* by Stephen Fry[17] on the other. De Camp has one man, single-handedly, pre-venting the Dark Ages after the Fall of Rome. Fry has time travelers who prevent the birth of Hitler, but create an even *worse* twentieth century. Deber sums up Card's position by quoting Columbus' last prayer in the third, better, reality: "There is no good thing that does not cost a dear price. . . . Happiness is not a life without pain, but rather a life in which the pain is traded for a worthy price. That is what You gave me, Lord."[18]

Card does not accept simple answers. He feels that, studying a prob-lem, we *can* ask: Is this solution worth the price? We can then pick up the little flashlight of our knowledge and insight and find our way, carefully, in the darkness. There may be an answer. The price may be worth it.

The Roots of *Pastwatch*[19]

Card had planned to have the book ready by 1992, the 500th anniver-sary of Columbus' voyage. It took longer, and the hardback edition came out in 1996. Card was irritated by things said and written that made Columbus either a saint or a devil. He felt that a different per-spective was needed.

Columbus did have a conscience. Now, if someone were there who could alert that conscience to see these natives as *people*, what might the result be? But, by itself that might not be enough. Perhaps someone should arrive earlier, to make the natives more ready for him. Perhaps a sabotage of his ships would keep him from returning to Europe.

And so the story developed.

A Parallel of Names in *Pastwatch* and *Enchantment*

The Native Americans who greeted Columbus called themselves "Taino." In our reality the Taino were destroyed by European weapons and diseases. The fictitious ninth-century Slavic kingdom in *Enchant-ment* is called "Taina." Card shows Taina as having disappeared from human history, only some of its folklore surviving.

Although these stories are different in their premises, both show good people (Ivan, Tagiri) who earnestly try to save whatever good things can be saved.

TIME TRAVEL IN CARD'S SHORT FICTION

In "Prior Restraint"[20] members of a Censorship Board from the future travel back to our day to stop publication of works that have serious negative effects in their time. In "Closing The Timelid"[21] thrill-seekers send their minds back in time into other bodies, in order to experience violent death, again and again. In "Clap Hands And Sing"[22] a old man's mind travels back into his youthful body to have one more day with a girl he knew. "Angles"[23] gives a new slant on the question of parallel universes. In "The Best Day"[24] a woman wants to keep one perfect day forever. Alas, she gets her wish!

Sometimes short works can say as much as long ones. Let us see some examples in the next chapter.

NOTES

1. Mark Twain, *A Connecticut Yankee in King Arthur's Court*, first published 1889 (New York: Bantam Classic Edition, 1981).

2. Orson Scott Card, *Enchantment,* paperback edition (New York: Ballantine, Del Rey, 1999), 125.

3. Personal interview, September 12, 2000.

4. Card, *Enchantment,* 158.

5. Card, *Enchantment,* 159.

6. This much-quoted saying appears to have originated in the article "Profiles of the Future," published by Arthur C. Clarke in 1962.

7. Card, *Enchantment,* 324.

8. Card, *Enchantment,* 336.

9. Card, *Enchantment,* 271.

10. Most of the material in this section comes from the interview cited in note 3.

11. Card, *Enchantment,* 417–419.

12. *Kirkus Reviews*, February 15, 1999.

13. Laura Esslinger, Winfield High School, *The Charleston Gazette Online,* July 15, 2000.

14. Orson Scott Card, *Pastwatch: The Redemption of Christopher Columbus,* hardback edition (New York: Tom Doherty Associates, Tor, 1999), 200.

15. Jonathan Deber, "The Seeds of Time Traveling," online, at the Hatrack River website (www.hatrack.com) under Student Papers, May 20, 1998. I have been unable, even with queries to the Hatrack River Forums, to discover who Jonathan Deber is, and whether he was a high school, college, or graduate student when he wrote this paper.

16. L. Sprague de Camp, *Lest Darkness Fall* (New York: Ballantine Books, 1939).

17. Stephen Fry, *Making History* (London: Hutchinson, 1996).

18. Card, *Pastwatch*, 345, cited by Deber, 6.

19. Just as with *Enchantment*, Card has three pages of acknowledgments. One that he cites particularly as "the book that made me want to write about Columbus" (Card, *Pastwatch*, 351) is *The Conquest of America* by Tzvetan Todorov (New York: Harper & Row, 1984). He also relies upon *Christopher Columbus* by Gianni Granzotto (Norman: University of Oklahoma Press, 1985). Along with other sources, he advises *The Tainos: The People Who Welcomed Columbus* by Francine Jacobs (New York: Putnam, 1992).

20. Orson Scott Card, "Prior Restraint, " *Maps in a Mirror: The Short Fiction of Orson Scott Card* (New York: Tom Doherty Associates, Tor, 1990), 74. Originally published in *Aboriginal Science Fiction*, September 1986, and reprinted in that magazine's annual anthology (1988). Also available on audio cassette, *Angles and Other Stories* (San Bruno, Calif.: Fantastic Audio, 2002).

21. Orson Scott Card, "Closing the Timelid," in *Maps in a Mirror*, 39–47. Originally published in *The Magazine of Fantasy and Science Fiction*, December 1979. Translated into French and published twice in that language.

22. Orson Scott Card, "Clap Hands and Sing," in *Maps in a Mirror*, 152–159. Originally published in *Best of Omni Science Fiction #3* (1982).

23. Orson Scott Card, "Angles," on audiotape, *Angles and Other Stories*. Also in *Doorways: Stories by Orson Scott Card* (Greensboro, N.C.: Hatrack River, 2002).

24. Orson Scott Card, "The Best Day," *Maps in a Mirror*, 374. Also available on audio cassette, *The Elephants of Posnam and Other Stories* (San Bruno, Calif.: Fantastic Audio, 2001). Originally a chapter in Card's novel *Saints*, pretending to be a story written by the lead character of that novel, Dinah Kirkham.

11

Shorter Fiction and Poems[1]

C'ard's particular talents are usually best shown when they get a chance to expand on the development of a person, or a relationship, or a society in novel length or longer. But no reader *always* wants the all-day reading experience, no matter how good it is. Sometimes we want one of these little jewels instead. We want to be taken captive by the story, be taken into a new realm of ideas. A story can do that as well as a novel. Sometimes even better.

THE PRIZE WINNER: "EYE FOR EYE"[2]

Mick Winger is seventeen years old and has killed many people. He never intended this, but when he is very angry his body puts off "sparks" that make cancers grow in others. He is trying to learn to control his temper. Unfortunately, the ones whom we love the best are often those who make us the most angry.

Mick discovers that his relatives are a backwoods Southern community descended from a Jacob Yow. They have inbred with each other, and consider the rest of humanity to be expendable. They justify their incest with perverted Bible interpretations, and have created babies so dangerous that they are boarded in orphanages, as Mick was, until the children are old enough to attempt control.

Mick is not pleased to discover incestuous, dirty, ignorant, murderous, religiously fanatic relatives. But if the Yows *can't* get him, and trust him, they will kill him. He can give cancer, but that wouldn't stop a bullet or a knife. A dissident branch of the Yow family has a different attitude. This "Roanoke" group wants to study the phenomenon. They are interested in research done in Sweden on powers of harming or helping others through the human bioelectric system.

Mick would prefer not to join either group, but that is not an option. The story is told from his viewpoint. The surprising ending is action-packed.

This novella was written on a dare. Card was driving to Roanoke with a fellow writer. Card made the "damfool" remark that "a *real* writer could come up with a story idea any time he felt like it" and he verbally roughed out the plot for "Eye for Eye."

The story was rejected twice, but it was finally published by *Asimov's*, with the cover illustration. "Eye for Eye" won the Hugo Award for the best novella of 1988. It also won the Japanese Science Fiction Award for the best in translation, and was also a finalist for the Bram Stoker Award in Horror Fiction. No other *short* work of Card's has been awarded to this extent.[3]

Issues of Life and Death

Almost every day that we live, we put our lives in the hands of others: We take a taxi; we get a prescription filled; we ride an elevator. As we acquire more responsibilities, more and more people put their lives in *our* hands. Heaven help them!

But there are two sides to almost every power: those with the power to kill may have life-giving powers also.

STORIES OF RELIGION: "SAVING GRACE," "SAINT AMY'S TALE," AND "HOMELESS IN HELL"

In "Saving Grace"[4] a child, Billy, who is paraplegic, discovers that the evangelistic healer, Bucky Fay, is a fraud. But when Billy is out in the park and is touched by a palsied child she is cured. So are many others who touch Billy. Word of the "crippled healer" spreads, and people come to him. Billy touches them, but takes no money until his mother quits her job to handle the crowds. Then he takes offerings *after* the healing, and just half of what is offered. He won't be another Bucky Fay.

Bucky Fay comes (complete with TV cameras and a very public repentance) begging for healing of his greed. Billy tries, but Bucky Fay continues to be a greedy hypocrite. Billy is never cured of paralysis. By the end he has happiness, of a sort.

There could not be a more unwilling healer than Billy. He gets so weary that he is almost—not quite—ready to lock the door. He doesn't need to "give God the glory" because it is *very* clear that wherever this power comes from, it surely doesn't come from Billy's righteousness, Billy's faith, Billy's intelligence, or anything whatever to do with Billy. As Billy himself puts it, "God ain't no cripple."

The Shock Technique in "Saving Grace"

In the beginning of "Saving Grace" the reader is prepared to receive a tale of religious hypocrisy or delusion. The first healing comes as a shock: This is a *real* healer! By being honest about the false, Card has given us a better understanding of the true. He shows that a true miracle can be found where it is least expected. As C. S. Lewis quotes from George Macdonald: "The altar must often be built in one place so that the fire from heaven may descend *somewhere else.*"[5]

In "Saint Amy's Tale"[6] an anti-archeologist tries to destroy all the artifacts of civilization in the hope that our descendants will learn nothing of us. But lies, legends, and truths are not so easy to destroy, and a religion is made of these. A false religion? False if taken literally, but it has much truth in it.

"Homeless in Hell"[7] gives an unusual glimpse of the afterlife, and of people there.

STORIES WITH HORROR: "A THOUSAND DEATHS," "KINGSMEAT," AND A FEW MORE

In "A Thousand Deaths"[8] a rebel against tyranny is executed, with his brain recorded so that it can be put into his clone. Then the clone (remembering every detail of the death) must give a speech, repenting his rebellion. If this speech is unconvincing, he will be executed again.

But one rebel cannot repent. Even after he has been hanged, boiled in oil, infected with rabies, dropped from heights, and other deaths, his true feelings come out, in spite of all that the executioners can do. The description of his death-agony is vividly detailed in the first death. Card's wife, Kristine, was unable to finish reading the story.

"Kingsmeat"[9] like so many of Card's works, imposes an ethical dilemma. A human world has been conquered by hideous aliens (known as "king" and "queen") who regard human beings as meat. The Shepherd is a human who harvests the meat for the king's table by painlessly cutting off someone's body part. Thus the person is maimed, but not slaughtered. Card has a description of the removal of one breast of a nursing mother.

The colony is rescued and the rescuers are astonished to find people alive. Humans are extinct in all the other worlds that were conquered by these aliens. Is the Shepherd a collaborator with the enemy, who deserves execution? Or is he a Savior to who should be honored? The ending is surprising, yet somehow seems inevitable.

Other Stories with Horror

"Freeway Games"[10] has no alien monsters. There is only the monster within each of us, perhaps closer to the surface than we might like to believe.

In "Fat Farm,"[11] being overweight and the struggle to lose weight is not treated comically. The desire to have a completely new body is appallingly fulfilled.

"Quietus"[12] is quiet horror, without violence. A man finds a coffin in his living room and he keeps remembering children, although he and his wife never had children.

Horror in Card's Early Stories

It worried Card that much of his early fiction was referred to as "cruel."[13] It was never his intention to be cruel; he is a kind and a gentle person. Like many other artists, he feels the need to depict what he hates. "Kingsmeat" was inspired by the thought of the dilemma of persons in concentration camps: Should one help the enemy by burying one's comrades? Or leave that last service to the uncaring, vicious, guards?[14]

CLOSEST TO ALL THAT CARD HAS TO SAY: "THE PORCELAIN SALAMANDER," "UNACCOMPANIED SONATA," AND OTHER FABLES

Card writes "If my career had to be encapsulated into only three stories, I believe I would choose 'The Porcelain Salamander,' 'Unaccompanied Sonata,' and 'Salvage' as the three that did the best job, together, of saying all that I had to say."[15]

"The Porcelain Salamander"[16]

A child named Kiren is miserable. Her mother died when she was born, and her father thoughtlessly cursed the baby, until she should lose something that she loves. Her muscles are weak, and she can barely walk and feed herself.

Her father repents his curse. When she is eleven, he comes home with a porcelain salamander that is constantly moving. If it ever stops moving, it will become lifeless. The salamander speaks to Kiren when they are alone. Her health improves; she goes for walks.

In the woods, Kiren and the salamander find themselves trapped. They try various means of escape, but it is finally clear that there is only one way. Although Kiren weeps, the salamander becomes motionless, stiff, and cold. Kiren, having no choice, climbs on top of what is now just a statue of a salamander, and escapes. Kiren is now strong.

Kiren grieves, but she comes to realize that the salamander's sacrifice was an eternal moment such as rarely comes. "And those who knew her well could almost see her gaze keep flickering about . . . as if she watched a bright, quick animal scamper by."

Love and Sacrifice in "The Porcelain Salamander"

The salamander keeps denying that he "loves" Kiren; he describes himself as a piece of porcelain that cannot "love" anyone. Yet, he gives the ultimate proof of love. And Kiren has to learn that grief must change to a calm, quiet celebration of the loved and lost.

Card's wife, Kristine, had playfully asked him for a bedtime story, and he arbitrarily chose to tell about a disgusting animal. Later, he made the story into a Christmas card.

"Unaccompanied Sonata"[17]

Little Christian Haroldson is a musical prodigy. He is taken away from his parents to live in a forest, cared for by unsinging servants. The only music that his Watchers will let him hear is

> birdsong, and windsong, and the crackling of winter wood; thunder, and the faint cry of golden leaves as they broke free and tumbled to the earth,

rain on the roof and the drip of water from icicles; the chatter of squirrels
and the deep silence of snow falling on a moonless night.

The entire story has the same lyrical quality as this passage.

He has the Instrument, a console with many keys, strips, levers, and
bars. On this, he composes original music uncontaminated by the music of any other composer. People come from afar to hear Christian's
music. One day, when Christian is older, one of these listeners smug-
gles Christian a recorder with the music of Bach. The Watchers detect
the difference in the music. Christian is condemned by a blind Watcher
to leave the forest and to live a life without music. "The world is too
perfect, too at peace, too happy for us to permit a misfit who broke the
law to go about spreading discontent."

He becomes a truck driver known as Chris. He delivers donuts to a
bar-and-grill that has an old, out-of-tune piano. He plays counterpoint
and variations on the familiar tunes that customers hum, working the
out-of-tune keys into his compositions. The customers love it, although
it makes them solemn, not merry. Then the blind Watcher appears, and,
with the greatest possible regret, cuts off Chris's fingers.

He goes to work on a road crew. His nickname is Sugar. Some of the
crew sing old Broadway tunes, Gospel, folk song, arias from Italian op-
eras. They all swear to keep Sugar's secret if he will make music for
them. Sugar makes up new songs, which the men say are "all wrong,
but I like the way [the songs feel] in my mouth." His songs are unfor-
gettable. Men transferred to other crews keep on singing them. The
blind Watcher appears again, and with a painless noninvasive tool, destroys Sugar's vocal chords.

Now Christian, with neither fingers nor voice, becomes a Watcher
himself. Watchers are always people like Christian, who could not be
stopped from creating. They will always do what must be done in the
kindest, most gentle way. There are not many Watchers, because most
people obey the law.

When he is old, he hears some teenagers with a guitar singing
"Sugar Songs," which they consider to be the best in the world. They
are sad songs, and the young people are happy. But they love the music because it was "written by a man who knows."

As the old man leaves them, he gives an unnoticed little bow.

The story is divided into sections: "Tuning Up," "First Movement,"
"Second Movement," "Third Movement," and "Applause," as if the
story itself were a symphony. Card asked himself the question: If I were
forbidden to write, would I obey? Some years after he had first asked
that, the story came "whole and complete from [his] typewriter" with
only spelling and punctuation changes needed. "Unaccompanied

Sonata" was a finalist for the Hugo award in 1980. Card, had been nominated for a major award every year since he began publishing (1977) but had never won. He felt sure that this was his only chance—he believed that this story was the best writing that he could ever do. Once again, someone else won the Hugo. (Since that time Card has won many awards of course, mostly for book-length works.)

He feels that it was an unconscious memory of "Tunesmith" by Lloyd Biggle, Jr. that was the quiet inspiration for this story, although the plots and themes are different.

"Salvage" in *Folk of the Fringe,* is the story of the treasure hunter who dives for hidden gold and comes up with other people's prayers. It was summarized, discussed, and the origin described in chapter 7.

"All That I Have to Say"

What has Card said in these three stories? He has said that life and love rightly understood include voluntary sacrifice. He has said that true creativity can never be stopped, although there may be a price to be paid. He has said that holiness cannot disappear because of war, or climate change, or anything else, as long as people pray.

These are stories about love, integrity, dedication, sacrifice, and faith. That is what Card has to say.

More Stories in the Style of Fables

"The Porcelain Salamander" and "Unaccompanied Sonata" (but *not* "Salvage") are more or less in the style of fable, or myth. Card has done other notable stories in this style.

In "Middle Woman,"[18] a woman is granted three wishes. But she unintentionally causes a disaster with the first, uses the second to undo the damage, and all her life long, she never uses the third one, but solves her problems by other means. This almost wrecks the dragon who granted her three wishes.

Magic Mirror[19] is short, published between hard covers as a picture book for adults. The illustrations are a combination of medievaloid and modern. The magic mirror is sometimes an old-fashioned large oval looking glass and sometimes an Internet screen.

Are Fables Easy or Hard to Write?

Card feels that "fables are devilishly hard to write . . . but . . . most satisfying. . . . It gives the author the delusion of having created something perfect, rather like a jewel cutter. . . . We can rarely tell, while cutting our little stones, whether we are working on a diamond, a garnet, or a zircon."[20]

ON AUDIOTAPE: "THE ELEPHANTS OF POSNAM" AND "FEED THE BABY OF LOVE"

In "The Elephants of Posnam,"[21] civilization has ended in worldwide plague that apparently leaves the few survivors sterile. With humanity no longer ruler of the earth, elephants take over. They migrate, fill every continent, and occupy the desolate human cities. They communicate with each other in rumblings below human hearing range.

In Posnam, Poland, a young boy and girl who matured sexually *after* the plague produce a child, born strange-looking. As he matures he develops into a combination of elephantine and human characteristics.

The story raises many questions and does not answer them all. It is told from the point of view of the father of the semi-elephantine boy. The architecture of Posnam, both the historic/beautiful and the communist/ugly forms the background of the story.

Card first thought of this story on an invited visit to Poland. His *Ender's Game* had been the first science fiction published there since the fall of Communism. He found it exciting to get to know the Polish people involved in the "re-creation and re-invention of their own society." By chance, he read a book about elephants while the Polish images were still fresh in his mind. When the story was done, he offered it first for publication in Poland, and the story was first published in Polish. It will be published in Spain, in both Spanish and Catalan. This audiotape version is the first "publication" in English.

"Feed the Baby of Love"[22] is the story of Rainie Pinyon, a wealthy, famous, bored singer and songwriter, who makes her way incognito across country and stops for a while in the town of Harmony, Illinois. She gets a restaurant job and discovers the neighborly cohesiveness, the close and easy, loving family bonding of small-town life.

She especially sees these things during an evening of a board game called Feed the Baby of Love, played at the house of Douglas Spaulding. She is envious, and wants to posses that kind of family love and friendly camaraderie. But there is no right way that she can have it, because of what she is, what she will never give up, and because of the honor of Douglas Spaulding.

The title comes from an actual board game developed by a friend of Card's. The plot, of Rainie Pinyon and the small town, had been in Card's mind for a long time. But can one make an interesting story out of an extramarital affair that *didn't* happen? When Card played the game he saw a way to do that.

Two years later Card was invited, along with about twenty other writers, to participate in an anthology of stories in honor of the author Ray Bradbury. The writers were invited to use settings and characters that Bradbury had invented. Card thought that most of the writers would base their stories on Bradbury's *Mars*.

But Card, instead, uses Bradbury's *Dandelion Wine*. This is about a young boy in the summer of 1928, in middle America. Card's story is set in the same small town in the 1990s. That young boy is now Grandpa, and he gives Rainie some sage old-man advice. Douglas Summer Spaulding, Grandpa's son, is the male lead of "Feed the Baby of Love."

Card would like to expand this story into a novel. But, so far, no publisher wants a *mainstream* novel by Orson Scott Card.[23]

POEMS

The general public hasn't seen much of Card's poetry, except "Prentice Alvin and the No-Good Plow."[24] In December of 2002 Card published a softcover book of just ninety-eight pages, called *Doorways*. This little collection has two stories (one written in 1982 as a Christmas gift for family and friends, not previously published)[25] and ten short poems.

The most moving of the poems is the one that opens the book as a memorial to Card's infant daughter, Erin Louisa, who was born and died on March 16, 1997:

O Hurried Guest

You did not see us on the night you came;
You did not answer when we spoke your name;
You barely stayed until the light of dawn;
Then traveled on.
O hurried guest, you could not know
The hospitality we meant to show,
The place we'd made for you, the tales we'd tell
Sweet Erinel.
What errand took you from our fireside?
Did you not hear us when we called and cried?

> Just once you came,
> As we will come someday where you abide;
> You'll see us, smile, and bid us come inside,
> Each one by name.[26]

Now, it is time to summarize what we have learned from Card's works, whether shorter or longer.

NOTES

1. Many of the items discussed or mentioned in this chapter can be found in Orson Scott Card, *Maps in a Mirror: The Short Fiction of Orson Scott Card* (New York: Tom Doherty Associates, Tor, 1990).

Some can also be found on audiotape: Orson Scott Card, *The Elephants of Posnan and Other Stories* and *Angles and Other Stories* (San Bruno, Calif.: Fantastic Audio, 2001). Each is a set of six audiotapes, recorded on both sides. There are also new stories on these tapes. Some of the stories are read by Card himself; some are read by his son Geoffrey Card or his daughter Emily Card. The rest are read by various readers.

2. Orson Scott Card, "Eye for Eye" in *Maps in a Mirror*, 456–490, and the afterword to "Eye for Eye" *Maps in a Mirror,* 532–533. Originally published in *Asimov's Science Fiction Magazine*, March 1987, 134–182. Also in *Tor Double Science Fiction Paperback* #27 (1990), along with "Tunesmith" by Lloyd Biggle, Jr. and a commentary on that story by Card, "How Lloyd C. Biggle, Jr. Changed My Life." And *The New Hugo Award Winners, Volume II* (New York: Baen, 1992).

3. "Hatrack River" (*Isaac Asimov's Science Fiction Magazine*, August 1986, 54–80) won the World Fantasy Award for Best Short Story of 1987. This story eventually became, without substantial alteration, the opening five chapters of *Seventh Son*, the first book in the Tales of Alvin Maker series. It is easy to see, when reading it, that "Hatrack River" is *not* a self-contained story, but the beginning of something longer. The short fiction anthology *Maps in a Mirror* won the Locus Award for the Best Collection of 1991. This was not an award to *one* story, but to an anthology of stories. Thus, "Eye For Eye" remains Card's only *self-contained*, shorter work, *considered by itself*, that has won a major award, although other stories have been among the finalists for major awards.

4. Orson Scott Card, "Saving Grace," in *Maps in a Mirror,* 446–455, and afterword to "Saving Grace, *Maps in a Mirror,* 531–532. Originally published in *Night Cry,* Fall 1987, 12–27.

5. C. S. Lewis attributes this remark to George Macdonald in *Letters to Malcolm* (New York: Harcourt, 1964), 117. Lewis does not give the exact source.

6. Orson Scott Card, "St. Amy's Tale," in *Maps in a Mirror*, 491–504, and afterword, 533–534. On audiotape, *Angles and Other Stories*. Originally published in *A Spadeful of Spacetime*, ed. Fred Saberhagen, (New York: Ace, 1981).

7. Orson Scott Card, *Homeless in Hell*, audiotape, *Angles and Other Stories*.

8. Orson Scott Card, "A Thousand Deaths" *Maps in a Mirror*, 140–151 and afterword to the same, *Maps in a Mirror*, 262–264. Originally published in *Omni*, December 1978, reprinted in *Best of Omni*, 2, 1981.

9. Orson Scott Card, "Kingsmeat" in *Maps in a Mirror*, 505–511, and afterword to the same, 534–535. Originally published in *Analog Yearbook*, 1978, and reprinted as a mass-market paperback (New York: Ace, 1978). Also, audiotape, *Angles and Other Stories*.

10. Orson Scott Card, "Freeway Games," in *Maps in a Mirror*, 46–56. Also, audiotape, *The Elephants of Posnan*.

11. Card, Orson Scott, "Fat Farm," in *Maps in a Mirror*, 31–38. Also, audiotape, *The Elephants of Posnan*.

12. Card, Orson Scott, "Quietus," in *Maps in a Mirror*, 16–25. Also, audiotape, *The Elephants of Posnan*.

13. Card, *Maps in a Mirror*, afterword to "A Thousand Deaths," 263.

14. Card, *Maps in a Mirror*, afterword to "Kingsmeat," 534.

15. Card, *Maps in a Mirror*, afterword to "The Porcelain Salamander," 424. When asked about this statement in my interview with Card on September 12, 2000, Card expressed surprise that he had said this. But he did not contradict it.

16. Orson Scott Card, "The Porcelain Salamander," in *Maps in a Mirror*, 301–306, and the afterword to the same, 424. Printed in *Expressionist* (Malibu, Calif.: Pepperdine University, 1994–1995). Also on audiotape, *The Elephants of Posnan*.

17. Orson Scott Card, "Unaccompanied Sonata," in *Maps in a Mirror*, 277–289, originally published in *Omni*, March 1979. Afterword to the same in *Maps in a Mirror*, 420–423. This afterword includes a reprinting from the essay "How Lloyd C. Biggle, Jr. Changed My Life" from the *Tor Double Science Fiction Paperback #27*. Also on audiotape, *The Elephants of Posnan*. Also published in *The 1980 Annual World's Best Science Fiction* (1980), *Best of Omni Science Fiction, #1* (1980), and *Fourth Book of Omni Science Fiction* (1985).

Finalist for Hugo Award, 1980. Finalist for Nebula Award, 1979. In *Storyteller: Orson Scott Card* (Woodstock, Ga.: Overlook Press, 2001), 296, Michael Collings quotes Card as saying of "Unaccompanied Sonata," "It's the truest thing I've ever written."

18. Orson Scott Card, "Middle Woman," in *Maps in a Mirror*, 307–309. Also on audiotape, *Angles and Other Stories*.

19. Orson Scott Card, *Magic Mirror: A Fable for Adults*, illustrated by Nathan Pinnock (Layton, Utah: Gibbs Smith, 1999).

20. Card, *Maps in a Mirror*, 427.

21. Orson Scott Card, *Elephants of Posnan and Other Stories*, audiotape set of six tapes. See note 1. The title story, with an introduction, is the first story on first tape. The story and introduction are both read by Card himself.

22. "Feed the Baby of Love" is the last story on the second side of the last tape, with an afterword. The story and afterword are both read by Card himself. The other selections on this set of tapes are read by other readers and have no introduction or afterword.

"Feed the Baby of Love" is also available in *The Bradbury Chronicles: Stories in Honor of Ray Bradbury,* ed. William F. Nolan and Martin H. Greenberg (New York: Penguin, 1992), 255–312.

23. In my interview with Card on September 12, 2000, I asked him: "What would you write just to please yourself, if you didn't have to consider what publishers would print, or what would sell well?" He described "Feed the Baby of Love" as a novel or a motion picture script and also another work of mainstream fiction, never written, called "Slow Leak."

24. Card, *Maps in a Mirror,* 589–600.

25. Orson Scott Card, "Dust," in *Doorways* (Greensboro, N.C.: Hatrack River, 2002), 47–94.

26. Card, *Doorways,* dedication page.

Conclusion

What Card Is Telling Us

THE TERRIBLE CHOICE

In most of Card's fiction there is the moment when someone realizes that there are no purely good choices left; the choice is between bad choices, but some not quite so bad as others. Card is willing to have you disagree with a character's choice, provided that you understand the agony of decision. To Card, there is no reason to write a story with easy choices. "It's no fun if it isn't hard."[1]

But this Terrible Choice is more than just "fun." G. K. Chesterton once wrote that the cross, the symbol of Christianity, could extend its arms to infinity because it contains at its heart a collision and a contradiction. The choices in Card's books are collisions and contradictions. Alvin carefully shapes manacles for the wrists of a slave child as a part of a scheme to free him forever.[2] The adult Ender meticulously tortures a friend to death so that the friend may be reborn into a greater life.[3] Tagiri reaches up to pull the switch that will obliterate seven centuries of human lives, saying, "I am killing everyone so that everyone may live. . . . I love you. . . . I love you all."[4]

In these collisions and contradictions someone "plays God." However, in the Christian tradition, God sacrifices himself. A decision to be like God is not to be undertaken lightly.

157

THE TALENTED YOUNG PERSON

At the heart of most of Card's fiction is a highly precocious boy or girl who relates better to adults than to most of his or her peers. This precocity can be either a blessing or a curse for the young person, and for his or her world, especially if the gifts are unusual. Ender is praised as a savior, and reviled as a xenocide. Peter, who could have been a curse, becomes something more benign as he matures. In Achilles, the precocious gifts are purely a curse, for everyone concerned including (ultimately) Achilles himself.

There is no gift that cannot be misused, whether "natural" or "magical." Even literacy, a priceless bond between eras and peoples, can be used to spread slander, as in *Rebekah*. Music, that lifter of the soul, can be used to destroy, as in *Songmaster*.

If the young person survives and becomes an adult, another young person often appears. Ender gets stepchildren. Alvin acquires the loyal friendship of Arthur Stuart. Tagiri has a daughter, Diko. The former child-hero becomes a mentor of another young and talented person.

These portrayals help explain why Card is a popular author among teens. Not all young people are precocious or talented, but most *wish* for it, in some capacity. "If only I could play ball like Larry, if I could write themes that always get an A as Susan does, if I grow up to be president, create a work of art that lives forever, or win a war." These are the dreams of youth. And those who are, in fact, aware that they have some real talent are coming to realize that this can be a mixed blessing, at best. Either way, talented or wishing for it, identification with the central character of a Card story is easy.

THE TEAM

It may be called an "army" or a "crew" or just "my friends," but in Card's books no hero, young or old, accomplishes any worthwhile goal alone. One leader cannot understand everything, and leaders make mistakes. Some sort of team is essential.

Just as a leader, such as Ender, Alvin, Nafai, or Tagiri, must mature from the precocious child to the youth, then to the adult, so the team matures as well, taking on a group character change in time. Over the course of three books Ender's stepfamily changes considerably, while keeping certain individual characteristics.

Sometimes members of the team must separate to do their work, as in *Pastwatch*. When this happens, the separated members form new teams in their new time and place, in much the same way that child-heroes who are grown mentor new child-heroes.

MALE AND FEMALE

The most intimate team, of course, is husband and wife. Card seems to take male–female equality of brains, purpose, judgment, and leadership ability so much for granted that he sees no need to defend this concept. The evenhanded partnerships of Bean and Petra, of Alvin and Peggy, of Nafai and Luet speak for themselves. In the case of Isaac and Rebekah, it is the wife who is correct, and the husband who is self-deceived.

Married life does not always run smoothly (neither does any other part of life) and adjustments, compromises, and forgiveness are needed. When Step Fletcher is inwardly enraged at his wife for manipulating him, he *forbids* himself to think about divorce, even in the most theoretical way.[5] When Ender's wife, Novinha, retreats into the religious Order of Children of the Mind of Christ, Ender doesn't plead or argue. He goes to the Order, finds her working in the field, picks up a hoe and weeds the vegetables with her.[6] The story of "Feed the Baby of Love" is about an extramarital affair that never happens; the potential lover is desirable, but the husband is committed to his family.[7]

In these examples it isn't love alone that triumphs, if by "love" we mean feeling that one's spouse is always lovable. It is decision, persistence, and commitment that win.

No one in Basilica (in the Homecoming Series) ever thinks of decision, persistence, and commitment in male–female relations. The choices there are between (a) commitment for just as long as two people find each other attractive or (b) a total, unrelenting, and repressive domination by the man. Basilica is a doomed society.

IT IS ESSENTIAL THAT WE TRY
TO UNDERSTAND EACH OTHER

Hive queens and humans, humans and native Lusitanians, Whites and Blacks, Whites and Reds, Israelites and Egyptians, Mormon Christians and other Christians, all stand at a point where one group, or both, try to enslave or exterminate the other one.

Are they are all just too wicked to share the world, or the galaxy, on an equal, peaceful basis? Perhaps a very few of them *are* that wicked. But most of them have simply not made the effort to understand the other, to see things from the other's point of view.

Sometimes it needs a repentant and reformed destroyer (an *ender*) to bridge the gap, just as it took a former persecutor of the Christian Church, Saul of Tarsus who became St. Paul, to save Christianity from extinction in its first century. A former destroyer is uniquely qualified to see both sides.

WE ARE NEVER ABANDONED; HELP IS ALWAYS THERE

These struggles and their resolution are never simple. The Terrible Choice must often be made. The divisions in family, in nation, in the churches, in the world, or between galactic species may seem beyond solution. But we don't struggle alone.

God is not mentioned by name in every book by Card, not even in most of them. But God is *always* there by implication, or under another name, guiding or protecting. Critics detect this presence of God, and they like or dislike Card the more for it, depending on the critic's own belief or disbelief.

Card tries to be neither an unrealistic optimist or an unrealistic pessimist. His hope is that, in the end, the results will be worth the struggle, the sacrifices. He holds to this hope, and holds us to it, without in the least minimizing the struggle or the sacrifices.

During the interview with this writer, mention was made of Stephen Fry and his book *Making History*, in which Fry says, "The point is that there is no point. That's the point."[8] Card responded at once, "If Fry believed that, he would not write books."

CARD'S PLACE IN THE ENDLESS CHAIN OF IMMORTAL THEMES

Sometimes a particular image comes down the ages from one writer to another.

A writer may not even realize that he is being unconsciously influenced by the image of an earlier one, but he transmits the image, in his own way, and later writers may, in turn, be consciously or unconsciously affected by him.

This writer suggested to Card that his book *Enchantment*[9] could be compared to The Chronicles of Narnia, seven books by C. S. Lewis, in which children from England travel back and forth between our world and the fantasy land of Narnia. In England, they are schoolchildren. In Narnia they are kings and queens by the favor of a divine figure. "What an interesting comparison!" exclaimed Card. It was clearly the first time that the similarity had consciously occurred to him. "Well . . . that's good."[10]

Lewis' Chronicles of Narnia also have much in common with certain books by the nineteenth century writer E. Nesbit, particularly *The Story Of The Amulet*. In this book, four time-traveling children inadvertently cause the Queen of Babylon to appear in the London of their day.[11] This can be compared to Queen Jadis, an evil witch, following two children into England, in their world, in *The Magician's Nephew*, a book in the Narnia series.[12] Then Card, in *Enchantment*, has the evil witch Baba Yaga following Ivan and Katerina into their own time.

The same chain of influence can be seen in another example. In Nesbit's *The Story of The Amulet*, the four children are in unfamiliar surroundings because of their mother's illness. They seek the other half of the amulet to attain their "heart's desire" that the family be together again. In Lewis' *The Magician's Nephew*, Digory's mother is dying; when he is in the magic land he is terribly tempted to get the fruit to heal her by unlawful means.

In Card's story "Dust" in the little book *Doorways*,[13] Enoch goes into a magic land to seek the dust that will heal his mother; but he must overcome certain obstacles.

E. Nesbit probably didn't begin these chains of images, and Card certainly will not end them. For this is exactly what Card is telling us in *Enchantment*: a story image (such as Sleeping Beauty) can live forever even when the source is forgotten.

And that's good.

CARD'S OWN HOPES FOR HIS READERS

This book began with a statement by Card on the meaning and purpose of his writing.[14] We will close with his own words once again, this time from his essay on Lloyd Biggle, Jr.'s story "The Tunesmith." When

Card was a child, the story affected him profoundly. Biggle never became a "big name" in science fiction, like Asimov, Clarke, or Heinlein. When Card rediscovered "The Tunesmith" as an adult and realized that this life-changing story was written by a relatively "minor" writer, this is his reaction:

> I knew that if I could write a story that would illuminate some hitherto dark corner in someone's soul and live on in [that soul] forever, then it hardly mattered whether my writing made me rich or kept me poor, put my name before the public or left me forgotten, for I would have bent the world's path a little. Just a little, yet all would be different from then on because I had done it. . . .
>
> If only a few were transformed . . . some of those [might] go on to tell their own tales, carrying part of mine with them. It might never end.[15]

NOTES

1. Orson Scott Card, *Characters & Viewpoint* (Cincinnati, Ohio: Writer's Digest Books, 1988), 19.

2. Orson Scott Card, *Prentice Alvin*, paperback edition (New York: Tom Doherty Associates, Tor, 1989), 269–274.

3. Orson Scott Card, *Speaker for the Dead*, paperback edition (New York: Tom Doherty Associates, Tor, 1986), 351–352.

4. Orson Scott Card, *Pastwatch: The Redemption of Christopher Columbus*, hardback edition (New York: Tom Doherty Associates, Tor, 1996), 235.

5. Orson Scott Card, *Lost Boys*, paperback edition (New York: HarperCollins, 1992), 286.

6. Orson Scott Card, *Children of the Mind*, paperback edition (New York: Tom Doherty Associates, Tor, 1996), 22.

7. Orson Scott Card, "Feed the Baby of Love" audiotape, *The Elephants of Posnam and Other Stories* (San Bruno, Calif.: Fantastic Audio, 2001). Also in *The Bradbury Chronicles: Stories in Honor of Ray Bradbury*, ed. William F. Nolan and Martin H. Greenberg (New York: Penguin Books, 1992), 255–312.

8. Stephen Fry, *Making History* (London: Hutchinson, 1996), 311.

9. See chapter 10.

10. Personal interview, September 12, 2000.

11. E. Nesbit, *The Story of the Amulet* (London: Puffin Books, 1959, 1996), chapter 8, 131–156.

12. C. S. Lewis, *The Magician's Nephew*, Chronicles of Narnia (New York: HarperCollins, 1955, 1983), chapters 6 and 7, 77–108.

13. Orson Scott Card, "Dust," in *Doorways* (Greensboro, N.C.: Hatrack River, 2002), 47–94. Privately presented as a Christmas gift to family and friends in 1982.

14. See the preface to this book, "In the Hands of the Savior".

15. Orson Scott Card, "How Lloyd Biggle, Jr. Changed My Life," a commentary on "The Tunesmith" by Lloyd Biggle, Jr., in *Science Fiction Double Paperback*, #27 (New York: Tom Doherty Associates, Tor, 1990), 112. This source contains "Eye for Eye" by Orson Scott Card and "The Tunesmith" by Lloyd Biggle, Jr.

Chronology of Events in the Life of Orson Scott Card*

August 24, 1951:	Born in Richland, Washington. Son of Willard Richards Card and Peggy Jane Park Card.
September 1951:	His family moves to San Mateo, California.
1954:	His family moves to Salt Lake City, Utah.
1957:	His family moves to Santa Clara, California. Begins wide-ranging reading.
1961:	At age ten, submits a story to two magazines. It is not accepted by either publication.
1964:	His family moves to Mesa, Arizona. He takes the role of Lyndon Johnson in the mock presidential debates in junior high school.
1967–1971:	His family moves to Orem, Utah in 1967, where his father is a professor at Brigham Young University. Card, at BYU High School, takes some college work while still a high school student, and enters college a year early.
	Writing: One play-script while in high school, nine play-scripts while in college. Submits short

---

*"Stories" is used here to include all works of less-than-novel length, whether short stories, novelettes, or novellas. In general, stories are ennumerated, but not mentioned by name unless they have won some award. "Books" (novel-length works) are mentioned by name.

story "The Tinker" for publication; it is rejected, with an encouraging note.

First inspiration for "Ender's Game" at this time, but nothing written.

1971–1973:   Mormon missionary in Sao Paulo, Brazil.

Writes the play "Stone Tables," which he sends back to BYU, where it is set to music and produced. (Rewritten as novel, in 1997.)

1973:   Returns to Utah, finishes college. Begins work as an assistant editor for *Ensign,* a Mormon publication. Continues to write plays, and other pieces, for the Mormon Church.

1975:   Attempts to begin theater company, which puts him into debt. Rewrites "The Tinker" and submits it to *Analog* magazine. Rejected, with encouragement.

1977:   Marries Kristine Allen. "Ender's Game" (the story, not the novel) published in *Analog.*

1977–1978:   Sixteen stories published.

1978:   Receives John W. Campbell Award for Best New Science Fiction Writer.

1979:   Eleven stories. Books: *Capitol, Hot Sleep,* and *A Planet Called Treason.*

1980:   Six stories. Book: *Songmaster.*

1981:   Poem: *Prentice Alvin and The No-Good Plow.* Wins first prize, Utah State Institute of Fine Arts (Long Poem Category).

1981–1983:   At University of Notre Dame, working on Ph.D. and teaching.

Three stories. Books: *The Worthing Chronicle* (a revision of *Capitol* and *Hot Sleep*) and *Hart's Hope.*

1983:   Ph.D. work abandoned in 1983. Moves to Greensboro, South Carolina. Position as editor of *Compute!* magazine lasts less than a year.

1984:   Book: *A Woman of Destiny* (later retitled *Saints*) published.

1985:   Association for Mormon Letters Award for *A Woman of Destiny.* One story. Book: *Ender's Game* (the novel).

1986:   Awards for *Ender's Game*: Nebula, Best Novel; Hugo, Best Novel; Edmund Hamilton/Leigh

Brackett Award: Best Novel. Three stories, including "Hatrack River" (later, the beginning of *Seventh Son*). Book: *Speaker for the Dead*.

1987: Awards for *Speaker For The Dead:* Nebula, Best Novel Hugo, Best Novel. Locus Award, Best Novel. World Fantasy Award for Best Short Story, "Hatrack River." Six stories, including "Eye For Eye" Books: *Seventh Son* and *Wyrms*.

1988: *America's Witness for Christ:* (The Hill Cummorah Pageant: Palmyra, NY). Awards for "Eye for Eye": Hugo Award, Best Novella. Japanese Science Fiction Award. Books: *Red Prophet, Characters & Viewpoint*. Books revised and/or retitled: *A Woman of Destiny* as *Saints; A Planet Called Treason* as *Treason*

1989: Best Fantasy Novel, Locus Magazine Awards: *Red Prophet*.

Five stories. Books: *Prentice Alvin, Folk of the Fringe* (story collection), *The Abyss* (novelization of a motion picture).

1990: Three stories. Books: *How to Write Science Fiction and Fantasy; Maps in a Mirror: The Short Fiction of Orson Scott Card; The Worthing Saga* (final revision of *Capitol, Hot Sleep,* and *The Worthing Chronicle*). Reprint: "Eye for Eye," Tor Double, with "Tunesmith" by Lloyd Biggle, Jr. and an essay by Card, "How Lloyd Biggle, Jr. Changed My Life."

1991: Locus Magazine Award, Best Collection: *Maps in a Mirror*.

Four stories. Book: *Xenocide*.

1992: One story. Books: *The Memory of Earth, Lost Boys,* and *The Call of Earth*.

1993: Book: *A Storyteller in Zion: Essays and Speeches*.

1994: One story. Books: *The Ships of Earth* and *Lovelock* (Mayflower Trilogy, Book 1, with Kathryn Kidd).

1995: One story. Books: *Earthfall, Earthborn,* and *Alvin Journeyman*.

1996: Books: *Pastwatch: The Redemption of Christopher Columbus, Children of the Mind,* and *Treasure Box*.

1997: *Barefoot To Zion* (musical drama).

Book: *Stone Tables* (former musical play of his, rewritten as novel).

1998:   On a list of "Best SF before 1990" *Locus*, November 1998, 11, Card's name is listed ninth. Two stories. Books: *Homebody, Heartfire*.

1999:   Geffen Award (Israel) for *Pastwatch: Redemption of Christopher Columbus*.

Three stories, in print. (Card begins to post stories on his website, some new, some older. These will not be enumerated unless they appear in print, or on tape, also.) Books: *Enchantment, Ender's Shadow*.

2000:   Grand Prix de l'Imaginaire (France) for *Enchantment*.

Books: *Shadow of the Hegemon*, and *Sarah*.

2001:   Set of tape recordings: *The Elephants of Posnan and Other Stories*. Book: *Rebekah*.

2002:   Set of tape recordings: *Angles and Other Stories*. Books: *Shadow Puppets*. Also, *First Meetings*, collection of three stories, one new: "Polish Boy."

One additional story in print. *Doorways*, short collection of stories and short poetry. One story, and all the poetry newly published here.

Scheduled for publication in 2003:   *The Crystal City* (Book 6, Tales of Alvin Maker). Story, "Teacher's Pest," paperback edition of *First Meetings*, and on audiotape. At least two more new stories in 2003, in anthologies. In progress: *Leah and Rachel* (Book 3, Women of Genesis), *Shadow of the Giant*. (Book 4, The Shadow Books), *Rasputin*. (Book 2, The Mayflower Trilogy). Under consideration: A book to link the Shadow Books and The Speaker Trilogy together. Books or stories in the Pastwatch Universe: On Noah, and on Eden.

This chronology does not attempt to cover all poetry, stage plays, video and audio plays, essays, reviews, or published letters. For a virtually complete listing of all works of Orson Scott Card (to the year 2000) consult *Storyteller: Orson Scott Card* by Michael R. Collings (Woodstock, Ga.: Overlook Connection Press, 2001)

Appendix

"God's Army"* by Geoffrey Card

Geoffrey Card, eldest son of Orson Scott Card, is a former missionary and is now creating electronic games in Washington State. He was impressed by the honesty of Richard Dutcher's fictional film based on typical experiences of Mormon missionaries. After Geoffrey Card wrote a review of the film, he asked for, and received, permission to do a novelization.

This group of young Mormons (called "Elders") come from all over the country and are now trying to "do something good" in Los Angeles. There are as many motives as there are individuals. Many motives are mixed with the young person's own personal or family problems. There is a tradition of practical jokes in the group (especially jokes played on newcomers, or "greenies"). In one case, there is the stupidest kind of intellectual pride. There are mistakes that are somewhere between hilarious and tragic: For example, two missionaries try to explain the doctrine of Eternal Marriage to a potential convert just when his wife is screaming at him.

The intellectually proud member loses his faith—not just his Mormon orientation, but belief in any kind of Christianity or in God—and he leaves. The truest "saint" in the group is literally a dying man. Yet,

---

*A novelization of the motion picture of the same name by Richard Dutcher (Salt Lake City, UT: Exel Entertainment Publishing, 2001).

with all the absurdities, failures, and tragedies, good *is* done in Los Angeles. True inner enlightenments and actual instances of divine guidance occur. There are not only baptisms and reformed lives, but a healing miracle of a convert.

Even more than the film does, Geoffery Card makes the case that when God succeeds it is not through *our* brilliant and dedicated efforts but, often, *in spite* of those efforts, making use of our failures. Orson Scott Card's works have often implied this. His son Geoffrey makes the matter explicit.

Index

The designation "book," "story," "drama," and so forth refers to a work authored by Orson Scott Card and discussed in this book, unless otherwise stated (e.g., *Ender's Game* book, not Card, Orson Scott, *Ender's Game*, book. But Twain, Mark, *The Prince and The Pauper*, book.) All titles should be assumed to be fiction unless otherwise designated.

Fictional characters are listed by the first name, or nickname, if that is the one most often used, or the only one used (e.g., Achilles. Anamarie Boagente.). They are listed by the title (e.g., Admiral Brown) if that is the usual, or only, designation. They are listed by the last name first if the last name is the one most often used (e.g., Carpenter, Timothy. Graff, Captain).

Historical characters, even if their lives are changed by alternate history, are usually listed with the last name first (e.g., Adams, John, in alternate history of Tales of Alvin Maker).

Biblical characters are listed as given in the Holy Bible. When Card has supplied a name where the Bible has none, the term "supplied name" is used (e.g., Lot's wife. *See* Qira. Qira, biblical, supplied name of Lot's wife).

There are cross-references designated by *See* for other forms of proper names.

All characters, events, devices, and the like should be assumed to be entirely fictional unless designated "actual," "historical," or "biblical."

Caution: This index does not attempt to cover all titles, characters, or events in the works of Orson Scott Card; only those mentioned in this book.

Aaron, biblical, in *Saints*, 87–89, 93
abolitionists: historical (Quakers) in
    Homebody, 129; in alternate history
    of Tales of Alvin Maker, 52
Abraham, biblical, in Women of
    Genesis series, 79–81, 82
Abram, biblical. *See* Abraham
Abyss, book, novelization of a motion
    picture, xxi, 33, 167
Achilles, in The Shadow Books,
    15–25, 158
Adams, John, historical, in alternate
    history of Tales of Alvin Maker, 49
Admiral Brown, in "Teacher's Pest," 4
African-Americans in Tales of Alvin
    Maker. *See* Blacks
Akma, in *Earthborn*, 64–67
Akmaro, in *Earthborn*, 64–67, 69
Alai, in *Ender's Game*, and The
    Shadow Books, 5, 7; as Caliph, 22
alternate history: in short stories, 143;
    of history since the time of
    Columbus, 139–142; of the North
    American Frontier, 41–56
Alvin Journeyman, book, 167. *See also*
    Tales of Alvin Maker
Alvin (known as Alvin Miller, Alvin
    Smith, and Alvin Maker), in Tales
    of Alvin Maker, 41–56, 157, 158, 159
"America," story in *The Folk of the
    Fringe*, 107–108
America's Witness for Christ. See Hill
    Cummorah Pageant
American Library Association, 12
Analog Science Fiction and Fact, actual
    magazine, xvii–xviii
Anderson, Poul, story, "Call Me Joe,"
    xv
angels (also known as sky people),
    intelligent species on Earth four
    million years: in the future,
    Earthfall and *Earthborn*, 62–67
Angles and Other Stories, audiotape
    collection, 154n1, 168
"Angles," story on audiotape, 143

Anna Kirkham, in *Saints*, 97
Anamari Boagente, in "America,"
    107–108
Ansett, in *Songmaster*, 116–119
ansible, in *Ender's Game*, *Ender's
    Shadow*, device imagined by
    Ursula LeGuin, 6, 13n4
anthropology, compared to
    imperialism and missionary work,
    35
Anton's Key, genetic alteration, in
    The Shadow Books, 18, 21
"any sufficiently advanced
    technology is indistinguishable
    from magic" (attributed to Arthur
    Clarke) and the converse, 136–137
Apologists. *See* biblical fiction,
    approaches to
Appalachee, state in alternate North
    America, in Tales of Alvin Maker,
    42
appearance versus reality, 128–129
Arthur Stuart, exiled king in
    alternate history, in Tales of Alvin
    Maker, 42, 48
Arthur Stuart, loyal friend of Alvin
    Maker, in Tales of Alvin Maker,
    47–49
Asimov, Isaac, The Foundation
    Trilogy, series, 71
Atomic bombing of Japan, historical:
    compared to destruction of
    bugger world in *Ender's Game*,
    10–11. *See also* World War II
awards won by Orson Scott Card:
    Association of Mormon Letters,
    xxi, 166; Edmond
    Hamilton/Leigh Brackett
    Memorial Award, xx, 119, 167;
    Geffen Award, (Israel) 168; Grand
    Prix de l'Imaginaire, (France) 168;
    Hugo Award, xxi, 12, 36, 146, 167;
    Japanese Science Fiction Award,
    146, 167; John W. Campbell
    Award, Best New Science Fiction

Writer, xx, 12, 166; *Locus* Magazine Award, 36, 154n3, 167, 168; Nebula Award, xxi, 12, 36, 167; Utah State Fine Arts, Long Poem Category, 54, 166; World Fantasy Award, 154n3

Baba Yaga, in *Enchantment*, 135, 137
background of a story can be as interesting as the plot, 100
baptism, in *Lost Boys*, 102, 105
Barefoot to Zion, historical musical drama, xxiv, 168
Basilica, a starship in The Homecoming Series, 62, 66
Basilica, city on Planet Harmony, in The Homecoming Series, 59–62, 66–67
Battle of the Belt, in *Ender's Game*, 6, 7
Battle School, in *Ender's Game* and *Ender's Shadow*, 4–5, 15–16
Bean, in *Ender's Game* and Shadow Books, 5, 7, 15–25
Bear, in *Enchantment*, 135, 137
Beliefnet, actual online column, xxiv
Bellamy Mansion, (Dr. Calhoun Bellamy) in *Homebody*, 129–132
Bennett, John C., historical, in *Saints*, 98
"Best Day, The" story, 143
best friend, in Tales of Alvin Maker. *See* Unmaker
Bethuel, biblical, in Rebecca, 81–82
Betsy Fletcher, in *Lost Boys*, 100
Bible. *See* Holy Bible
biblical fiction, approaches to, 93–94. *See also* irony in biblical fiction
Biggle, Lloyd, Jr., story, "The Tunesmith," xv, 162, 167
Billy, in "Saving Grace," 146–147
birthright, in Women of Genesis series. *See* literacy
Bishop, Michael, review, xix

Blacks, African-Americans in Tales of Alvin Maker, 51–52. *See also* Arthur Stuart, loyal friend of Alvin Maker
Blake, William, historical, in alternate history of Tales of Alvin Maker. *See* Taleswapper
blessings, in *Lost Boys*, 102–103
Bonaparte, Napoleon, in alternate history of Tales of Alvin Maker, 53
Bonzo, in *Ender's Game*, and *Ender's Shadow*, 5–6, 16
Book of Mormon, Books of Nephi and Alma as model for The Homecoming Series, 71
Bradbury, Ray, book, *Dandelion Wine*, 152–153
Brazil and Brazilians: actual, in life of Orson Scott Card, xvii; of the future in Shadow Books, 19; of the future, Brazilians in space, in Speaker Trilogy. *See also* Lusitania, present day and of the future; "America," short story
Briseus, character in "Iliad," epic poem by Homer, name applied to Petra by Bean, 21
Brown, Admiral. *See* Admiral Brown
Brown, Theresa. *See* Theresa Brown (Wiggin)
Bucky Fay, in "Saving Grace," 146–147
buggers, enemies of humanity: in "The Polish Boy," "Teacher's Pest," *Ender's Game*, *Ender's Shadow*, 3–17. *See also* hive queen
bull-calf, obscene god of the Hyksos, historical, possibly biblical, 89, 93

Caliph. *See* Alai
Call of Earth, The, book, 61–62, 167
Calvin Miller, in Tales of Alvin Maker, 44, 49
Cannan, land of, biblical: as "promised land," in *Stone Tables*,

89; in Women of Genesis series, 79–84

Capitol, book, xviii, xx, 166

Card, Charles Benjamin, 1983–2000, xiv, xx, xxii–xxiii, 126–127

Card, Emily Janice, xiv, xix, xxii

Card, Erin Louisa, xxiii, 153

Card, Kristine Allen, xiv, xix, xxii, 147,149, 166

Card, (Michael) Geoffrey, xiv, xix, xxiii; "God's Army," novelization of a motion picture, 171–172

Card, Orson Rega, 1891–1984, xiii

Card, Orson Scott, life of, xii–xiv, 165–169; Sycamore Hills Writers Workshop, 109, 126–127; teaching writing of speculative fiction at University of Utah, 119–120; Whitman, Prof. Charles, role in development of *Stone Tables*, 92

Card, Peggy Jane Park, xiv–xv

Card, Willard Richards, xiv–xv

Card, Zina Margaret, xiv, xv

Carpenter, Timothy, in *The Folk of the Fringe*, 105–106, 109

Carthage, Illinois, historical, in *Saints*, 98

Catholic Bishop on Lusitania, in The Speaker Trilogy, 34

Catholics and Catholicism, 3. *See also* Catholic Bishop on Lusitania; Children of the Mind of Christ, fictitious religious order; Sister Carlotta

Characters & Viewpoint, book, nonfiction, 167

Charles Banks Kirkham Family Organization, fictitious research source in *Saints*, 99

Charles ("Charlie") Kirkham, in *Saints*, 97–98

Children of the Mind, book, 168. *See also* Speaker Trilogy, The

Children of the Mind of Christ, fictitious religious order in The Speaker Trilogy, 34, 159

China and the Chinese: in the future, in The Shadow Books, 19–20; on planets in space. *See* Path, a planet in The Speaker Trilogy

Christ. *See* Jesus Christ

Christian Haroldson ("Chris" and "Sugar") in "Unaccompanied Sonata," 149–151

church, 103, 104, 100–111

City of God. *See* Puritans

City of Women. *See* Basilica, city on Planet Harmony

civilization: a theme in *The Folk of the Fringe*, 108; invented by women, for women, in The Homecoming Series, 67

"Clap Hands and Sing," story, 143

cloaks. *See* disguises

"Closing The Timelid," story, 143

Collings, Michael R., nonfiction book, *Storyteller: Official Guide to the Works of Orson Scott Card*, ix–x, xxi, xxiv, 126

Columbus, Christopher, historical and in alternate history, *Pastwatch*, 139–142

Command School, *Ender's Game*, and *Ender's Shadow*, 6–9, 16–17

communism, collapse of. *See* Soviet Union, fall of, 1989

community, a theme in *The Folk of the Fringe*, 108

Cooper, Verily. *See* Verily Cooper

Cormier, Robert, book, *I Am The Cheese*, xx

Cranning Call. *See* Wyrms

Crown Colonies, in alternate North America, Tales of Alvin Maker, 42

Crystal City, The, Alvin's vision and goal, Tales of Alvin Maker, 44–46

Crystal City, The, book, due for publication in 2003, 168

Darakemba, city in *Earthborn*, 64–67

DeAnne Fletcher, in *Lost Boys*, 100–104, 125–126

death, crucifixion, and resurrection images in *Homebody*, 131

Deaver Teague, in *The Folk of The Fringe*, 105–107, 108–109

Deber, Jonathan, student paper, 142, 143n15

deCamp, Sprague, book, *Lest Darkness Fall*, 142

deception, almost as serious as war, 36

Delaney, Sylvie. *See* Sylvie Delaney

descolada, disease of Lutsitania in The Speaker Trilogy, 31–32

Deseret, future state of, in *The Folk of The Fringe*, 104–108

Devil. *See* Satan

diggers (also known as earth people), intelligent species on Earth four million years in the future, *Earthfall* and *Earthborn*, 62–67

Diko, in *Pastwatch*, 140–141

Dinah Kirkham (also known as Dinah Handy, Dinah Smith, Dinah Young, Sister Dinah, and The Prophetess), in *Saints*, 97–99

disguises, theme in The Homecoming Series, 70–71

divine inspiration, 79, 80, 81, 82, 85, 90, 93, 102–103. *See also* prayer

Don Lark, in *Homebody*, 129–132

Doorways, small soft-cover book, collection of stories and poems, 156n25, 168

Douglas Spaulding. *See* Grandpa Douglas Spaulding

Douglas Summer Spaulding, in "Feed The Baby of Love," 152–153

Doyle, Arthur Conan, Sherlock Holmes stories, 99

dread, contrasted with terror and horror, 133

dreams: in "America," 107–108; in The Homecoming Series, 62–63, 65–66, 68

"Dust," story in *Doorways*, 161

earth people. *See* diggers

Earth, Planet: four million years in the future, in The Homecoming Series, 62–67; one century in the future, in *Ender's Game*, and The Shadow Books, 3–25; two centuries in the future, in *Pastwatch*, 139–141; unspecified centuries in the future, in *Songmaster*, 116–117

Earthborn, book, 64–67, 167

Earthfall, book, 62–64, 167

Eastern Orthodox Christianity, ninth century, 137

Easton, Tom, reviews, 71, 116

Egypt, biblical: in the time of Abraham, in *Sarah*, 79–80; in the time of Moses, in *Stone Tables*, 86–89, 91–92

Eight Bits, Inc., business in *Lost Boys*, 101, 103

Eight-Faced Mound, in Tales of Alvin Maker, 51

Ela Ribeira, in The Speaker Trilogy, 28, 29, 33, 35

Elemak, a character in The Homecoming Series, 60, 62–63, 68, 69

Elemaki, a people in The Homecoming Series, 62–64

Elephants of Posnan and Other Stories, audiotape collection, 154n1, 168

"Elephants of Posnan," story on audiotape, 152

Eliezer, biblical, in Women of Genesis series, 81, 82

Emma Smith, historical, in *Saints*, 98

Enchantment, book, 135–139, 160–161, 168

Ender (Andrew) Wiggin, in *Ender's Game*, in The Shadow Books, xxi, 3–13, in The Speaker Trilogy, xxi, 3–13, 15–17, 21, 27–38

Ender's Game, the book, xvi, xxi, 3–14, 24, 166

"Ender's Game," the novelette, xviii, xxi, 11–12, 36, 166

Ender's Shadow, 168. *See also* Shadow
    Books, The
"Enemy gate is *down*," in *Ender's
    Game,* and *Ender's Shadow,* 5, 7,
    11, 16
Esau, biblical, in *Rebekah,* 82–84
Esslinger, Laura, student's review,
    139, 143n13
evil, misfortune, why does God
    permit, 100–101
"Eye For Eye," prize-winning story,
    145–146, 167

"50 WPM," story, 24
fables, 148–152
Faith Miller, in Tales of Alvin Maker,
    42
false religion. *See* obsessive
    compulsive disorder (OCD)
fantasy: as exaggeration, 53–54;
    medieval style, 41, 119–122;
    modern ghost story, 41, 125–134;
    on the North American frontier,
    41–56
"Fat Farm," story, 148
Father Mikal. *See* Mikal the Terrible
Fay, Bucky. *See* Bucky Fay
Fears, Lizzy. *See* Lizzy Fears
Fears, Quentin. *See* Quentin Fears
"Feed The Baby of Love," story on
    audiotape, 152–153, 159
feminine and masculine, 62, 67, 159
Ferret, in *Songmaster,* 117
fidelity, 152–153, 159
"Fifty Words Per Minute." *See* "50
    WPM"
First meetings, collection of stories,
    13n1, 168
firstborn of Egypt, death of. *See*
    Passover
Fletcher, Betsy. *See* Betsy Fletcher
Fletcher, DeAnne. *See* DeAnne
    Fletcher
Fletcher, Jeremy. *See* Jeremy Fletcher
Fletcher, Robbie. *See* Robbie Fletcher

Fletcher, Step. *See* Step Fletcher
Folk of The Fringe, The, collection of
    stories, 104–109, 167
Folktales. *See* Enchantment
"For Quim and Christ," in *Xenocide,*
    32–33
"Forest of Waters," group of stories
    in *The Worthing Saga,* xxi
forgiveness, 64–67, 69
Formics. *See* buggers
freedom, best but risky, 69
"Freeway Games," story, 148
fringe, habitable area after the Six
    Missile War, *The Folk of The Fringe,*
    104–108
"Fringe, The" story in *The Folk of the
    Fringe,* 105–106, 108–109
Fry, Stephen, book, *Making History,*
    142, 160
Fugitive Slave Treaty, (same as
    historical Fugitive Slave Act,) in
    Tales of Alvin Maker, 48

Gaballufix, in The Homecoming
    Series, 60–61, 68
Gallowglass, in *Lost Boys,* 100–101
Gershom, biblical, in *Stone Tables,* 89
"Gloriously Bright" (early chapters
    of *Xenocide* published separately),
    38n8
God as "God" or "The Lord," 79–95,
    160. *See also* miracle; playing God;
    prayer
god named God. *See* Hart's Hope
God, under another name, 74, 160.
    See also Keeper of Earth; Outside;
    Someone in Charge
gods in *Hart's Hope. See* Hart's Hope
godspoken. *See* obsessive compulsive
    disorder (OCD)
golden calf. *See* bull-calf
golden plow, in Tales of Alvin Maker,
    45–48
Graff, Captain, in *Ender's Game,* 3, 4,
    6, 8

Grandmother, in *Treasure Box*, 127–128

Grandpa Douglas Spaulding, in "Feed The Baby of Love," 153

Greensboro, North Carolina: a century in the future, in *Ender's Game*, 5, 8; actual, in life of Orson Scott Card, xx–xxi; in "Homebody," short story, 129–132; in "Lost Boys," short story, 126

greensong. *See* Reds (Native Americans)

Grego Ribeira, in The Speaker Trilogy, 28, 29, 32–33

grotesque, use and risk of, 122–123

Hagar, biblical, in *Sarah*, 2–3, 84

Han Fei-tzu, in *Xenocide*, 30–31

Handy, Matthew. *See* Matthew Handy

Haroldson, Christian. *See* Christian Haroldson

Hart, The. *See* Hart's Hope

Hart's Hope, book, 119–121, 166

Harubel, biblical, name supplied, leader of opposition to Moses in *Stone Tables*, 89

Hatrack River, in Tales of Alvin Maker, 42, 45, 46

"Hatrack River," story, 154n3, 167

Hatshepsut, Pharaoh, historical and possibly biblical: foster mother of Moses in *Stone Tables*, 86–87, 89, 90–91, 91–92

heartfire, 46, 51

Heartfire, book, 168. *See also* Tales of Alvin Maker

Hegemon, The, fictitious book by Ender Wiggin. *See Hive Queen and The Hegemon, The*

Hegemon, office of, in *Ender's Game* and The Shadow Books, 3, 9, 17, 19, 22

Heptarch, ruler, in *Wyrms*, 121

Hersey, John, book, *The Wall*, 99

High Room (of the Songhouse). *See* Songmaster of the High Room

Hill Cummorah Pageant, *America's Witness for Christ*, xxiv, 167

Hio River, Ohio River in Tales of Alvin Maker, 47

Hittite wives of Esau, biblical, in *Rebekah*, 83, 84

Hive Queen and The Hegemon, The, fictitious book by Ender Wiggin, 9

hive queen, bugger survivor, *Ender's Game*, in The Shadow Books, in The Speaker Trilogy, 8–9, 12, 25, 33. *See also* buggers

Hive Queen, The, fictitious book. *See Hive Queen and The Hegemon, The*

Holy Bible: Exodus, 86–96; Genesis, 79–86; Gospel of Matthew, 29, 100–101, 121. *See also* biblical fiction, approaches to; crucifixion, death, resurrection, images in *Homebody*; irony in biblical fiction

Homebody, book, 129–132, 168

Homecoming Series, The, 57–72, 158–159, 167

"Homeless In Hell," story, 147

hope versus despair in our imperfect choices, 140–142

Horace Guester, in Tales of Alvin Maker, 47–48

horror, (contrasted with dread and terror). *See* dread

Hot Sleep: The Worthing Chronicle, book, xviii–xix, xx, 166

"How Lloyd Biggle, Jr., Changed My Life," essay, xv, 161–162, 167

How To Write Science Fiction and Fantasy, nonfiction book, 119–120, 132, 167

Human, (name of a piggy), in The Speaker Trilogy, 32, 157

humility with daring (in contrast to pride), 89–90

Hyksos, historical conquerors of
    Egypt, possibly pharaohs in time
    of Joseph, in *Stone Tables*, 86. *See
    also* bull-calf

I.F. (International Fleet), defenders of
    Earth in bugger wars: in *Ender's
    Game*, and *Ender's Shadow*, 3, 4, 15
Imakulata, nation on a distant planet
    in *Wyrms*, 121
imperialism, compared to missionary
    work and anthropology, 35
"In The Dragon's House," story, 132
Index, (of the Oversoul) in The
    Homecoming Series, 61
India, a century in the future in The
    Shadow Books, 19, 20, 24
International Fleet. *See* I.F.
"Inventing Lovers on the Phone,"
    story, 132
"Investment Counselor," story, 27
irony: in biblical fiction, 85; in The
    Shadow Books, 23–24
Irrakwa (Iroquois native Americans
    in alternate history, in Tales of
    Alvin Maker), 50
Ishmael, biblical, in *Sarah*, 80, 81, 84
Islam, Islamic countries, Muslims, a
    century in the future in The
    Shadow Books, 20, 22. *See also* Alai
Isaac, biblical, in Women of Genesis,
    81, 82–83, 84, 86
Issib, in The Homecoming Series, 60
Ivan Smetski, in *Enchantment*, 135–139

Jacob, biblical, in *Rebekah*, 82–84
Jamie Teague, in *The Folk of the
    Fringe*, 105
Jane, computer personality, in The
    Speaker Trilogy, 27, 28
Japanese, on planets in space in the
    future in The Speaker Trilogy, 37
Jason Worthing, in *Capitol, Hot Sleep:
    The Worthing Chronicle, Worthing
    Saga*, xviii–xix, xxi–xxii

Jeremy Fletcher, in *Lost Boys*, 102–103
Jesus Christ: foreshadowing of, 86,
    91; name used in unconscious
    blasphemy; quoted by Quim in
    The Speaker Trilogy, 29. *See also*
    death, crucifixion, and
    resurrection images in *Homebody*;
    "For Quim and Christ"
Jethro, biblical, in *Stone Tables*, 87, 89,
    90
Jocabed, biblical, in *Stone Tables*,
    supplied name of Moses' birth
    mother, 86, 87, 90
John Kirkham, in *Saints*, 97
John Paul Wiggin (Wieczorek),
    "Polish Boy," "Teacher's Pest,"
    Shadow Books, 3, 4, 22
Joshua, biblical, in *Stone Tables*, 88, 90
Josif, in *Songmaster*, 117
Judaism, 137

Katerina, Princess, in *Enchantment*,
    135–138
Keeper of Earth, (God, or a heavenly
    power), 59, 64–67, 70
Kept, The, religion of Darakemba in
    Earthborn, 64–67, 69
Kidd, Kathryn, collaborator with
    Card in Mayflower Trilogy. *See
    Lovelock*
Kimball, Heber, in *Saints*, 97
"Kingsmeat," story, 148
Kirkham, Anna. *See* Anna Kirkham
Kirkham, Charles. *See* Charles
    ("Charlie") Kirkham
Kirkham, Dinah. *See* Dinah Kirkham
Kirkham, John. *See* John Kirkham
Kirkham, O. *See* O. Kirkham
knacks, 41, 49–50, 53–54
"know, think, choose, do," Bean's
    maxim in *Ender's Shadow*, 16, 23
knowledge, lasting through time,
    136, 160–161
Kirill, Saint, historical, in
    Enchantment, 136

Laban, biblical, in *Rebekah*, 81, 82, 84

Lake Bonneville, in the future in *The Folk of the Fringe*, 105

land-sense. *See* Reds (Native Americans), in Tales of Alvin Maker

Lanik Mueller, in *Treason*, 115–116

Lark, Don. *See* Don Lark

Latter-Day Saints. *See* Mormons and Mormonism

Leah and Rachel, forthcoming book, 94, 168

Lewis, C. S., Chronicles of Narnia, *Magician's Nephew*, 160–161

"lies we live will . . . be confessed in the stories we tell," 126–127

limited nuclear war. *See* Six Missile War

Lissy, in *Homebody*, 131

literacy, as the holy birthright, 81–85

"Little Doctor" (Molecular Detachment Device, or M.D. Device,) 7, 17, 28, 30, 33

Little Mothers, life-cycle stage of native Lusitanians, The Speaker Trilogy, 32, 35

Lizzy Fears, in *Treasure Box*, 127

Locke, Peter Wiggin's net identity, 8, 17, 19

Lord Peace, in *Wyrms*, 121

Lost Boys, book, xxi, 100–104, 110. 126–127, 132, 167

"Lost Boys," story, 126–127

Lot, biblical, in *Sarah*, 79–81

Lot's Wife. *See* Qira

Love: in *Ender's Game*, in The Shadow Books, and The Speaker Trilogy, 23, 37; in shorter works, 148–151

Lovelock, book, 73, 167

Luet, in The Homecoming Series, 60, 61, 62, 64, 67

Lusitania, planet with native life, settled by humans, in The Speaker Trilogy, 27–36

M.D. Device. *See* "Little Doctor"

MacDonald, George, attributed quotation from sermon, 36

Machiavelli, Niccolò, Machiavellian thinking, 19–20

Madeleine ("Mad"), in *Treasure Box*, 127–129

Magic Mirror, very short, hard-cover picture book, 151, 168

Magic. *See Enchantment*, book. *See also Hart's Hope*, book; Tales of Alvin Maker

Maker, (person with extraordinary abilities,) 41–56

Manager of Earth, office in *Songmaster*, 117

Manchester, England, historical, in *Saints*, 97

manna, biblical, in *Stone Tables*, 88–89

Maps in a Mirror: The Short Fiction of Orson Scott Card, collection, 154n1, 167

Masks. *See* disguises

materialism as a belief, 137–138

Matthew Handy, in *Saints*, 97

Mayflower Trilogy. *See Lovelock*

Mazer Rackham, in *Ender's Game*, 3, 6, 7, 8

Mebbekew, in The Homecoming Series, 60, 68

Memory of Earth, The, book, 57–61, 167

Mick Winger, in "Eye For Eye," 145–146

middle people, term for humans in *Earthborn*, 63–64, 65

"Middle Woman," story, 151

Mikal The Terrible, Emperor in *Songmaster*, 116–117

"Mikal's Songbird," novelette, 118–119

miracle, 34–35, 88–89, 93, 146–147

Miro, in The Speaker Trilogy, 28, 29

misfortune. *See* evil, misfortune, why does God allow

missionary work: compared to
     imperialism and anthropology, 35.
     See also Heber Kimball, in *Saints*;
     Card, (Michael) Geoffrey, God's
     Army
Mississippi River, in *Saints*, 97
Mizzipy River, Mississippi River in
     Tales of Alvin Maker, 42, 51
Mohamedans. *See* Islam, Islamic
     countries, Muslims
Molecular Detachment Device, or
     M.D. Device. *See* Little Doctor
Monson, Sam. *See* Sam Monson
Moozh, General, in The
     Homecoming Series, 61–62
Mormons and Mormonism, 4, 97–112.
     See also Book of Mormon as a
     model for The Homecoming Series
Moses, biblical, in *Stone Tables*, 86–91
Moses' birth mother. *See* Jocabed
Mothertree, in The Speaker Trilogy, 32
Motiak, King of Darakemba, and
     sons of Motiak, in The
     Homecoming Series, 64–67
Mount Moriah, biblical, in *Sarah*, 81
Mount Sinai. biblical, (also called
     Holy Mountain) in *Stone Tables*,
     88, 91
Mueller, Lanik. *See* Lanik Mueller
murder, controversy, 61, 68
music, power of, 116–119, 149–151

Nafai, a character in the The
     Homecoming Series, 57–64, 68,
     159
Nafari, a people in The Homecoming
     Series, 64–67
Napoleon. *See* Bonaparte, Napoleon
Native Americans: actual, and in the
     future. *See* "America," short story;
     in two different alternate
     histories. *See* Pastwatch: The
     Redemption of Christopher
     Columbus; in alternate history of
     Tales of Alvin Maker. *See* Reds

Nauvoo, Illinois, historical, in *Saints*,
     97
Nesbit, E., book, *The Story of The
     Amulet*, 160–161
New England, in alternate history of
     Tales of Alvin Maker. *See* Puritans
Noah, biblical: book under
     consideration, 168; in Women of
     Genesis series, 79, 81
Novinha, in The Speaker Trilogy,
     28–29

"O Hurried Guest," short poem, 153
O. Kirkham, fictitious researcher of
     Saints, 98–99
obsessive compulsive disorder
     (OCD), 30–31, 34, 36
Old Peg, in Tales of Alvin Maker,
     47–48
Olhado, in The Speaker Trilogy, 28–29
Ollie, in "Pageant Wagon," 106–107
"On Sycamore Hill," Author's Note,
     in *The Folk of the Fringe*, 109
optimism. *See* hope versus despair
Orthodox Church. *See* Eastern
     Orthodox Christianity
Outside, (God), 34–35
Overseer, in Tales of Alvin Maker. *See*
     Unmaker
Oversoul, planet-ruling computer in
     The Homecoming Series, 57–70

Pabulog, and sons of Pabulog, in
     Earthborn, 64–65
Pacific Island cultures, on planets in
     space in The Speaker Trilogy, 37
pacifist versus patriot. *See* patriot
     versus pacifist
"Pageant Wagon," story in *The Folk of
     the Fringe*, 106–107, 109
parallel universes. *See* alternate history
Passover, in *Stone Tables*, 88
*Pastwatch: The Redemption of
     Christopher Columbus*, book,
     139–142

Path, a planet in The Speaker Trilogy, 30–31

Patience, character in *Wyrms*, 121–122

patriot versus pacifist, 9–11

Peace, character in *Wyrms*. *See* Lord Peace

Peggy Guester, also known as Margaret Larner or Peggy Smith, 45–47, 52, 159

pessimism. *See* hope versus despair

Peter Wiggin, brother of Ender, 4, 5, 8, 9, 19–20, 22

"Peter," copy of Ender's brother, created from Ender's memory in The Speaker Trilogy, 30

Petra, 5, 7, 20, 21, 24

Pharaoh(s) of Egypt, historical and biblical: from Exodus; in Genesis, 79–80. *See also Stone Tables*

piggies, natives of Lusitania in The Speaker Trilogy, 27–28, 31–33, 35–36

pillar of cloud by day, pillar of fire by night, in *Stone Tables*, 88–89

Pinyon, Rainie. *See* Rainie Pinyon

plagues of Egypt. *See* Passover

Planet Called Treason, A, book. *See Treason*

Planet Earth in the future. *See* Earth, Planet, in the future

Planter, Lusitanian native in The Speaker Trilogy, 33

playing God, 10, 157

Poke, in The Shadow Books, 15, 16, 19

Poland, in the future: in "Elephants of Posnan," 152; in "Polish Boy," 3

"Polish Boy," story, 3, 168

polygamy, historical, in *Saints*, 97, 110

"Porcelain Salamander, The" story, 148, 151

porquinhos. *See* piggies

Porschet, Alma Jean, master's thesis, 56n16, 56n17

power-hunger, 127–128

prayer, 34–35, 87, 101–102, 142. *See also* divine inspiration

"Prentice Alvin and the No-Good Plow," long poem, 54, 166

Prentice Alvin, book, 167. *See also* Tales of Alvin Maker

pride, (in contrast to humility with daring,) 90

Princess Katerina. *See* Katerina, Princess

principle of celestial marriage. *See* polygamy

"Prior Restraint," story, 143

prohibition, historical, in *Homebody*, 129

Prophet, The, brother of Ta-Kumsaw (Tecumseh): in alternate history of Tales of Alvin Maker, (also called Shining Man) 43, 44, 51. *See also* Reds

Puritans, in alternate history of Tales of Alvin Maker, 45

purity, 129

Qing-jao (also known as Gloriously Bright), in The Speaker Trilogy, 30–31

Qira, biblical, supplied name of Lot's wife, in *Sarah*, 79, 80–81

Quakers (abolitionists), in *Homebody*. *See* abolitionists

Quara, in The Speaker Trilogy, 28, 33

Quentin Fears, in *Treasure Box*, 127–128

Quetzalcotl, Mexican myth, in "America,"107–108

"Quietus," story, 148

Quim, in The Speaker Trilogy, 28, 32–33

racial prejudice. *See* Arthur Stuart

Rackham, Mazer. *See* Mazer Rackham

rads, (radical regeneratives), 115–116
Rainie Pinyon, in "Feed The Baby of
    Love," 152–153
Rasa, in The Homecoming Series, 60,
    61, 67–68
Rasputin, (forthcoming book), 73, 168
Rebekah, biblical, in *Rebekah*, 81–85,
    122–123
Rebekah, book, 81–84, 122–123, 168.
    See also Women of Genesis series
rebuilding, as metaphor, 131–132
Red Prophet, book, xii, 167. *See also*
    Tales of Alvin Maker
Red Sea, in *Stone Tables*, 88. *See also*
    miracle
Reds, in alternate history of Tales of
    Alvin Maker, 49–51. *See also* The
    Prophet, brother of Ta-Kumsaw
    (Tecumseh); Ta-Kumsaw
Renault, Mary, book, *The King Must
    Die*, 120
Rejectionists. *See* biblical fiction,
    approaches to
retelling in fiction stories from
    history, legend, myth and sacred
    writing, 71–72
revenge. *See* vengeance
Riktors Ashen, in *Songmaster*, 116–117
Robbie Fletcher, in *Lost Boys*, 100, 104
Robert Kirkham, in *Saints*, 97
Roman Catholics and Roman
    Catholicism. *See* Catholics and
    Catholicism
Rotterdam, Netherlands, in the
    future of The Shadow Books, 15
Russia, in the future of The Shadow
    Books, 17, 20

"Saint Amy's Tale," story, 147
Saints, book, xxi, 97–99, 166
Sally, in *Treasure Box*, 128–129
Salt Lake City, Temple Square: actual,
    in life of Orson Scott Card, xv; in
    the future of *The Folk of the Fringe*.
    See "Salvage"

"Salvage," story in *The Folk of the
    Fringe*, 105, 151
Sam Monson in "America," 107–108
Sarah, biblical, in *Sarah*, 79–81, 84–86
Sarah, book, 79–81, 168. *See also*
    Women of Genesis series
Sarai. *See* Sarah
Satan, 91. *See also* temptation;
    Unmaker
"Saving Grace," story, 146–147
science fiction and fantasy to express
    religious views, xi–xii, 72
seventh son of a seventh son born
    under a caul, 43. *See also* Alvin
Seventh Son, book, 167. *See also* Tales
    of Alvin Maker
Shadow Books, The, xvii, 13, 15–25
Shadow of the Giant, (forthcoming
    book) 25, 168
Shadow of the Hegemon, 168. *See also*
    Shadow Books, The
Shadow Puppets, 168. *See also* Shadow
    Books, The
Shakespeare, William, drama, *King
    Lear*, xx
Shedemei, in The Homecoming
    Series, 61–62, 63–64, 65–66, 67
Shepherd, The, in "Kingsmeat," 148
Ships of Earth, The, book, 62, 167. *See
    also* Homecoming Series, The
Shirer, William, nonfiction book, *Rise
    and Fall of the Third Reich*, xv
simulator, 7, 16
Singers, students at the Songhouse,
    in *Songmaster*, 116
Sister Carlotta, in The Shadow
    Books, 15, 17–19, 20, 21
Six Missile War, in *The Folk of the
    Fringe*, 104–108
skeptics, religious, dishonesty of
    some, 70
sky people. *See* angels
slave finders, in Tales of Alvin
    Maker, 48–49
slavery, 47–49, 51–52

Sleeping Beauty. *See Enchantment*

Smetski, Ivan. *See* Ivan Smetski

Smith, Joseph, historical, in *Saints*, 97, 98, 99; life of, as the "skeleton" for the character of Alvin Maker, 54–55

Snow, Eliza, historical, one of several models for Dinah Kirkham in *Saints*, 98–99

Sodom, biblical, in *Sarah*, 80–81

somec, starship sleep drug, in The Worthing Books, xviii–xix

someone in charge, (God), 52–53

Songbirds, exceptional Singers from the Songhouse in *Songmaster*, 116–118

Songhouse, The, on planet Tew, in *Songmaster*, 116–117

"Songhouse," novella, 119

Songmaster, book, xx, 116–119, 122–123, 166

Songmaster (of the High Room), in *Songmaster*, 116, 117

Soviet Union, fall of, in 1989, historic, in *Enchantment*, 135

Spaulding, Douglas Summer. *See* Douglas Summer Spaulding

Spaulding, Douglas, Grandpa. *See* Grandpa Douglas Spaulding

Speaker for the Dead, book, xvii, xxi, 167. *See also* Speaker Trilogy, The

Speaker of Death. *See Speaker for the Dead*

Speaker Trilogy, The, series, xxi, 12–13, 25, 27–37,157, 158, 159, 167–168

Spenser, William, epic poem, "The Faerie Queen", 54

Starmaster, (Starmaster's cloak), in The Homecoming Series, 62, 63, 70

Starways Congress, in The Speaker Trilogy, 30–31, 33

Step Fletcher, in *Lost Boys*, 100–104, 125–126; identification with Orson Scott Card, 104, 111n15

Steuben, fictional city in North Carolina in *Lost Boys*, 125

Stevie Fletcher, in *Lost Boys*, 100–104, 125–126

Stilson, in *Ender's Game*, xv–xvi, 4, 6

Stone Tables, musical play, xvii, xxiv, 166

Stone Tables, novel, 86–92, 93–94, 168

Storyteller in Zion, book, essays, speeches of Orson Scott Card, 110, 167

Sweet Sisters. *See Hart's Hope*

Sylvie Delaney, in *Homebody*, 130–132

Tagiri, in *Pastwatch*, 140–141, 158

Taina, fictitious ninth-century kingdom in the Ukraine in *Enchantment* 135–136

Taino, historical and in alternate histories of *Pastwatch*, 142

Ta-Kumsaw (Tecumseh) in alternate history of Tales of Alvin Maker, 50–51. *See also* Reds, in alternate history of Tales of Alvin Maker

Tales of Alvin Maker, series, xxi, 44–56, 157, 158, 159, 167–168

Taleswapper, William Blake in alternate history of Tales of Alvin Maker, 43

"Teacher's Pest," story, 4, 168

Teague, Deaver. *See* Deaver Teague

Teague, Jamie. *See* Jamie Teague

temptation, 101

terror, contrasted with dread and horror. *See* dread

Tew, planet in *Songmaster*, 116, 117

Thailand, in future, in The Shadow Books, 18

Thane, Elsworth, Williamsburg series, xv

that power, (God), 137

Theresa Brown, (Wiggin,) "Teacher's Pest," "Ender's Game," in The Shadow Books 4, 22

Third Invasion (of human–bugger war), 6–8, 15–17

"Thousand Deaths, A" story, 147

time travel, 135–143

Timothy Carpenter. *See* Carpenter, Timothy

"Tinker, The" story, xvii, xx, xxi–xxii

Tlaxcalans, historical, in alternate history in *Pastwatch*, 139. *See also* Native Americans in two alternate histories of *Pastwatch*

torch, 45–47. *See also* Peggy Guester

Treason, book, xiv, 115–116, 166–167

Treasure Box, book, 127–129, 168

trees or rivets (difference between fantasy and science fiction,) xviii

True Name, The, in Tales of Alvin Maker, 51–52

Truman, Margaret, series of books about murders in Washington, D.C. area, 100

Tutmose, I and III, historical and possibly biblical, 86, 88, 89

Twain, Mark, books: *A Connecticut Yankee in King Arthur's Court*, 135–136; *Personal Recollections of Joan of Arc*, 99; *The Prince and The Pauper*, xv

"Unaccompanied Sonata," story, 149–150

understanding each other is essential, xiii, 35–36, 67–68, 69, 159–160

United States, in alternate history of Tales of Alvin Maker, 42

Unmaker, The, in Tales of Alvin Maker, 43–44, 49

Ur, ancient country, biblical and historical, 79

Utah, in the future of *The Folk of the Fringe*. *See* Deseret

Valentine Wiggin, sister of Ender, 4, 5, 8, 30. *See also* Young Val

vengeance, futility of, 18, 37, 64–67, 69

Verily Cooper, in Tales of Alvin Maker, 49

Vesey, Denmark, historical, in alternate history of Tales of Alvin Maker, 52

Vietnam War, as stimulus for *Ender's Game*, 11

Vigor Church, frontier town, 43

Vigor Miller, in Tales of Alvin Maker, 42–43

Visitor. *See* Unmaker

Volemak, in The Homecoming Series, 60–61, 63, 67–68

Volescu, in The Shadow Books, 21

Wang-mu, in The Speaker Trilogy, 30–31

Washington, George, in alternate history of Tales of Alvin Maker, 42

weaving, as an image of divine purpose, 53

Webster, Daniel, in alternate history of Tales of Alvin Maker, 49

Weird Sisters in *Homebody*, 130, 131

"West," story in *The Folk of the Fringe*, 105, 110

Wieczorek family, (later, Wiggin). *See* "Polish Boy"

Wiggin, Andrew. *See* Ender (Andrew) Wiggin

Wiggin, John Paul (Wieczorek). *See* John Paul Wiggin

Wiggin, Peter. *See* Peter Wiggin

Wiggin, Theresa Brown. *See* Thresa Brown (Wiggin)

Wiggin, Valentine. *See* Valentine Wiggin

Winger, Mick. *See* Mick Winger

Woman of Destiny, A. *See* Saints

Women of Genesis series, 79–86, 92–94, 168

World War I, historical: books about training pilots as stimulus for *Ender's Game*, 11

World War II, historical: actual, in career of Orson Scott Card's father, xv; in commentary on *Ender's Game*, 10–11; in The Shadow Books, comparison to imagined future,19

Worthing Chronicle, The, book, xx, xxi, 166

Worthing, Jason. *See* Jason Worthing

Worthing Saga, book, xxi, 167

writing of speculative fiction, a detailed example. *See Hart's Hope*

Wyrms, book, xxi, 12, 167

Xenocide, book, 167. *See also* Speaker Trilogy, The

Young, Brigham, historical, in *Saints*, 98, 99

"Young Val," sister of Ender as he remembers her when they were young, created from Ender's mind in The Speaker Trilogy, 30

Zeforah, biblical, in *Stone Tables*, 87, 90

About the Author

Edith S. Tyson, now retired, served her community as a general reference and young adult librarian. She is a former instructor of English at the University of New Mexico, and later, Clarion University of Pennsylvania. She also taught religious studies at the University of Michigan, and served as a community resource teacher at an alternative high school in Ann Arbor, Michigan. Ms. Tyson holds a master of arts degree from the University of Michigan, Ann Arbor, and a master's degree in library science from Clarion University of Pennsylvania.

Edith Tyson has been a teacher, book reviewer, writer, and public librarian, having the special responsibility of selecting and programming literature for teens. She has organized and reorganized a church library, taught Sunday school, trained Sunday school teachers, given lectures, and conducted workshops.

She began telling stories at the age of twelve to her nieces and nephews, and her primary hobby continues to this day to be reading and engaging in good conversation with family and friends. She has four grandchildren and resides in northeast Ohio.